SCOLIOSIS

THE USURPATION OF
RICHARD THE THIRD

THE USURPATION OF RICHARD THE THIRD

DOMINICUS MANCINUS
AD ANGELUM CATONEM
DE OCCUPATIONE REGNI ANGLIE
PER RICCARDUM TERCIUM
LIBELLUS

TRANSLATED AND WITH AN INTRODUCTION
BY
C. A. J. ARMSTRONG

ALAN SUTTON
1989

ALAN SUTTON PUBLISHING LIMITED
BRUNSWICK ROAD · GLOUCESTER

ALAN SUTTON PUBLISHING INC.
WOLFEBORO · NEW HAMPSHIRE · USA

This reprint has been authorised by the Oxford University Press
COPYRIGHT © OXFORD UNIVERSITY PRESS 1969
THIS EDITION PUBLISHED 1984
REPRINTED 1989

BRITISH LIBRARY CATALOGUING IN PUBLICATION DATA

Mancini, Dominic
Usurpation of Richard III.—2nd ed.
1. Richard III, *King of England*
I. Title   II. De occupatione Regni Anglie
per Riccardum Tercium libelius. *English*
942.04'6'0924   DA260

ISBN 0-86299-135-8

Cover pictures: Left, Richard III, right, Edward V;
design based on an idea by Geoffrey Wheeler.

Printed and bound in Great Britain by
The Guernsey Press Co. Ltd., Guernsey, Channel Islands.

PREFACE

WHEN in 1936 I edited the text of Mancini, the history of fifteenth century England was, notwithstanding the notable work of certain scholars, an undoubtedly neglected field of study: a field moreover which many would-be workers were deterred from entering by the commonly reported saying that the nature of the source-material was unpromising. Happily, the intervening years have witnessed an increasing pre-occupation on the part of historians with the English—and indeed European—fifteenth century. This fact by itself alone has necessitated the re-writing of the introduction and of the historical notes accompanying this edition of the *De Occupatione Regni Anglie*; and I can but hope that the new *apparatus* to the text takes into full account the remarkable achievements of historical research undertaken since the 1930s. In our country this re-valuation of the fifteenth century owes, in my own opinion, more to the teaching, lecturing, and writing of the late K. B. McFarlane than to any other individual.

Inevitably many of those whose advice assisted me in preparing the first edition of this book have since then gone to their reward. Among the dead I remember with especial gratitude, Sir Maurice Powicke, Seymour de Ricci, Charles Hignett, and Daniel Callus O.P. It is therefore with all the greater pleasure that I turn to thank those of my friends, who not content with helping me in the 1936 publication have since then generously contributed toward my studies. I am thinking particularly of Professor Emeritus V. H. Galbraith, Gervase Mathew O.P., Dr. R. W. Hunt, and Professor R. Weiss. To Professor Weiss I owe an exceptional debt for he continually revives for friends and general readers alike the literary relations between early-Renaissance Italy and late-Gothic England.

I have enjoyed the advantage of hearing on various subjects the views of Dr. B. P. Wolffe about the fifteenth century, and in this connexion I am also indebted to Mr. J. R. Lander. Dr. D. E. Rhodes has likewise placed at my disposal his massive knowledge of fifteenth century English printing and book collecting.

There are not a few others whose welcome assistance on subjects of many sorts receives, I trust, in my footnotes an acknowledgment that their learning and kindness deserve.

C. A. J. A.

CONTENTS

Bibliography	xi
Historiographical note to the English narrative sources	xvii
Sigla	xxii
Introduction	1
Dominic Mancini	1
Angelo Cato	26
The Manuscript and its language	50
Text and translation	56
Historical notes to the text	106
Appendix: Richard III as seen by another foreign traveller, Nicolas von Poppelau	136
Index	139

BIBLIOGRAPHY

The entries marked below with an asterisk are discussed further in the historiographical note which follows the bibliography

Auctarium Chartularii Universitatis parisiensis, ed. C. Samaran and A. van Moë, vol. iii, *Liber Procuratorum Nationis alemanniae*, 1935.

BASIN, THOMAS: *Historia Caroli VII et Ludovici XI*, ed. J. Quicherat, 4 vols. (S. H. F.), Paris, 1855–9. This edition is in course of being superseded by that of Charles Samaran.

— *Histoire de Louis XI*, ed. and transl. by Charles Samaran, vol. i, 1963; vol. ii, 1966 (Classiques de l'Histoire de France au Moyen Age) *in progress*.

BERNARD ANDRÉ: 'Vita Henrici VII', being pp. 3–77 of *Memorials of King Henry VII*, ed. J. Gairdner (R.S.), London, 1858.

BORGIA, S.: *Memorie istoriche della pontificia città di Benevento*, 3 vols., Rome, 1763–9.

BURCHARDUS, JOHANNES: *Diarium*, 1483–1506, ed. L. Thusane, 3 vols., Paris, 1883–5.

Calendar of Patent Rolls preserved in the Public Record Office: Edward IV, 1461–7, Stationery Office, London, 1897. *Edward IV, Henry VI, 1467–77*, 1900. *Edward IV, Edward V, Richard III, 1476–85*, 1901.

Calendar of State Papers and MSS. existing in the Archives and Collections of Milan, ed. A. B. Hinds, vol. i, Stationery Office, London, 1912.

Calendar of State Papers and MSS. relating to English Affairs existing in the Archives and Collections of Venice, ed. Rawdon Brown, vol. i, Stationery Office, London, 1864.

CALMETTE, J. and PÉRINELLE, G.: *Louis XI et l'Angleterre, 1461–83* (Mémoires et documents publiés par la Société de l'Ecole des Chartes, xi), Paris, 1930.

CANNAVALE, E.: *Lo Studio di Napoli nel Rinascimento*, Turin, 1895.

CASPAR, WEINREICH: 'Danziger Chronik', being pp. 725–800, vol. iv, *Scriptores Rerum Prussicarum*, ed. T. Hirsch, 4 vols., Leipzig, 1861–70.

CATO, ANGELO: *De Cometa* [Naples, Sixtus Riessinger, 1472], 4to. Paris, B.N., Rés. R.1306 (*Gesamtkatalog der Wiegendrucke*, no. 6385).

Cely Papers, ed. H. E. Malden, (C.S., third series, vol. i), London, 1900.

CHARVET, C.: *Histoire de la sainte Eglise de Vienne*, Lyons, 1761.

— *Supplément à l'histoire de l'Eglise de Vienne* [simultaneously published].

* *Chronicles of London*, ed. C. L. Kingsford, Oxford, 1905.

[*A*] *Collection of Ordinances and Regulations for the Government of the Royal Household from Edward III to William and Mary*, printed for the Society of Antiquaries, London, 1790.

†COMINES, PHILIPPE DE: *Mémoires*, ed. J. Calmette and G. Durville, 3 vols. (Classiques de l'Histoire de France au Moyen Age), Paris, 1924–5. [This edition is intended except when otherwise stated.]

— *Mémoires*, ed. D. Sauvage, Paris (G. du Pré and J. de Roigny), 1552, fol., B.M. 1866.e.1.

— *Mémoires*, ed. Mlle E. Dupont, 3 vols. (S.H.F.), Paris, 1840–7.

— *Mémoires*, ed. B. de Mandrot, 2 vols., Paris, 1901–3.

— *Lettres et négociations de Philippe de Commines*, ed. Baron Kervyn de Lettenhoven, 3 vols., Brussels, Académie royale de Belgique, 1867–74.

Complete Peerage of England, Scotland..., by G.E.C., new edition revised by V. Gibbs, H. A. Doubleday and others, 12 vols., London, 1910–59.

COPINGER, W. A.: *Supplement to Hain's Repertorium Bibliographicum*, 2 parts, London, 1895–1902.

Coventry Leet Book or Mayor's Register, ed. M. D. Harris, 2 parts (Early English Texts Society, nos. cxxxiv, cxxxv), London, 1907–8.

CROCE, B.: 'Il personaggio italiano che esortò il Commynes a scrivere i Mémoires: Angelo Catone' in his *Vite di avventure, di fede e di passione*, Bari, 1936, pp. 161–78.

DELISLE, L. V.: *Le Cabinet des MSS. de la Bibliothèque impériale*, 3 vols., Paris, 1868–81.

†Although there are strong arguments for adopting the form 'Commynes' (see *Mémoires*, ed. Calmette, t. i. p. i. no. 3) it seems preferable to use, as does the catalogue of the British Museum, the standard orthography of the place-name Comines (Nord, arr. Lille, cant. Quesnoy-sur-Deule) since this lordship provided the family with its patronymic.

Dépêches des ambassadeurs milanais en France sous Louis XI et François Sforza, ed. B. de Mandrot, 4 vols. (S.H.F.), Paris, 1916–23.
Dictionnaire de la Noblesse, ed. Aubert de la Chenaye Desbois (third edition), 19 vols., Paris, 1863–77.
DU CLERCQ, JACQUES: *Mémoires 1448–67*, ed. Baron de Reiffenberg, 4 vols., Brussels, 1823.
EMDEN, A. B.: *Biographical register of the University of Oxford to 1500*, 3 vols., Oxford, 1957–9.
—— *Biographical register of the University of Cambridge to 1500*, Cambridge, 1963 [referred to below as A. B. Emden, *Oxford*, and A. B. Emden, *Cambridge*, respectively].
EUBEL, C.: *Hierarchia Catholica Medii AEvi*, 3 vols., Monasterii, 1898–1910.
Excerpta historica, ed. S. Bentley, London, 1831.
FABRICIUS, J. A.: *Bibliotheca latina mediae et infimae aetatis*, tom. vi, Florentiae, 1858.
* FABYAN, ROBERT: *New Chronicles of England and France*, ed. H. Ellis, London, 1811.
FAVA, M. and BRESCIANO, G.: *La Stampa a Napoli nel xv secolo*, 2 vols., Leipzig, 1911–12, in *Sammlung Bibliothekswissenschaftlicher Arbeiten*, ed. K. Haebler, serie. 2. Bd. xvi.
FREYTAG, F. G.: *Adparatus litterarius*, 3 vols., Leipzig, 1752.
FUETER, E.: *Geschichte der neueren Historiographie*, 3rd ed., Munich, 1936.
GAGUIN, R.: *Roberti Gaguini epistolae et orationes*, ed. L. Thuasne, 2 vols., Paris, 1903–4.
Gesamtkatalog der Wiegendrucke, ed. Kommission für den Gesamtkatalog der Wiegendrucke, 7 vols., Leipzig, 1925–38 [unfinished].
GODEFROY-MÉNILGLAISE, MARQUIS DE: *Les Savants Godefroy*, Paris, 1873.
GRAFTON, RICHARD: *Grafton's Chronicle, or History of England*, 2 vols., London, 1809 [see also under HARDYNG].
* *Great Chronicle of London*, ed. A. H. Thomas and I. D. Thornley, London, 1938.
GREGORIUS ARIMINENSIS: *Lectura super primum librum sententiarum*, Paris, 1482, fol. (Pellechet, 1165), Paris, B.N., Rés. D.54.
GUAINERIUS, ANTONIUS: *Tractatus de febribus*, Neapoli [Bertold Rying], 1474, fol. (Copinger, 2803), B.M., I.B.29383.

HAIN, L.: *Repertorium bibliographicum*, 2 vols., Stuttgart, 1826–31.
HALL, EDWARD: *Hall's Chronicle*, London, 1809.
HARDYNG, JOHN: *The Chronicle of John Hardyng . . . Together with the Continuation by R. Grafton*, ed. H. Ellis, London, 1812.
HILL, Sir G. F.: *Corpus of Italian Medals of the Renaissance before Cellini*, 2 vols., London, 1930.
* Historia Croylandensis: 'Historiae Croylandensis Continuatio', being pp. 449–592 of vol. i, *Rerum anglicarum scriptorum veterum*, ed. W. Fulman, Oxon., 1684.
Historie of the Arrivall of Edward IV in England and the finall Recoverye of his kingdomes from Henry VI, ed. J. A. Bruce (C.S.), London, 1838.
Household Books of John, duke of Norfolk and Thomas, earl of Surrey, 1481–90, ed. John Payne Collier, Roxburghe Club, London, 1844.
Household of Edward IV, ed. A. R. Myers, Liverpool, 1959.
'Household of Queen Elizabeth Woodville 1466–7', A. R. Myers, *Bulletin of the John Rylands Library*, l (1967) 207–35.
IVES, E. W.: 'Andrew Dymmock and the papers of Antony earl Rivers 1483–3', *Bulletin of the Institute of Historical Research*, xli (1968) 216–25.
Joachimsen, P.: *Geschichtsauffassung und Geschichtschreibung in Deutschland unter dem Einfluss des Humanismus*, Berlin, 1910.
KENDALL, P. M.: *Richard the Third*, London, 1955.
* KINGSFORD, C. L.: *English Historical Literature in the Fifteenth Century*, Oxford, 1913.
KRISTELLER, P. O.: *Iter italicum. A finding list of uncatalogued or incompletely catalogued humanistic manuscripts of the Renaissance in Italian and other libraries*, 2 vols. London and Leiden, 1963–7.
LA MARCHE, OLIVIER DE: *Mémoires*, ed. Beaune et d'Arbaumont, 4 vols. (S.H.F.), Paris, 1883–8.
LANDER, J. R.: 'The treason and death of the duke of Clarence: a re-interpretation' *Canadian Journal of History*, ii (1967) 1–28.
Letters and Papers illustrative of the reigns of Richard III and Henry VII, ed. J. Gairdner, 2 vols. (R.S.), London, 1861–3.
Letters and Papers illustrative of the Wars of the English in France during the reign of Henry the Sixth, ed. J. Stevenson, 2 vols. (R.S.), London, 1861–4.

Lettres de Charles VIII, ed. P. Pélicier and B. de Mandrot, 5 vols. (S.H.F.), Paris, 1898-1905.

Lettres de Louis XI, ed. J. Vaesen and E. Charavay (S.H.F.), Paris, 11 vols. 1883-1909.

MANCINI, DOMINIC: *De quatuor virtutibus libellus*, Paris, J. Higman, 1484, xi, Kal., jan. (Hain 10630). Paris, B.N., Rés. m. Yc. 179 and 199.

MARINIS, TAMMÀRO DE: *La Biblioteca napolitana dei Re d'Aragona*, 4 vols., Milan, 1946-52.

— 'Nota su Angelo Catone di Benevento', *Miscellanea di scritti di bibliografia ed erudizione in memoria di Luigi Ferrari*, Florence, 1952, pp. 227-32.

MAZZATINTI, G.: *La Biblioteca dei Re d'Aragona in Napoli*, Rocca S. Casciano, 1897.

MESUE, JOHANNES [Yūhuannā ibn Māsawaih]: *Practica de medicinis*, Neapoli [Bertold Rying], 1475, fol., (Hain, 11117), Paris, B.N., Rés. Te. 1716.

MOLINET, JEAN: *Chroniques*, ed. G. Doutrepont and O. Jodogne, 3 vols. (Acad. roy. de Belgique, classe des Lettres, Coll. des anciens auteurs belges), Brussels, 1935-7.

* MORE, ST. THOMAS: 'History of King Richard the Third', *Complete Works of Saint Thomas More*, ed. R. S. Sylvester, ii, Yale University Press, 1963.

MYERS, A. R.: 'The character of Richard III', *History Today*, iv (1954) 511-21. See also *Household of Edward IV*, and *Household of Queen Elizabeth Woodville 1466-7*.

NICHOLS, J. G.: *Grants etc. from the Crown during the Reign of Edward the Fifth* (C.S.), London, 1854.

NOTAR, GIACOMO: *Cronica di Napoli*, ed. P. Garzilli, Naples, 1845.

OSLER, Sir W.: *Incunabula medica*, Oxford, 1923.

PASSERO, GIULIANO: *Storie in forma di Giornali*, ed. V. M. Altobello, Naples, 1785.

Paston Letters, ed. J. Gairdner, 6 vols., London, 1904.

PELLECHET, M.: *Catalogue général des incunables des bibliothèques publiques de France*, 3 vols., Paris, 1897-1909.

PHARÈS, SYMON DE: *Recueil des plus célèbres astrologues*, ed. E. Wickersheimer, Paris, 1929.

Registrum Thome Bourgchier, ed. F. R. H. du Boulay, Oxford, 1957 (*Canterbury and York Society*, liv).

REICHLING, D.: *Appendices ad Hainii Copingeri repertorium bibliographicum, additiones*, vi fasciculi, Munich, 1905–11.
[A] *Relation or rather a true account of the Island of England*, ed. C. A. Sneyd (C.S.), London, 1847.
RHODES, D. E.: *John Argentine, Provost of King's, his Life and Library*, Amsterdam, 1967.
* ROSS, JOHN: *Historia regum Anglie*, ed. T. Hearne (2nd ed.), Oxford, 1745.
— *Rows Roll*, ed. W. Courthope, London, 1859.
Rotuli parliamentorum; ut et petitiones, et placita in parliamento, 6 vols. [ed. J. Strachey, London, 1767–77].
ROWSE, A. L.: *Bosworth Field and the Wars of the Roses*, London (Macmillan), 1966.
ROYE, JEAN DE: *Journal... connu sous le nom de chronique scandaleuse 1460–83*, ed. B. de Mandrot, 2 vols. (S.H.F.), Paris, 1894–6.
ROŽMITÁLA A BLATNÉ, JAROSLAV LEV: *Commentarius brevis et iucundus itineris atque perigrinationis... a domino Leone... de Rosmital et Blatna*, ed. K. Hrdina, Academia scientiarum et artium bohemica, Prague, 1951.
— *Des böhmischen Herrn Leo's von Rosmital Ritter-Hof-und Pilger-Reise durch die Abendlande 1465–67*. Stuttgart [auf Kosten des literarischen Vereins], 1843.
Short-title Catalogue of Books printed in England, Scotland and Ireland, 1475–1640: ed. A. W. Pollard and G. R. Redgrave, London, 1926.
SILVATICUS, MATTHAEUS: *Liber cibalis et medicinalis Pandectarum*, Neapoli [Arnold of Brussels], 1474 (prima Aprili), fol., (Hain, 15194), B.M., IC.29360.
Stonor Letters and Papers, 1290–1483, ed. C. L. Kingsford, 2 vols., (C.S., 3rd series, xxix and xxx), London, 1919.
STOW, JOHN: *A survey of London*, ed. C. L. Kingsford, 2 vols., Oxford, 1908.
THUASNE, L.: See GAGUIN, R.
TRINCHERA, F.: *Codice aragonese*, 3 vols., Naples, 1866–74.
TRITHEMIUS, JOANNES: *Liber de scriptoribus ecclesiasticis*, Basiliae [J. Amerbach], 1494, fol., Bodleian, Auct Q, 1, 3, 7.
TUMMULILLIS, ANGELO DA SANT'ELIADE: *Notabilia temporum*, ed. C. Corvisieri, Rome, 1890.

* VERGIL, POLYDORE: *Anglicae historiae, libri xxvii*, ed. Antonius Thysius, Lugduni Batavorum, 1651.
WARKWORTH, JOHN: *Chronicle of the first thirteen years of the reign of Edward IV*, ed. J. O. Halliwell (C.S.), London, 1839.
WAVRIN, JEHAN DE: *Anchiennes Cronicques d'Engleterre*, ed. Mlle E. Dupont, 3 vols. (S.H.F.), Paris, 1858–63.
WEISS, R.: *Humanism in England during the Fifteenth Century*, (3rd ed.), Oxford, 1967.
* WORCESTER, WILLIAM: 'Annales Rerum Anglicarum', being pp. 743–93, vol. ii, pt. 2, *Letters and Papers illustrative of the Wars of the English in France during the reign of Henry the Sixth*, ed. J. Stevenson, 2 vols. (R.S.), London, 1864.
York civic Records, vol. l, ed. Angelo Raine (*Yorkshire archaeological Society*, Record Series, xcviii, 1938).

HISTORIOGRAPHICAL NOTE
TO THE ENGLISH NARRATIVE SOURCES

TAKING the narrative sources as a whole C. L. Kingsford's, *English Historical Literature in the Fifteenth Century*, Oxford, 1913 remains indispensable. Nevertheless in the course of the fifty-five years since its publication its author's judgements have necessarily undergone revision. Among the sources mentioned below, this is particularly true in the case of the *Annales* attributed to William Worcester, the *Great Chronicle of London* and the *Anglica Historia* of Polydore Vergil.

Annales rerum anglicarum, reputedly by William Worcester

K. B. McFarlane in 'William Worcester: A preliminary survey' (*Studies presented to Sir Hilary Jenkinson*, ed. J. Conway-Davies, Oxford, 1957, pp. 196–221 and especially pp. 206–7) has demonstrated why these miscellaneous notes of uneven historical value can no longer be safely ascribed to Worcester. However, it seems preferable to retain the conventional label and to refer in the present work to William Worcester, *Annales*, rather than to designate this source, the shortcomings of which have long been familiar to historians, as the false- or *pseudo*-Worcester.

Historia croylandensis continuatio

For the circumstances in which this the only serious monastic

chronicle of the time was composed see Sir Goronwy Edwards, 'The second continuation of the Crowland Chronicle: was it written in ten days?', *Bulletin of the Institute of Historical Research*, xxxix (1966) 117–29. The same article contains some shrewd criticism regarding the possible authorship of this chronicle.

Historia regum Angliae and the *Rows* or *Rous Roll* of John Ross of Warwick

John Ross of Warwick was an important antiquary but a second rate historian of the period. With reference to Mancini's work the most useful assessment of the *Historia regum Angliae* is to be found in Professor R. S. Sylvester's introduction pp. lxxi–lxxii of the *Complete Works of Saint Thomas More*, ii (see below under More). For the English and Latin forms of the *Roll* see the appraisal and bibliography in A. R. Wagner, *A Calendar of English mediaeval Rolls of Arms*, London, 1950, pp. 116–20.

Great Chronicle of London

The editors Dr. A. H. Thomas and the late I. D. Thornley produced (introduction, pp. xli–lxix) serious reasons for thinking that the *Great Chronicle* should be assigned to Robert Fabyan. Accordingly it can now be regarded as his major historical compilation, while the chronicle published over his name by William Rastell in 1533 (*ib.* p. xlvi, and *Short Title Catalogue . . . 1475–1640*, compiled by A. W. Pollard and G. R. Redgrave, Bibliographical Society, 1926, no. 10660) and finally edited in 1811 by H. Ellis may be relegated to a secondary place. In their introduction to the *Great Chronicle* (p. lxx) the editors modify certain opinions expressed by C. L. Kingsford (*English Historical Literature in the Fifteenth Century*, p. 99) relating to the city chronicle contained in British Museum, Cotton MS. Vitellius A xvi. This chronicle published by Kingsford (*Chronicles of London*, Oxford, 1905, pp. 153–263) though decidedly less interesting than the *Great Chronicle* can not be disregarded as a parallel London source for the reigns of Edward IV, Edward V, and Richard III.

Polydore Vergil, *Anglica Historia*

In Renaissance Europe Vergil was an accepted authority on English history. The historical value of his work for his own day and for the late fifteenth century has been re-assessed and re-

instated by Professor Denys Hay in 'The Manuscript of Polydore Vergil's *Anglica Historia*', *English Historical Review*, liv (1939) 240–51; 'The Life of Polydore Vergil of Urbino', *Journal of the Warburg and Courtauld Institutes*, xii (1949) 132–51, and *The Anglica Historia of Polydore Vergil 1485–1537* (Camden Series, lxxiv, 1950), introduction pp. ix–lxiii. It should be noted that Vergil's account of the reigns of Edward IV and of Richard III was written, not merely drafted, no later than 1512–13. The *terminus ad quem* for the date of Vergil's narration of Richard III's usurpation therefore appreciably antedates the *terminus a quo* for dating the composition of More's account of the events of 1483 (*Anglica Historia of Polydore Vergil 1485–1537*, pp. xv, xli). In Vergil's lifetime three editions of his history, the first two only covering the period up to 1509, were published: Basle, 1534, Johannes Bebelius, fol.; Basle, 1546, Michael Isingrin, fol.; and Basle, 1555, Michael Isingrin, fol. The third, the 1555 edition, was reprinted at Basle by Isingrin in 1557 and by Thomas Guérin at Basle in 1570. The three Basle editions are all alike, rare books of which examples are seldom found outside the greater libraries. I have therefore quoted from the more widely available Leiden 1651 second reprint (the first had been at Ghent 1556–8) of the 1546 Basle edition. The Leiden publication was prepared for the press by A. Thysius as editor.

Sir Thomas More's *History of Richard III*

The present state of the question regarding the composition and character of More's history has developed out of two studies of A. L. Pollard 'Sir Thomas More's Richard III', *History*, xvii (1932–3) 317–23 and, the more specialized, 'Making of Sir Thomas More's *Richard III*', in *Historical Essays in honour of James Tait*, Manchester, 1933, 223–38. Professor P. M. Kendall's critique of More in *Richard the Third* (appendix I, 'Who murdered the Little Princes?') which was almost exclusively concerned with More's allegations against Richard III as the murderer of his nephews 'The Princes', has been superseded by the judicious appraisal of More's historical work by Professor R. S. Sylvester in the introduction to his edition of the *Complete Works of Saint Thomas More*, ii, Yale University Press, 1963. Professor Sylvester has left little doubt that the 'History' must have been written

down between the years 1514 and 1518 (pp. lxiii–lxiv). There remains, however, the disquieting question as to the provenance of More's information, a question relevant to any study of Mancini, since, as Professor Sylvester remarks, 'Mancini's treatise substantiates More's History in many points of detail' (p. lxxiii). Indeed, as will be seen from a comparison of the historical notes appended to the text (pp. 106–35), the information furnished by Mancini is at times closer to that of More than to the work of authorities such as the Croyland chronicler or Polydore Vergil.

SIGLA

B.I.H.R.	*Bulletin of the Institute of Historical Research*
B.M.	British Museum
C.D.I.H.F.	*Collection de documents inédits sur l'histoire de France*
C.S.	*Camden Society*
E.H.R.	*English Historical Review*
H.M.C.	*Historical Manuscripts Commission*
Paris B.N.	Paris, Bibliothèque nationale
P.R.O	Public Record Office
R.S.	*Rolls Series*
S.H.F.	*Société de l'histoire de France*

All dates given are according to the new style, unless otherwise stated.

INTRODUCTION
DOMINIC MANCINI

AT the end of the fifteenth century the Roman family of the Mancini had its home near the Via Lata.[1] It was in seventeenth century France through a marriage with a kindred but humbler family, that of Mazzarini, that the Mancini enjoyed their greatest prosperity. By marrying Hieronyma Mazzarini, sister of cardinal Mazarin, Michel Laurent Mancini gained a liberal share of the cardinal's favour. The family assumed the name of Mancini-Mazzarini; and on it was bestowed the duchy of Nevers. The cardinal's nephew, Philippe Julien Mancini-Mazzarini (1641–1707), duke of Nevers, was interested in the history of his ancestors and he applied part of his ample means to research on the subject. At his command deeds and notarial acts were inspected in several Italian cities but more particularly in Rome, where documents preserved in the Capitol and the parish registers of S. Maria-in-Via Lata and Ara Coeli yielded him much information. The work done for him was embodied in a voluminous annotated genealogy,[2] according to which Dominic Mancini was the son of Alexander Mancini, who died at a great age in 1491, and of Ambrosina Fabii, his wife. Legal transactions relating to family affairs in 1478 and 1491 that mentioned the name of Dominic were noticed by the genealogists whom the duke of Nevers employed. Otherwise their notes on Dominic Mancini were chiefly concerned to emphasize the value of his latin poems *De quatuor Virtutibus* and *De Passione Domini*, which by the late seventeenth century must have been generally forgotten. Dominic Mancini was born not later than 1434. Indeed he thought of himself by 1484 as having reached old age; and, after making allowance for the earlier onset of age in previous generations, he can scarcely then have been less than fifty. This reference to his age comes from his Latin poem *De quatuor Virtutibus* (first published December 1484) and a passage in the same work leaves no doubt that he was then in orders. The

---

[1] J. Burchard, *Diarium*, iii. 33.
[2] Paris, B.N. Dossiers bleus 422 (MS. français 29967), Mancini, ff. 1–32. This genealogy in abridged form was published in *Dictionnaire de la Noblesse*, xiii. 87–98.

actual words he used *votum fidei, religioque sacra* strongly suggest that he belonged to the regular rather than to the secular clergy.[1]

The evidence, such as it is, points to a literary career which achieved success beyond the Alps rather than in Italy. It can be assumed that he was in France, probably at Paris, not later than 1482. In August of that year there was published in Paris the *Lectura super primum librum Sententiarum* of Gregorius Ariminensis, edited by Guillaume Milet a professor of the Paris faculty of theology; and to this book Mancini contributed a preliminary commendatory poem in Latin.[2] Apart from the consideration that the editor or printer was unlikely to have selected an entire stranger to recommend the book, it is probable that Mancini had been in Paris for some time before 1482, since the contents of his Latin verses show him as keenly interested in a series of events that disturbed academic life in Paris between 1474 and 1482.

The publication of this the first edition of Ariminensis coincided with the end of a period during which the philosophers and theologians at Paris belonging to the party of so-called Ancients or Realists had maintained supremacy thanks to their adroit use of royal intervention on their own behalf. The rival academic faction of Moderns or Terminalists, popularly known as Nominalists, had been silenced by royal authority while the writings of their masters were consigned to locked cupboards. Indeed Ariminensis (Gregorio da Rimini), the *magister distincionum*, was singled out for especial condemnation when Louis XI, in 1474, prohibited Nominalist teaching. This ban was lifted in 1481 though it was not until 17 May 1482 that the manuscripts of the Terminalist masters were officially allowed to be taken out from confinement.[3] Since the ban came into force in 1474 the printing press had made progress in Paris and had already given evidence of its potentiality. The first impression of Ariminensis in August 1482 was, therefore,

---

[1] *De quatuor Virtutibus* (1484) f. 3. Reprinted by Thuasne *Gaguini Epistole*, ii. 215–16.

'non etiam sanctus quo ascribor postulat ordo, et votum fidei religioque sacra.'

[2] This poem is printed on f. 1ᵛᵒ of the 1482 edition.

[3] C. E. Bulaeus, *Historia Universitatis parisiensis*, 6 vols., Paris, 1665–73, v. 739, 747–8. C. M. Jourdain, *Index chronologicus Chartarum pertinentium ad historiam Universitatis parisiensis*, Paris, 1862, p. 297. J. Salabert, *Philosophia Nominalium vindicata*, Paris, 1651, pp. 54–70.

something of a manifesto on the part of the now triumphant Nominalists utilizing the press to display their rewon freedom.

These then were the events that Dominic Mancini celebrated in his verses which praised Ariminensis as the unconquerable master and extolled the *via moderna* as the supreme philosophical method.[1]

At the foot of his sprightly introduction to the weighty questions of Ariminensis, Mancini described himself as a 'most eloquent orator, a poet laureate and a palatine count'. It is not impossible that the dignity of a poet laureate was conferred on him by Frederick III on one of the imperial visits to Italy.[2] These were evidently titles that he brought with him from Italy; but Mancini, whether from personal humility or because of Gallic scepticism relinquished their use in his subsequent publications. Indeed Gaguin, who accorded the title of laureate to the least reputable of his correspondents, did not extend it to Mancini.[3]

At present the evidence for the visit of Mancini to England rests exclusively on his *De Occupatione Regni Anglie*. To date the length of his stay, there is only available the *terminus ad quem*, which was shortly after 6 July 1483, when he was recalled to France by Angelo Cato, archbishop of Vienne.[4] It may be assumed that Mancini was still in Paris during May 1482 when the locked up texts of the Nominalists were officially released and perhaps as late as August of that year when Ariminensis was printed. This

[1] Qui fuerat iussus Gregorius ante tacere
     Liberius toto nunc datur ore loqui;
     Nec quia tot tacuit lustris est gutture raucus

     Quare age cum liceat sacras nunc tollere voces
     Et liceat medio iam resonare foro
     Hunc pete, sacrarum tendis qui ad culmina rerum;
     Hunc pete, quem studiis altius ire iuvat

     Impugnat si quid, non est defendere tutum;
     Si quid defendat quis nocuisse potest?
     Cumque labent alii doctores, sepe repulsi
     Hic tenet immotum turris ut alta caput.

     Reddidit hunc nobis Ludovici gratia regis,
     Reddidit et dogma, a nomine nomen habens.

Super primum librum Sententiarum (1482) f. 1vo.

[2] On his 1469 visit he granted for cash many such titles. *Diario ferrarese*, ed. G. Pardi, p. 56 (*Rerum italicarum scriptores*, 1938).

[3] Thuasne, *Gaguini Epistole*, ii. 272.

[4] See below, p. 104, l. 12.

supposition would accord fairly well with the retrospective summary that he provides of the reign of Edward IV.[1] Indeed this summary looks as if it was written by someone who had only been in England during the last few months of that king's life.

It would be more interesting to know why he came to England. Of course Italian men of letters had long been wont to visit the country in hopes of finding profitable employment for their talents; and two such men Pietro Carmeliano and Stefano Surigone were in England about this time.[2] Nevertheless there are grounds for thinking that Mancini was sent to England by Cato. In the first place there is the passage in the introduction, which Mancini addressed to Cato, where he alludes to the information he collected about English affairs. He starts this passage with the words *qui tua causa laborem non refugiebam*,[3] as though he had received some commission from his patron to gather information in England. The mere fact that Cato could recall Mancini quickly from England does to some extent pre-suppose that he sent him there. At this time the influence of Cato on Louis XI of France, as that king's physician and councillor was considerable. After the death of Cato an official inventory was compiled of the state papers found among his possessions. This list shows that he was very intimately associated with the domestic and foreign affairs of the French crown at the close of the reign of Louis XI.[4] The king was always avid for information and the favour and pre-eminence which he accorded to his councillors largely depended on the quality and quantity of the information with which they could provide him. There is then some likelihood that Cato either sent Mancini to England to produce a report on the situation there, at a time when relations between the courts of England and France were becoming increasingly strained, or that he asked Mancini, who was going to England for some other business, to prepare a memorandum.

During the summer of 1482 there was ample opportunity for Mancini to have crossed the Channel with one or other official

[1] See below, pp. 60–68.
[2] For Carmeliano see below, p. 19, n. 1. Surigone probably left England shortly after 1478, which was the publication date of the elegy which he wrote for Caxton in praise of Chaucer. R. Weiss, *Humanism in England during the Fifteenth Century*, p. 139.
[3] See below, p. 56, l. 12. [4] See below, p. 38.

party bound for England, as the recent death of Mary of Burgundy and arrangements for the payment of Edward IV's pension intensified the normal diplomatic exchanges. Besides there were other missions which might equally well explain his arrival in England during the latter part of 1482. On 27 August 1482 Pope Sixtus IV dispatched four briefs to England, one each to the king and to his brother Richard duke of Gloucester and the other two addressed to Thomas Rotherham, archbishop of York, and to William lord Hastings respectively.[1] Angelo Cato was a former pupil of the pope and when in July 1482 the king of France nominated him to the archbishopric of Vienne he successfully appealed to a long-standing friendship with Sixtus IV in order to obtain papal provision.[2] What between royal and papal favour Cato would have had little difficulty in having Mancini included in one of these missions going to England in the latter part of 1482.

The records of the English Crown do not appear to register either the arrival or the departure of Mancini. Letters of passage granted during July 1483 to a few distinguished foreigners were indeed enrolled; but the supervision of English ports was seemingly lax, since, later in 1483 after the revolt of the duke of Buckingham in the autumn of that year, Richard III was obliged to require keepers of ports to observe the rule of preventing the departure of anyone not holding a royal permit.[3] On returning to France Mancini was evidently with Cato for a certain length of time, since he was able to give frequent accounts to his patron, the archbishop of Vienne, of what he had observed in England.[4] Certainly, it is quite probable that when he addressed his opuscule to Cato from Beaugency[5] on 1 December 1483, Mancini was staying in the archbishop's household.

Mancini no doubt continued to maintain a reasonably close connexion with the archbishop of Vienne, for it is significant that Cato has left what appears to be an autograph *ex-libris* dated 1 May 1486 in a copy of the edition of Ariminensis printed in

---

[1] Calmette and Périnelle, *Louis XI et l'Angleterre*, pp. 251–2, 395–6, pièce justificative, no. 83.
[2] See below, p. 39.
[3] B.M. Harleian, MS. 433, ff. 107ro, 135vo, 139vo.
[4] See below, p. 56, l. 8.
[5] See below, p. 104, l. 15.

1482 to which Mancini had contributed the preliminary verses.[1] From his published work the *De quatuor Virtutibus*, which appeared in Paris at the end of 1484, it is possible partly to reconstruct the society which Mancini cultivated following his return from England. The book itself was dedicated to another Italian, Federico da Sanseverino, bishop of Maillezais,[2] and a son of an exiled Neapolitan baron of the Angevin faction, Roberto da Sanseverino. The family was not unimportant given the general situation in France and Italy; and the *De quatuor Virtutibus* contained a rather fulsome tribute to Roberto and some epigrams exchanged between Mancini and his son the bishop of Maillezais.[3]

Printed as an appendix to the 1484, 1488, and 1492 Paris editions of the *De quatuor Virtutibus* there was a miscellany of Latin verse addressed to some of the leading figures in and around the French court of the young Charles VIII including a poem *De prima etate Caroli regis*.[4] Among those to whom Mancini addressed his verse were the chancellor, Guillaume de Rochefort,[5] Jean de Rély,[6] the grave and reformist confessor of the king and, a rather different personality, Claude de Vaudrey,[7] a knight of the county of Burgundy a renowned hero of the battle-field and the tilt-yard. There was also a satirical piece against the fallen favourites of Louis XI.[8]

In Paris literary society in so far as it was sedate and semi-official found at that time a leader in Robert Gaguin, the general of the Trinitarian order. His classical and historical interests, his travels and his correspondence combined to make of him a widely known personality.[9] It is to this society that Mancini with his correct Latin and moral views most naturally belonged. His own acquaintance with Gaguin may have originated over a question of adjacent property. Mancini either owned himself or managed,

---

[1] Paris, B.N., Rés. D.54, sig. a i.
[2] Eubel, *Hierarchia Catholica*, ii. 22, 204. There is frequent mention of Roberto da Sanseverino in contemporary Italian narrative sources.
[3] *De Quatuor Virtutibus* (1484), ff. 3vo–4vo, 25vo, 26, 32ro.
[4] *Ib*., ff. 30ro–31vo.   [5] *Ib*., ff. 28–9vo.   [6] *Ib*., f. 29vo.
[7] *Ib*., ff. 26vo–27ro.   [8] *Ib*., ff. 27ro–28vo.
[9] The introduction of L. Thuasne to his *Gaguini Epistole* and A. Renaudet, *Preréforme et Humanisme à Paris*, Paris, 1916, *passim* give a good idea of this small but not necessarily narrow society.

perhaps in the interests of his order, a piece of land planted with fruit trees, and these—as is their universal custom—gradually extended over neighbouring ground, which in this case belonged to Gaguin or to the Trinitarians.[1] At first Mancini adopted a highly correct attitude and wrote to Gaguin admitting his right to cut off the branches or to gather their fruit. However, he soon regretted his admission and he again wrote to Gaguin this time lamenting the mutilation of the trees and pleading for a reprieve. With generosity rare among gardeners, let alone men of letters, Gaguin granted the request and complimented his correspondent on his Latin style.[2]

An unpublished Latin poem by Mancini describes in some detail the literary 'salon' gathered around Gaguin. The unanimity of his guests in submitting their work to the criticism of their host was equalled only by the tactful comments of Gaguin, as their master.[3] Doubtless it was due to Gaguin that Mancini was included in the *De Scriptoribus ecclesiasticis* of Trithemius, who invited Gaguin to forward to him the names and qualifications of those deserving a place in his repertory of authors. Abbot Trithemius was in many respects a German equivalent of Gaguin, for the two men were devoted to the cause of christian humanism, the same field of study as that in which Mancini himself laboured. There is no evidence to show that Gaguin ever did submit the name of Mancini, although it is known that he, Gaguin, did recommend the name of two other acquaintances for a mention in the *De Scriptoribus* of Trithemius.[4]

The entry itself in the *De Scriptoribus* represents the so far unique contemporary notice on Mancini. It runs as follows:

'Dominicus Mancinus, vir in divinis scripturis admodum eruditus, et in secularibus litteris egregie doctus, metro excellens et prosa, ingenio subtilis et clarus eloquio. Scripsit quaedam probata opuscula quibus nomen suum divulgavit. E quibus ego legi dumtaxat tractatum illum quem eleganti metro composuit. *De Passione Domini, lib. i*, "Non hominum laudes". Scripsit alia.

---

[1] The properties controlled by Gaguin, in one capacity or other, have been identified by Thuasne (*Gaguini Epistole*, i. 52, 99, 116).
[2] *Ib.*, ii. 214–17.
[3] Paris B.N., Cinq Cents de Colbert, MS. 484, ff. 436ro–437ro.
[4] Thuasne, *Gaguini Epistole*, i. 399–404.

8   INTRODUCTION

Vivere adhuc dicitur et varia conscribere sub Maximiliano rege nobilissimo: anno domini quo nos ista scripsimus MCDXCIV.'¹

The notice does not contain anything startling about Mancini; but the reference to his work in prose is interesting since the *De Occupatione Regni Anglie* is his only piece in prose so far known. The comment *clarus eloquio* suggests that he was not merely a timid scholar. The *probata opuscula* apply presumably to his two printed publications the *De quatuor Virtutibus* and the *De Passione Domini*, the second of which Trithemius had read. The *De Passione Domini*, in what appears to be its earliest edition, is undated. It is also undedicated. However it was probably printed at Paris during the 1480s.² In the absence of evidence pointing to subsequent literary output on the part of Mancini it is worth noting that in 1494 Trithemius heard that Mancini was still alive and still engaged on literary work, 'varia conscribere'. The notice of Trithemius must also serve as an epitaph on Mancini, for after 1494 nothing more is heard of him; and whatever the date of his death it probably occurred before 1514.³

As has already been said it looks from what Mancini wrote about himself in the *De quatuor Virtutibus* that he was not only in orders but a member of a religious order.⁴ Although nothing in the notice by Trithemius is inconsistent with this view, it is disappointing that Trithemius omitted to be precise. Trithemius himself was a Benedictine monk, and he took a justifiable pride in the illustrious men, particularly the scholars and authors, who had adorned the Benedictine order.⁵ Had he heard that Mancini was also a Benedictine it is improbable that Trithemius would not have recorded the fact. There may be a clue to the order to which Mancini belonged in a few lines of some Latin verse which he addressed to Robert Gaguin. In the course of a rather strained and obscure metaphor, Mancini characterizes the muses accompanying Gaguin as clad in white wool, while those on his own side

¹ *Liber de Scriptoribus ecclesiasticis*, (1494) f. 139ʳᵒ.
² See below, p. 11, n. 1.
³ In a notarial act summarized in the seventeenth century genealogy, referred to above, p. 1, a partition of family property in 1514 does not mention Dominic Mancini while making provision for his two brothers (Paris B.N., MS, français, 29967, f. 26).
⁴ See above, p. 2, n. 1.
⁵ See his *De Viris illustribus ordinis Sancti Benedicti, Libri iv*, edited and printed by Gervinus Calenius, Cologne, 1575, fol.

wore black.[1] Since Gaguin was the general of the Trinitarians, an order whose habit was white, it is probable that Mancini was seeking to symbolize the order to which Gaguin belonged; and, if this supposition be admitted, there can remain little doubt that the dark or black habit represented the order of which Mancini was himself a member.

The colour black would suggest the Benedictines, the black monks, but the silence of Trithemius on this point is scarcely encouraging. There remain, among the more notable congregations of the period, the two Augustinian orders of canons and hermits. Both of these wore a black habit, which each of them claimed to have been specially instituted by St. Augustine. The fact that Mancini was chosen to write the preliminary verse introducing the first printed edition of Gregorio da Rimini (Gregorius Ariminensis) seems at first sight to indicate that Mancini belonged to the order of Augustinian Hermits. Indeed Gregorio da Rimini had been a fourteenth-century general of the Augustinian Hermits; and by the second half of the fifteenth century that order had come to regard his philosophy as closely identified with its own teaching. By the end of the Middle Ages the larger religious orders were identifying themselves more closely with the teaching of their particular doctors. For long each order had striven to spread its characteristic philosophy by means of the works of its own representative thinkers. This rivalry was perhaps intensified by the invention of printing; but at least the tendency among the orders toward intellectual specialization is borne out by the numerous early editions of notable scholastics in the publication of which contemporary members of the same orders played a part.[2] As a matter of fact the first edition of

[1] Hospita musarum domus est tua fida mearum,
Roberte: at musis regia celsa tuis.
Nec patet hospitio tantum mihi nocte dieque
Omnibus at doctis semper aperta viris.
Distingunt habitus varii sed utrasque sorores
Fusca tegit nostras, candida lana tuas.
Paris B.N., Cinq Cents de Colbert, MS. 484, f. 436ro (late fifteenth-century humanistic hand).

[2] Of the editions of Aquinas where Hain gives the editor's name, one is the work of a Carmelite and at another both a Benedictine and a Dominican collaborated; but the others are all by Dominicans (Hain, nos. 1337, 1338, 1339, 1387, 1389, 1417, 1418, 1442, 1452, 1475, 1477, 1490, 1504, 1505, 1517, 1528, 1535, 1540). If Penketh, an Augustinian Hermit, was the earliest editor of Scotus,

Ariminensis, that published in Paris in 1482, to which Mancini contributed the preliminary commendatory verses, was not prepared for the press by an Augustinian. Its editor was Guillaume Milet, later a secular canon of Saint-Sauveur at Blois and chaplain to Louis duke of Orleans.[1] However, it may have seemed advisable to Guillaume Milet, since he himself was not an Augustinian Hermit, to have a member of that order write an elegant and laudatory Latin poem to recommend Ariminensis to his fellow Augustinians.[2] It is true that the name of Dominic Mancini is not to be found among the records of the Augustinian Hermits of this period preserved in the central archives of the order in Rome.[3]

Nevertheless he may possibly have been a member of the order in view of these two scraps of evidence:

(i) that on his own, admittedly obscure, statement he belonged to an order wearing a black habit,[4] and

---

the Franciscan order provided nearly all the editors of the other incunabel editions recorded by Hain (nos. 6419, 6422, 6423, 6425, 6448, 6450, 6451, 6454). Johannes de Bacone and Guido Terrena were among the most respected masters of the Carmelites; and both editions of works by Johannes de Bacone printed before 1500 were prepared by Carmelites (*Gesamtkatalog der Wiegendrucke*, nos. 3150, 3151) and the same was true of the early sixteenth-century editions of Guido Terrena (Cosmas de Villiers a Sancto Stephano, *Bibliotheca carmelitana*, 2 vols., Orleans, 1752, i. 290, 507, 584). The commentary on Aristotle's Physics by the well-known Servite, Urbano da Bologna (Urbanus Averroista), was first printed in 1492 at Venice under the auspices of Antonio Alabanti, general of the Servite order (Hain, no. 16097). Aegidius Romanus, to an even greater extent than Ariminensis, was the acknowledged master of the Augustinian Hermits, and almost all the pre-1500 editions of Aegidius, whose editors can be ascertained, were prepared by Augustinians (*Gesamtkatalog der Wiegendrucke*, nos. 7195, 7197, 7205, 7206, 7208. J. F. Ossinger, *Bibliotheca augustiniana*, Ingolstadt, 1768, pp. 89, 411, 603, 749, 894).

[1] In 1498 Milet was described by a notary as aged about fifty-five (*Procédures politiques du règne de Louis XII*, ed. M. De Maulde, (C.D.I.H.F.) Paris, 1885, pp. 1007-8).

[2] It is significant in this connexion that the editor, who was an Augustinian Hermit, of the edition of Ariminensis printed in 1500 at Valencia chose to reproduce Mancini's poem, and that the same is true of the edition printed at Venice in 1503 (Reichling, v. 8-9).

[3] I have to thank the Rev. D. Gutiérrez, O.S.A., who was so friendly as to undertake on my behalf extensive, though fruitless, research in the registers of the order between 1458 and 1495 in the Archivio generale at Santa Monica, Rome.

[4] The Augustinian Canons also wore a black habit; but Mancini's poem on Ariminensis provides internal evidence which does not suit the suggestion that he himself was a canon. Indeed he does not shrink from comparing Gregorio da Rimini with Saint Augustine, whom he treats as the founder of the order to

(ii) that the *editio princeps* of Gregorio da Rimini was prefaced by commendatory verses of his composing.

Mancini was a most successful author appealing not only to the tastes of his own but also to those of the succeeding generation. This statement may be safely affirmed without undertaking a detailed bibliography of his *De quatuor Virtutibus* or of his *De Passione Domini*. A bibliography such as this would be outside the scope of the present study; but Mancini's contemporary and posthumous reputation is amply confirmed by the catalogues of major libraries.[1]

His success[2] was due in varying degree to his style, to his

which Gregorio belonged namely the Hermits (the entire poem, but with errors is reprinted by Joseph Würsdörfer, *Erkennen und Wissen nach Gregor von Rimini*, Münster-i.-W., 1917, p. 9). However both the Canons and the Hermits claimed Augustine as their founder, and in 1477 when the question arose whether a statue of the saint in Milan cathedral should represent him as a Canon or Hermit, a quarrel broke out between the two orders. In 1481 Ambrosius de Cora upheld the claims of the Hermits in a spirited defence printed at Rome, but burned on the petition of the Canons of the Lateran. By 1484 the controversy so annoyed Sixtus IV that he ordered the parties to desist. J. F. Ossinger, *Bibliotheca augustiniana*, pp. 261–2; L. Empoli, *Bullarium Ordinis Eremitarum S. Augustini*, Rome, 1628, pp. 321–4.

[1] See in particular *British Museum General Catalogue of Printed Books, Photolithographic Edition to 1955*, vol. 151, cols. 573–4 and *Catalogue général des livres imprimés de la Bibliothèque nationale* [Paris], t. civ, cols. 1052–4. The *De quatuor Virtutibus* was first printed by Johannes Higman 22 December 1484 at Paris and there again by Georg Mitelhuss in 1488 and 1492. The second and third but not the first edition are in the British Museum. It was printed in Germany as early as 1488 at Leipzig (Reichling. i. 166). In the Netherlands editions appeared in 1535 and 1540 at Antwerp (Wouter Nijhoff and M. E. Kronenburg, *Nederlandsche Bibliographie van 1500 tot 1540*, 2 vols., The Hague, 1923, 1940, i. 528; ii. 604). For the 1520, 1523, 1570 publications in England and the English translations by Alexander Barclay see *Short-title Catalogue*, nos., 17241, 17242, 17243. The earliest editions of the *De Passione Domini* were printed in Paris but without indication of printer, place, and year (*Catalogue général, loc. cit.*). Editions before or about 1500 appeared at Angoulême, Poitiers, and Rouen (*ib.* and Copinger, pt. 2, vol. i, no. 3806): in Germany at Leipzig in 1500 (Hain, no. 10639): in the Netherlands at Deventer 1510 (Nijhoff and Kronenburg, *op. cit.*, i. 528) and at Antwerp *Dominici Mancini Poemata, Hieronymi Vallensis patavini Jesuidos, vel de Dominica Passione, lib i Opera Theodori Poelmanni edita*, 1559. In his introduction Poelmann states (pp. 2–3) that he bought Mancini's work off an Antwerp pedlar and was so impressed by the quality of the neglected poem that he published it. It was also printed at Cracow in 1525. K. Estreicher, *Bibliografiia polska*, 29 vols., Krakow, 1870–1933, xxii (1908) 109.

[2] The *De quatuor Virtutibus* and still more the *De Passione Domini* is extant in manuscripts which to all appearances were copied from printed texts; an example of the inter-changeability of type and script at this period. The *De*

choice of subjects and to his stock of ideas. His Latin, if not scintillating, was good and fluent. The prosody of his verse was correct; and, if it lacked the crispness and tenderness of a Politian, it may, on that account, have gained a wider circle of readers. The subject matter, whether moral, as in the *De quatuor Virtutibus*, or devotional as in the *De Passione Domini*, was equally traditional; but in the pre-Reformation period each could count on an increasing number of readers. The ideology, which inspired Mancini's published works, was also inherited and derivative; but its presentation in classical metre won for it an immediate public.

The *De quatuor Virtutibus* restated the sound advice of an already abundant literature aiming at the improvement of private and public morals.[1] If Mancini was theological in his approach to the cardinal virtues, his special merit consisted in applying them to education and the social graces. An interesting feature is the marked abhorrence with which Mancini censured the violent man in public life[2] as though he were still recovering from the shock of what he had lived through in England. The respect for truth

---

quatuor Virtutibus was copied at Lindau in 1499 (*Verzeichniss der Handschriften der Stiftsbibliothek von St. Gallen herausgegeben auf Veranstaltung des katholischen Administrationsrathes des Kantons St. Gallen*, Halle, 1875, p. 295) and read by a schoolmaster to his class, and the *De Passione Domini* in the same year was transcribed at Zittau (A. Podlaha, *Manuscrits du Chapitre de Prague, F-P.*, Prague, 1922, no. 1347). Early sixteenth-century copies of the *De Passione Domini* are recorded at the following libraries: Berlin, *codices electorales*, 993 (ii) see *Handschriften-Verzeichnisse der königlichen Bibliothek zu Berlin*, Bd. xiii (1905) 1276; British Museum, Add. MS. 19050, ff. 58, 95–8; Einsiedeln, *Codices monasterii Einsidlensis*, Leipzig, 1899, no. 317; Montbéliard, *Catalogue général des Manuscrits des Bibliothèques publiques de France-Départements*, xiii (1891) no. 104; and Munich, Bayerische Staats-Bibliothek, *codices latini*, 12115. There must be many more.

[1] Cf. the popularity of the *De quatuor Virtutibus* falsely attributed to Seneca frequently printed in the fifteenth century (Hain, nos. 14614–32).

[2] In the section devoted to Justice:

> 'Non etiam ut magnus fias te dede rapinae
> Nam neque quo regnes ius violare licet,
> Nec tantum a iusto violentia longius absit'.
> *De quatuor Virtutibus*, f. 11ro.

And again in the section devoted to Magnanimity:

> 'Qui patriam insultat:violat qui publica iura
> Non vir magnanimus ille putandus erit.
> Est audax potius, temerarius, impius, amens,
> Est quidquid possit lingua referre mali.'
> *Ib.*, f. 12vo.

he recommended should have made of him a good reporter[1]; but had he observed another of his precepts, that foreigners should not concern themselves with what went on in the countries which they visited, he could scarcely have gathered the information to write the *De Occupatione Regni Anglie*.[2]

When in England Mancini looked at the houses of London merchants with interest and admiration[3]; but nowhere in the *De quatuor Virtutibus* is the inherited mediaeval outlook more striking than in the passage where the author condemns the common morality of trading.[4] On the other hand he was sufficiently a man of his own times to recommend the professions of the architect and of the physician[5]—the second perhaps out of regard for his patron Angelo Cato. Not that Mancini was always so deferential to him, since the *De quatuor Virtutibus* contains several passages expressing scepticism or disapproval of astrology.[6] This work then, which was not an original piece of classical scholarship seeing that the references to the Ancients were hackneyed, was conservative without being reactionary. Its emphasis on politeness and the social aspects of the virtues furnished it with a secular appeal that successfully withstood the advent of Protestantism.[7]

In the same Latin hexameters as the *De quatuor Virtutibus* the *De Passione Domini* recounted the Passion while adhering strictly to the narrative of the Evangelists. The literature of the Passion,

---

[1] *Ib.*, f. 9vo.
[2] 'Ipse peregrina si forte moraris in urbe
  Nullius urbane sit tibi cura rei,
  Sed tantum proprii maneat tibi cura negoci
  Ne tibi quis dicat: advena vade foras.'
  Ib., f. 22ro.
[3] See below, p. 102, l. 32.
[4] 'Mercator tenuis: sordidus ipse quoque est
  Quisquis emit merces: illas subitoque revendit
  Periurus: vanus semper is esse solet,
  Nil autem vano et periuro turpius extat,
  Namque homines fraudat, negligit ille deos
  Atsi mercator magnus sit mercis opime
  Ut puto non magno vertitur ille probro'.
  De quatuor Virtutibus, f. 25ro.
[5] *Ib.*, f. 25ro.
[6] E.g. 'Quid prodest varios stellarum inquirere cursus
  Quid res et causas noscere inepte petis?'
  Ib., f. 7vo.
[7] An edition was printed in London in 1638 (*Short-title Catalogue*, no. 17240) and in Germany so late as 1691 (Freytag, *Adparatus litterarius*, iii. 10).

abundant throughout the Middle Ages, was still increasing at the time of the introduction of printing; and the object of Mancini was to offer a scholarly and classical framework for a devotion otherwise dependent on Books of Hours or Primers. An analogy between the latter and the *De Passione* is a poem addressed to Our Lady following on the main work just as the Hours of the Virgin are appended to the Canonical. It is easy, therefore, to see that the *De Passione* had little chance of re-publication within Protestant Europe. It did, however, contribute to the text of the so-called *Great Passion* published in 1511 at Nuremberg which accompanied the splendid woodcuts of Albert Dürer.[1]

To remember that the author of the works in Latin verse was one and the same as the writer of the *De Occupatione Regni Anglie* might be hard, even though the occasional verses appended to the *De quatuor Virtutibus* display an interest in current affairs, were it not for a common trait of objectivity which runs through the writing of Mancini. The *De quatuor Virtutibus* is devoid of personal and romantic reminiscences and free likewise of any embellishment of one particular virtue. The *De Passione Domini* is a faithful transcription into Latin hexameters of the account left by the Evangelists without additions from apocryphal sources or from private mysticism. Of the three the *De Occupatione Regni Anglie* is the most pronouncedly objective. Mancini, who was writing a report or a narrative treatise of a dynastic revolution, hides himself entirely behind the facts which he relates. He was scrupulous in avoiding considerations foreign to his subject matter and in refraining from the use of historical data as a pretext for ethical reflection.[2]

His attitude towards his task as a narrator was rare among his contemporaries, for if the humanist school decried the moralizing of chroniclers, it did so only to expatiate on neo-classic virtues infinitely remote from the realities of the time. Significantly enough he employs direct speech only once and then briefly.[3] Instead of acquainting the reader with the motives of statesmen under the travesty of a set speech drawn from a classical model,

[1] *Impressum per A. Durer*, Nurnberge, 1511, B.M., 7, f. 3 (2).
[2] With one exception, the comment on Hasting's death. See below, p. 90, l. 19.
[3] See below, p. 74, l. 1.

Mancini prefers to explain in his own words the actions which he has to account for. This treatment confers a certain individuality on each incident in his short account of the reign of Edward V.

Although there is no reason to think that the surviving manuscript of the *De Occupatione Regni Anglie* is from Mancini's own hand, the division into chapters and the chapter-headings may be ascribed to him. The older historical works of which the texts were not divided into chapters were often provided with chapter headings in preparation for printing[1]; but there is no reason for thinking that our manuscript was prepared with a view to publishing. Rather do the divisions into chapters draw together and articulate the text of the *De Occupatione*. The same method had already been employed, on a larger scale, by Aeneas Sylvius, Piccolomini, in historical composition.[2]

The unity of the *De Occupatione* is certainly disturbed by the lengthy account of the court of Edward IV, about which Mancini must have possessed some direct information; and the symmetry of the central theme—Richard of Gloucester's usurpation—is impaired by the chapter concerning the topography of London.[3] The digression about sanctuary and the details regarding the equipment of English common soldiers had some contribution to make to the main topic.[4] The remarks on London are rather poor notes of any traveller.

On the other hand nothing could be less like a traveller's diary than Mancini writing on the political events. He omitted, quite intentionally, a description alike of Edward IV's funeral or of Richard III's coronation. He excluded the details of public affairs, which feature so largely in chronicles, memoirs, and travellers' reminiscences that delight in reproducing minutiae such as the number of attendants waiting upon a queen.[5] It must be assumed

---

[1] Histories in Latin, for example those of Aeneas Sylvius Piccolomini and of Thomas Basin, were in the second half of the fifteenth century normally produced with division into chapters (Joachimsen, *Geschichtsauffassung in Deutschland*, pp. 28–36). A vernacular work such as the *Mémoires* of Comines although frequently printed before was not divided systematically into chapters until the edition of Denis Sauvage, historiographer of Henry II, published in 1552.
[2] Joachimsen, *op. cit., loc. cit.*
[3] See below, p. 100. [4] See below, pp. 78. 98.
[5] E.g. the account of Elizabeth Woodville's public appearances given by Gabriel Tetzel of Nuremberg (Rosmital, *Ritter-Hof-und Pilger-Reise*, p. 156).

that Mancini did not readily understand English, perhaps not at all, so that he had no capacity to summarize the proclamations cried in London[1] to which he refers and which would have been such precious historical evidence.

By far the most remarkable omission is the absence of any portrait of Richard duke of Gloucester. One has only to consider how much the literary appeal of the work would have stood to gain from a description of Richard's appearance,[2] and moreover how easy would have been the conventional picture of a tyrant grasping power, in order to feel some respect for Mancini's reticence concerning the external appearance of the man whose political actions he described. The otherwise unaccountable decision to exclude even a sketch of Richard becomes intelligible only if Mancini had no opportunity to observe him sufficiently. It is noticeable that the narrative grows less detailed as it approaches Richard's final occupation of the throne on 26 June 1483; and there are grounds for supposing that while Mancini had sources of information regarding Edward IV and Edward V he never secured a reliable informant to tell him about Richard III. He apparently preferred to remain silent when reliable sources of information failed him.

The brevity, select material, and sober style besides a certain air of practical utility apparent in the treatise of Mancini exhibit some similarity with diplomatic reports, which are common enough in the fifteenth century alike from Italian and non-Italian sources.[3] The similarity is not fortuitous since he, like the authors of diplomatic relations, was writing an extended memorandum on the orders and for the instruction of a superior. All the same

---

[1] See below, p. 90, l. 23.

[2] This omission is to some extent repaired by the brief description of King Richard left by Nicolas von Poppelau. See below, p. 137.

[3] The *De Occupatione* is slightly earlier than the published series of Venetian diplomatic relations; but the Venetians for over a century had required reports from their representatives abroad and their merchants as much as their diplomats were accustomed to describe the countries which they visited (Marco Foscarini, *Della Letteratura veneziana*, Padua, 1752, pp. 409–12. *Relazioni degli Ambasciatori veneti al Senato*, ed. E. Alberi, serie prima, vol. i, p. xx). The empirical diplomatic methods of northern Europe often produced better results than the systematic diplomacy of the Italians; and the same is partly true of diplomatic relations. See as a non-Italian example the 'Relation de l'ambassade envoyée par Philippe le Bon en Portugal 1428–9' published by L. P. Gachard in his *Documents inédits concernant l'histoire de Belgique*, Brussels, 1833–5, ii. 63–91.

there exists a distinction between the *De Occupatione Regni Anglie* and the official relations. In the first place Mancini was writing what was at best only a semi-official report for the information of Angelo Cato, who, however influential, was not a sovereign head of state. It is more pertinent to note that, although Mancini is not known to have composed another historical work, he evidently wrote the *De Occupatione* consciously as an historian, not as a diplomatic correspondent.

Relations designed as memoranda for statesmen aimed necessarily at achieving an effect of finality by reducing as far as possible the course of events to a static situation. Mancini's outlook was, however, looking for change; and nowhere is this characteristic more evident than at the termination of his treatise, when as his knowledge of events ended abruptly he was left thinking what sort of a ruler Richard III might turn out to be.[1]

There seems in the *De Occupatione Regni Anglie* little trace of animus or prejudice—save for the assumption that the duke of Gloucester was all along aiming at the crown—and, apart from the ecclesiastics such as Bourchier, Rotherham, and possibly Morton, the leading personalities among the lords, with the exception perhaps of Rivers, are delineated as avid for power and pleasure. For an author of successful moral and devotional works, he is remarkable for having recorded events from a wholly human and secular standpoint. The divine and supernatural are nowhere involved. Holy orders[2] and rights of sanctuary are considered exclusively in the light of their relevance to current affairs.[3]

Both Dominic Mancini and Philippe de Comines wrote at the behest of Angelo Cato. The former was an ecclesiastic and an Italian while the latter was a layman and a Fleming. Mancini, so far as we know, wrote exclusively in Latin, whereas Comines the run-away Fleming, whose career was made by Louis XI, wrote in French, a language which he handled far better than most Frenchmen. Mancini and Comines were both anxious to show that they regarded men's actions and motives objectively. Mancini, whose published work was to earn for him a reputation as a moralist, refrained equally from cynicism and moralization when dealing with historical events. On the contrary Comines the layman could

---

[1] P. 104, l. 10.   [2] P. 90, l. 16.   [3] P. 80, l. 5.

scarcely ever resist the pleasure either of recounting events as a hard-bitten man of the world or of drawing edifying and trite conclusions from the lessons of history.

The *De Occupatione* has several not altogether negligible defects. It was perhaps understandable that Mancini should be unsound on English geography. His view of events was unmistakeably that of a foreign visitor who had been in London throughout his stay in the country. Equally pardonable was his failure to discover that English lords did not necessarily hold the bulk of their lands in those places which provided them with their principal titles.[1] More disappointing was his failure to provide some factual detail about the assembly at Westminster which connived at the deposition of Edward V and accepted Richard of Gloucester's claim to the throne.[2] However the most serious historiographical flaw in Mancini's text was his disregard of chronology. It was bad enough to get the exact date of King Edward's death wrong by two days, but his omission to give the dates of the month when describing important events like the death of Hastings constitutes a serious blemish. Certainly the humanist trained historians paid as little attention as possible to chronology[3]; and even an exceptional representative of this school of historiography such as Polydore Vergil seems to keep to a minimum his references to actual dates in the text of his work. Still Mancini displays the worst side of the literary approach to history, when he contents himself with expressions such as *paucis post diebus*[4] or when at the conclusion of his work he provides in a rather round about way a clue to the lapse of time covered by his narrative between the death of King Edward and the coronation of King Richard.

As a rule Mancini does not disclose the sources of his information; but it looks as though he enjoyed during the last period of Edward IV's reign direct access to the court or at least had an informant who did so. If this informant had been one of the great lords, either ecclesiastical or lay, whom Mancini mentions it is difficult not to think that his narrative would have been in certain

---

[1] See below, p. 70. Historical notes to the text, no. 36.
[2] See below, p. 96, l. 29.
[3] Fueter, *Geschichte der neueren Historiographie*, p. 19.
[4] See below, p. 82, l. 11.

respects more precise. Pietro Carmeliano¹ could have introduced Mancini to the court and could certainly have told him something about the literary education of the young Edward V. In any event it may be assumed that the story of the strategem adopted by the Genoese commanders to escape from the fleet commanded by Sir Edward Woodville was recounted to Mancini by an Italian probably himself attached to the Genoese merchants in England.²

The only time that Mancini attributes specific information to an individual, whom he names, is when he appeals to John Argentine as having stated—'referebat Argentinus medicus'—that the young king, Edward V, felt himself to be awaiting death in the Tower.³ Although he does not claim that Argentine had told him personally of the king's premonition, Argentine is in fact among the various Englishmen whom Mancini mentions by name the one most likely to have given him confidential information. While Hastings or the bishop of Ely on account of their high rank and office were, quite apart from reasons of discretion, unlikely to impart confidences to a visiting foreign clerk, there was no such social gulf between the two clerics Argentine and Mancini. Argentine may have wanted the truth about his former master, Edward V, to become known abroad and can have had little, at least in the immediate future, to expect from Richard III. What is more Argentine on his own showing knew at least some Italian or rather Venetian; and this is a particularly relevant point if, as

---

[1] On whom see R. Weiss, *Humanism in England during the Fifteenth Century*, pp. 139, 169–72, 176. The verses in praise of spring which Carmeliano presented to Edward, then Prince of Wales, were dated Easter Day (7 April) 1482 from Rolls House so that it is natural to suppose that Carmeliano was employed in some capacity in the chancery at Rolls House. B.M., Royal MS. 12A, xxix, appears to be the presentation copy. Carmeliano is better known for another Latin poem on St. Catherine, addressed to Sir Robert Brackenbury, constable of the Tower under Richard III. Bodleian, Laud MS. 501 [apparently the author's own copy] contains in the preface (ff. 1–2) the well-known eulogy of Richard III. An undated edition of the *De quatuor Virtutibus* (B.M., 8406, d.19: Bodleian, Arch Ae 99) contains on the title-page a few lines of Latin verse by Carmeliano in praise of Mancini and his work as though to suggest that the two men were known to each other.

This edition has neither printer's name nor place of publication, but it should be attributed to Richard Pynson at London. The date is less certain, but on typographical grounds it can be assigned to about 1520. This information I owe to the kindness of Dr. D. M. Rogers of the Bodleian Library.

[2] See below, p. 86.   [3] See below, p. 92, l. 14.

seems probable, Mancini knew little or no English.[1] Argentine's connexion with Italy is known from his curious preference for inscribing in all his books and manuscripts save one his name and ownership written in the Italian of Venice.[2] This use of the Venetian form of Italian points to a sojourn at the university of Padua, a not unlikely place for an Englishman interested in medicine to visit; and if, as Dr. Rhodes conjectures, Argentine's visit to Italy took place at a time between 1473 and 1476[3] he would have acquired what knowledge he had of the language prior to Mancini's visit to England.

Similarly the only time when Mancini records an historical circumstance, which he claims to have witnessed himself, is when he goes out of his way to state that he saw men weep in talking of Edward V after the king's disappearance in the Tower.[4] This report of the uncontrolled grief evoked by the disappearance of Edward V and Richard duke of York is relevant to another question, that of the moral sentiments and standards current among their contemporaries. One of the hardest tasks facing a historian is to determine what were at any given period the issues which aroused pity or indignation, or in other words to decide in which directions earlier generations were sensitive rather than relatively callous. The sources available for the English fifteenth century do not lend themselves readily, apart from rare exceptions mainly devotional and domestic in character,[5] to this type of investigation.

It is always easy to postulate that different moralities at different times governed the behaviour and feelings of men; but this sort of explanation belongs to the category of facile assumptions liable to be punctured by a notorious and well-attested historical fact. Pre-modern sentiment toward the young differed considerably from that of recent generations. One has only to remember that the forcible marriage of children by their parents for the material

---

[1] See above, p. 16.
[2] D. E. Rhodes, *John Argentine Provost of King's, his Life and Library*, Amsterdam, 1967, p. 12. See also below, n. 89.
[3] *Ib.* p. 12.   [4] See below, p. 92.
[5] For example Margery Kempe's autobiographical account of her religious experiences (*The Book of Margery Kempe*, ed. S. B. Meech and H. E. Allen, *Early English Text Society*, original series, 1940, 212) and the last letter written by William de la Pole, duke of Suffolk, to his son printed *Paston Letters*, ii. 142–3.

gains of dowry and dower was accepted practice throughout society. However the killing of children for reasons of State was regarded with aversion; and in fact it was one of the rumours—probably unfounded—raked up against the unpopular John Tiptoft, earl of Worcester, at the time of his execution[1] in 1470. That royal children could not disappear in the Tower without arousing compassion is sufficiently confirmed by the testimony of Mancini. Nothing could have been more circumspect in all matters relating to the disappearance of Edward IV's sons than the official attitude during the reign of Henry VII[2]; but the act of attainder passed against Richard III in King Henry's first parliament 1485-6 contained one very unusual charge that of 'shedding infants' blood'.[3] By this date attainders of the losing side in the latest trial of strength were conventional in form; and words so abnormal such as these can only be understood as an appeal to popular sentiment for the lost Edward V and his brother.

The period was one in which the Holy Innocents were held in reverence and some fear. The day of the week on which their feast fell was deemed to be unlucky throughout the forthcoming year—their blood still crying to heaven.[4] All the more interesting then to note that the *marginalia* written, apparently in Henry VII's reign, in the *Great Chronicle of London* against the crucial passage for the disappearance of the Princes run as follows: *Innocentes, Mors Innocentium*.[5] King Henry's court astrologer, William Parron, when embarking on the delicate question of the Princes' death in the course of an astrological exercise dedicated to the king, chose as the relevant chapter heading, *De innocentibus*.[6]

[1] Vespasiono da Bisticci, *Vite di Uomini illustri del secolo XV*, ed. P. d'Ancona and E. Aeschlimann, Milan, 1951, pp. 227-8.

[2] C. A. J. Armstrong, 'An Italian astrologer at the court of Henry VII', *Italian Renaissance Studies, A Tribute to the late Cecilia M. Ady*, London, 1960, pp. 447-9.

[3] *Rotuli Parliamentorum*, vi. 276a.

[4] On this superstition, current in England, e.g. the day of Edward IV's coronation, see J. Huizinga 'Een merkwaardig bijgeloof, Onnoozele Kinderen, als ongeluksdag', *Tien Studien*, Haarlem, 1926, pp. 240-8; and in the author's *Verzamelde Werken*, iv (1949) 212-18. I do not know of this valuable study having been translated into English or French.

[5] *Great Chronicle*, pp. xxii, 234, 236. At about the same date a similar notation in the manuscript B.M. Vitellius A, xvi, published by Kingsford *Chronicles of London*, p. 191, 'The Deth of the Innocentes'.

[6] Armstrong, *op. cit.*, p. 448, n. 5. quoting Oxford, Bodleian, Selden Supra, MS. 77, ff. 17vo, 18ro.

In January 1484 the chancellor of France, Guillaume de Rochefort, when addressing the States-General assembled at Tours, accused Richard III of murdering his nephews, the sons of Edward IV.[1] The point of the chancellor's speech was to rally support behind the new king of France, the young Charles VIII, so as to preserve royal authority, which was seriously jeopardized by the reaction against the absolutist government of the late king, Louis XI. In the course of his speech which congratulated his hearers alike on the continuity of the French royal succession and on the loyalty of themselves and their countrymen to the reigning house the chancellor somewhat complacently directed their attention to the very different conditions prevailing in England where disloyalty was rife leading to the frequent deposition and murder of kings culminating in the recent and extraordinary crime of Richard III. The allusion to English conditions, though sufficiently startling since the two kingdoms were not officially or actively at war, was in keeping with the tradition of fifteenth-century French reaction to the insecurity of the English crown. French opinion had never wholly recovered from the shock of Richard II's deposition less than three years after his marriage to Isabelle de France. The 'regicidal proclivities of the English'[2] had been acidly commented on in 1444 by no less a person than Jean Jouvenel des Ursins; and subsequently another councillor of Charles VII, Noël de Fribois, produced a catalogue of murdered English monarchs.

Against a background such as this and allowing for the circumstances in which the States-General were convened the chancellor's accusation against Richard III may be better understood, but it remains—at any time and place—an amazing outburst for an official allocution.[3] The French chancery was not prone to

[1] J. Masselin, *Journal des Etats-généraux de France tenus à Tours en 1484*, C.D.I.H.F. (1835), p. 38, and see below, p. 24, n. 1.

[2] An expression borrowed from Mr. P. S. Lewis, a Welshman, whose valuable study 'Two pieces of fifteenth-century Political Iconography' (*Journal of the Warburg and Courtauld Institutes*, xxvii [1964] 317–20) first drew attention to this theme in contemporary French opinion.

[3] 'Satis sit e proximis Anglis proferre testimonium. Aspicite, quaeso, quidnam post mortem regis Eduardi in ea terra contigerit, ejus scilicet jam adultos et egregios liberos impune trucidari et regni diadema in horum extinctorem, populis faventibus, delatum.' From this point the chancellor reviewed the violent course of English history since the Conquest. J. Masselin, *Journal des Etats-généraux de France tenus à Tours, loc. cit.*

random utterances; and everything else known about Guillaume de Rochefort indicates a learned and rather staid personality,[1] who would scarcely have committed himself to such a statement unless he possessed special intelligences in respect of the subject matter.

Mancini may very well have contributed directly or indirectly to the chancellor's information on the subject. In the first place, there was Angelo Cato, the recipient of Mancini's treatise, who as a former councillor of Louis XI and as archbishop of Vienne could have ready access to the chancellor. At a slightly later date Cato and the chancellor's brother, Gui de Rochefort, were members of the same literary circle in Paris. The whereabouts of Cato in January 1484 are uncertain; but early in March 1484 he was summoned in a professional capacity, that of physician, from Tours to attend Louis duke of Orleans, who had fallen ill on the way from Orleans to Blois.[2]

As for Mancini, he finished his study of Richard III's usurpation on 1 December 1483 at Beaugency,[3] where Charles VIII and his court were staying from 9 November to 22 November 1483 when the king removed to Notre-Dame-de-Cléry[4] on the opposite left bank of the Loire. Here save for a short visit to nearby Orleans the king and court remained for the first half of December 1483, during which period the chancellor was at hand presiding over the royal councils.[5] Evidence for any connexion between Mancini and Guillaume de Rochefort, chancellor of France, rests exclusively on three poems which Mancini addressed to the chancellor and which were printed in 1484.[6] The chancellor indeed was a man of literary interests and frequented in so far as his duties permitted

---

[1] J. Mangin, 'Guillaume de Rochefort, conseiller de Charles le Téméraire et chancelier de France', *Ecole des Chartes, Positions des Thèses*, 1936, pp. 117-23. For the scholarship and political ideas of Guillaume de Rochefort see F. Saxl, 'The classical inscription in Renaissance Art and Politics', *Journal of the Warburg and Courtauld Institutes*, iv (1940-1) 37-42.

[2] R. Maulde-la-Clavière, *Histoire de Louis XII*, Paris, 1890, ii. 87.

[3] Loiret; arr. Orleans.

[4] Modern, Cléry. Loiret; arr. Orleans; can. Beaugency. See the itinerary of Charles VIII in P. Pelicier, *Essai sur le gouvernement de la dame de Beaujeu*, Paris, 1882, p. 292.

[5] 'Procès verbaux de cinq séances du grand conseil du roi Charles VIII tenues au mois de décembre 1483, communication de M. Rossignol', *Bulletin du comité de la Langue, de l'Histoire et des Arts de la France*, iii (1855-6) 248, 250, 254, 257.

[6] See above, p. 6, n. 5.

the circle of scholars around Robert Gaguin in Paris to which Mancini also belonged. Judging from these three poems, Mancini had found in Guillaume de Rochefort a kind and helpful friend.

If the verses of Mancini are admissible evidence of some acquaintance existing about this time between himself and the chancellor, the two men were at least geographically close to one another in November and December 1483 when Mancini finished his treatise only a few weeks before the chancellor had to address the States-General in January 1484. The conviction of Mancini when he left England that King Richard either had or was about to rid himself of his nephews could, if communicated to Guillaume de Rochefort, have confirmed the chancellor's belief in King Richard's guilt, a belief based presumably on other reports about which we at present know nothing.

While the chancellor of France was treating the States-General at Tours to his account of the latest murders in the English royal family coming on top of no less than twenty-six rebellions since the Conquest,[1] the earl of Richmond, the future Henry VII, recently returned from his abortive cruise off the south-west coast of England was waiting in Brittany for another chance to invade. During this period of nearly two years waiting in Brittany and ultimately in France the earl of Richmond had to study closely opinion at the courts of France and Brittany, if he was to avoid being handed over to Richard III let alone secure the help he required for a new expedition.[2] His success in understanding the

[1] 'Et si paulo altius ejus gentis [the English] historias repetamus, constabit vix duos aut ad summum tres reges quietos fuisse, sineque mutatione regnum assecutos, quin a populo facile in alienam sobolem veris relictis haeredibus, transferretur. Legimus siquidem quod post tempora Guillelmi, qui regionem illam armis vindicavit, haec ejus regni nona translatio est, et ab exordio instituti regni vicesima sexta.' J. Masselin, *Journal des Etats-généraux de France tenus à Tours en 1484*, p. 38. See also above, p. 22. Among his occasional verse printed with his *Libellus de quatuor virtutibus* in December 1484 Mancini published a piece 'De prima Etate Caroli regis Francorum Carmen undecasyllabum' which recalls the gathering of the States-General at Tours:

'Inde Turonam properant in urbem
Nobiles omnes: properatque clerus:
Et suos mittens popularis ordo
Convenit illuc.   *De quatuor Virtutibus*, Paris, 1484.

[2] As will be seen (below, p. 38, n. 5) Angelo Cato, Mancini's patron, was, judging from the papers in his possession, something of a specialist on Breton affairs among the councillors of the French king.

prevalent mood at the court of France is sufficiently proved by the fact that he sailed well equipped from Harfleur at the end of July 1485.[1]

No one then had better reasons than the earl of Richmond for getting to know the views about English kingship entertained by those who governed France for the young Charles VIII. He could not have failed to perceive the damage done abroad to the dignity and authority of the English crown by publicity given to murders within the royal house of England. The discreet silence regarding the fate of The Princes which Henry VII was to maintain has aroused astonishment and even encouraged suspicions that Henry himself may have had them put to death. This attitude seriously underrates King Henry's concern to rehabilitate the reputation of the English crown abroad. From the outset he cultivated intensely diplomatic relations with the courts of Europe; and no sooner had he children of his own to offer than he entered the dynastic marriage market in an eager search for promising matrimonial alliances between his own and other ruling houses. How damaging to the English crown, which Henry VII like every king of England identified with his own family, to afford the least publicity to the disappearance of a recent king and his brother whose sister was until her death in 1503 King Henry's queen and the mother of his children. Official publicity of that sort was not calculated to enhance the dignity of England let alone to encourage marriages into the English royal house.

If Mancini survived, as seems not impossible, to about 1500, he would have witnessed the diffusion of his writings devotional and moral; but thereafter his name though not so much his works fell into oblivion. In Italy, where none of his works were published, he was so far forgotten that by the mid-century his books were known only by hearsay and he himself was thought to have been a German.[2] Henceforth the compilers of bio-bibliographical dictionaries contented themselves with repeating in some form or

---

[1] *The Anglica Historia of Polydore Vergil*, ed. D. Hay, *Camden Society*, lxxiv (1950) 3. A. L. Rowse, *Bosworth Field and the Wars of the Roses*, 1966, pp. 206–14.
[2] Lilius Gregorius Gyraldus Ferrarensis, *Dialogi duo de Poetis nostrorum Temporum*, Florence, 1551, p. 76.

other the notice of Trithemius.¹ Moreri and Bayle the greatest of the seventeenth-century historical encyclopaedists ignored Mancini; and only with the rise of modern bibliographical studies in the eighteenth century did he receive attention from Fabricius and Freytag as the author of rare incunabels.²

ANGELO CATO

ANGELO CATO was a notable personality. His successful public career was based on his professional skill as a physician, at first in Naples, subsequently in France. His learned interests in astrology and philosophy were associated directly with medicine. If he was a friend of humanists his personal studies judging by his own writings and other scraps of evidence were remote from the humanists' passion for poetry and rhetoric. Other original aspects of his intellectual activity were his enthusiasm for publication by means of the printing press and his enlightened curiosity in contemporary history.

For several centuries Cato's reputation rested on reputedly well-attested examples of his success as an astrologer rather than on his responsibility for asking Comines to write the *Mémoires*. Admittedly his patronage of Comines resulted in this misleading reputation getting into circulation, for Denis Sauvage, the historiographer of Henry II of France, who produced the first critical edition of Comines's *Mémoires*, also published as a preamble to the text a ridiculous, though apparently quite genuine, sixteenth-century account of Cato.³ This source by asserting that Cato was a Neapolitan exile of the Angevin faction, who reached the court of Burgundy in the suite of Nicolas of Calabria, the Angevin aspirant to the hand of Mary heiress of Burgundy, effectively misled several generations of French historians.⁴ It⁵ was, however, mainly

---
[1] Conrad Gesner, *Bibliotheca universalis*, Zurich, 1545, ff. 214–15. Josias Simler, *Bibliotheca*, Zurich, 1574, p. 173. Antonio Possevino, *Apparatus sacer*, Venice, 1603–6, i. 416.

[2] Fabricius, *Bibliotheca latina*, v. 13; Freytag, *Adparatus litterarius*, iii, 8–10.

[3] Comines, *Mémoires*, ed. Sauvage, sig. aa v, aa vi.

[4] For the French editors of Comines see B. de Mandrot, (1901–3) 1, l. n. 1. Benedetto Croce, *op. cit.*, p. 163 points out that the older Italian historians of the Neapolitan provinces divided Cato's public career among three persons of the same name, since they were so perplexed in bringing together his multifarious activities.

[5] This piece of historiographical trash was composed from the recollections of

concerned with Cato's powers of divination. Thus, Cato had told Louis XI at Tours of the death of Charles the Bold on the very day and hour that the duke of Burgundy succumbed at the battle of Nancy.[1] Similarly, as regards Guillaume Briçonnet, one of the authorities upon whose evidence the account published by Denis Sauvage reposed, Cato had warned him in advance of the risk of death by crossing a dangerous ferry; and in the event Briçonnet only just escaped by hanging on to an overhanging willow-branch when the boat duly overturned. More spectacular as an example of long-range prediction Cato had foretold to Guillaume Briçonnet that he, then a married man, would end his career as a prelate and would only narrowly miss becoming pope.

Comines had been far too circumspect to introduce marvels of this sort into his *Mémoires*. Instead he briefly reported that he had heard Frederick, prince of Taranto, declare that Cato had written reports to Italy several days before the engagements at Grandson and Morat forecasting correctly the defeat in each battle of Charles the Bold at the hands of the Swiss. With his habitual caution, Comines contented himself with saying that according to some people the advice which Cato proffered to Frederick of Taranto was instrumental in deciding him, the prince, to leave the camp of Charles the Bold on the eve of the battle of Morat. This was, at worst, a pardonable piece of flattery on the part of Comines to Angelo Cato for whom after all he was writing his *Mémoires*.[2]

Jean Briçonnet, son of Guillaume Briçonnet, Jean-François de Cardonne and Renaldo d'Albiano, a pro-Angevin Neapolitan exile dwelling in France. The first two are well authenticated. When it was written Jean-François de Cardonne (ob. 1526) was dead already and Jean Briçonnet, who lived until 1548, was still alive (*Catalogue des actes de François Ier*, v [1892] 807–8: G. Bretonneau, *Histoire généalogique de la maison des Briçonnets*, Paris, 1621, p. 41). The memorandum then was according to its own internal evidence written down between 1526 and 1548.

[1] The battle was fought on 5 January 1477: on the following 9 January Louis XI writing to the seigneur de Craon was still sceptical regarding the death of Charles the Bold, *Lettres de Louis XI*, vi. 112.

[2] 'Ledit prince [Frederick] print congié dudit duc [Charles] le soir devant la bataille [Morat], en obeissant au commandement du roy son père [Ferrante, king of Naples], car, à la première bataille [Grandson] s'estoit trouvé comme homme de bien. Aussi disent aucuns qu'il usa de vostre conseil, monsr. de Vienne [Angelo Cato]. Car je luy ouy dire et tesmongner, quant il fut arrivé devers le roy [Louis XI] et au duc d'Astoly, appelé le conte Julio, et plusieurs autres que, de la première et seconde bataille vous en avyez escript en Ytalie

Possibly Comines was at this point making a discreet allusion to Cato's acknowledged skill in astrological prediction of events. On the other hand Comines may equally well be paying tribute to the capability of Cato for diagnosing by normal rational standards the probable outcome of an impending military encounter. After all Cato's master, Frederick prince of Taranto, was not alone in choosing to quit the Burgundian camp before Morat rather than risk another conflict with the Swiss under the dubious generalship of Charles the Bold. Anthony Woodville, Earl Rivers, who to our knowledge had no occult advice about the duke of Burgundy's military chances in the next battle, prudently withdrew from the duke's army shortly before the same battle of Morat (22 June 1476).[1]

Once only does Comines invoke the astrological powers of Cato, and this passage was apparently written or at least re-touched after the death of Cato, when it came to the succession (7 October 1496) of Frederick, formerly prince of Taranto, to the throne of Naples. In this context, Comines does indeed affirm that Cato had frequently assured him 'parlant par astrologie' that Frederick would become king. Of course judged by fifteenth-century standards, a forecast of this sort based on a personal horoscope astrologically considered would have been regarded as strictly scientific.[2] Indeed Cato himself in an original letter still extant and addressed to Pope Sixtus IV did not hesitate to remind him of the prediction which he, Cato, had long ago addressed to him from Benevento foretelling his elevation to the papacy.[3] Guillaume Briçonnet and Jean-François de Cardonne, two of the personalities named by Sauvage as his authorities for information relating to the occult powers of Cato, had been known to Comines, who as a hard-headed Fleming had however made a practice of avoiding the inclusion in his *Mémoires* of anything excessively irrational.

---

et dit ce qui en advint plusieurs jours avant qu'elles fussent.' *Mémoires*, ii. 118. The first person to credit Cato with predicting by astrology the overthrow of Charles the Bold, duke of Burgundy, was Symon de Pharès, himself a professional astrologer. Pharès, *Recueil des plus célèbres astrologues*, p. 265.

[1] *Dépêches des ambassadeurs milanais sur les campagnes de Charles le Hardi . . . de 1474 à 1477*, ed. F. de Gingins la Sarra, Paris and Geneva, 1858, ii, 233, 236.

[2] Comines, *Mémoires*, iii. 34.

[3] For this letter see below, p. 39, n. 3.

During the time that he occupied a chair in the university of Naples Cato described himself as *Angelo Cato Supinas de Benevento, philosophus et medicus*.[1] Indeed he was born at Supino near Frossinone within the Patrimony of Saint Peter and his family originated from Benevento, the papal enclave within the kingdom of Naples.[2] He was born presumably well before 1440 as by 1461 he was described officially as 'maestro nella medicina'.[3] His earliest known work is a medical treatise *Liber de Epidemia* of which the extant manuscript is dated 15 May 1464 and was offered to the magistrates of Benevento.[4] It looks as if at this date he was the municipal physician of the city of Benevento. Italian cities of the period not uncommonly demanded of their physicians a medical-astrological report in the form of an almanack of the year.[5]

Cato appears to have been one of the masters whom King Ferrante summoned to Naples when he reopened the university there, which had been shut for some years consequent upon the disturbances in the kingdom following the death of the king's father, Alfonso V of Aragon, in 1458. Cato was in receipt of 120 ducats' stipend for his lectures given in the academic year 1465-6[6]; but at first he seems to have been only off and on at the university of Naples, and in June 1469 he wrote from Benevento to Matteo dell'Acquila, an abbot of the Celestinian order and an Aristotelian philosopher, who taught at Naples from 1469 to 74.[7] The following year, however, Cato resumed his place at the university; and from 1470 until 1474, when he departed with King

---

[1] In the epistle dedicatory of his work *De Cometa*, 1472 (see below, p. 32) and in the dedication of his edition of Mesue, 1474. The medal dating from his residence in Naples omits, obviously for reasons of space, *de Benevento*. See plate facing p. 26.

[2] A critical consideration of the evidence in B. Croce, 'Il personaggio italiano che esortò il Commynes a scrivere i Mémoires: Angelo Catone', *Vite di avventure di fede e di passione*, Bari, 1936, p. 163.

[3] In a grant of land from the papal governor of Benevento, Borgia, *Memorie istoriche della pontificia città di Benevento*, iii. 397.

[4] In the title of this work he already describes himself as 'philosophus et medicus'. De Marinis 'Nota su Angelo Catone di Benevento' in *Miscellanea . . . in memoria di Luigi Ferrari*, p. 228.

[5] At Bologna the university was responsible for supplying the city with an annual prognostication of weather, harvests and epidemics, G. Zaccagnini, *Storia del Studio di Bologna durante il Rinascimento*, in *Biblioteca dell' Archivum romanicum*, serie 1, t. xiv, Geneva, 1930, pp. 55-7.

[6] Cannavale, *Lo Studio di Napoli*, pp. 11-14, document no. 13.

[7] *Ib.*, pp. 45-9. Tummulillis, *Notabilia temporum*, pp. 151-6.

Ferrante's second son Federigo on a journey abroad, Cato was paid, as indeed were all the regent masters and professors at Naples, out of the royal treasury, for his regular lectures on natural philosophy and astrology.[1]

It does not appear to be known at what date Cato took orders; but it is generally accepted that he began his career as a layman.[2] It is known that he left children and there is no good reason for thinking that they were bastards. Indeed they were mentioned in his will, without any qualification as to legitimacy as was normal in contemporary testamentary references to illegitimate children. His son Lucrezio subsequently caused his father considerable embarrassment, by his political opposition to King Ferrante, Cato's old patron, but instead of disclaiming him as illegitimate Cato did his best to smooth over the affair with the Neapolitan royal family.[3]

At Naples he was in close connexion with the court of the ruling Aragonese dynasty. His association with princes and politics was henceforth to be an enduring feature of Cato's life. He became one of the court physicians of King Ferrante of Naples[4] for whom he composed a curious work on poisons designed to provide an antidote for every conceivable case whether accidental or criminal.[5] His scholarly interest in manuscripts, which remained with him into old age, was no doubt fostered in the splendid collection of the Aragonese library at Naples of which he was also a curator.[6] His first printed publication was dedicated to John of Aragon,[7] a son of King Ferrante whom his father put into orders at a tender age; and througha ccompanying Federigo, another of the king's sons, on a journey beyond the Alps, he, Cato, was able to seize the chance of a brilliant career in France.

[1] Cannavale, *op. cit.*, documents nos. 23, 43, 68, 87, 109, 132, 157, 187, 720, 751, 768, 792, 829, 842, 864. In his dedicatory epistle addressed to King Ferrante of his edition of Silvaticus he, Cato, shows himself fully aware of the fact that his stipend was paid to him direct by the Crown, *op. cit.*, f. 1ro. See also Croce, *op. cit.*, p. 164, n. 6.

[2] See a discussion of the question by Croce, *op. cit.*, p. 164.

[3] See below, p. 46.

[4] Mesue, *Practica de medicinis*, (1475) f. 1vo.

[5] Apparently only extant in a seventeenth-century manuscript copy Vienna, Nationalbibliothek, Cod. 11245 (*Tabulae Codicum MSS. praeter graecos et orientales in Bibliotheca Palatina vindobonensi asservatorum*, ed. Academia Caesarea vindobonensis, vi. [Vienna, 1873] 296).

[6] Vienna, Nationalbibliothek, Cod. 11245, ff. 55ro, 60ro.

[7] Eubel, *Hierarchia catholica*, ii. 19. *Gesamtkatalog der Wiegendrucke*, no. 2309. De Marinis, *La Biblioteca napoletana dei Re d'Aragona*, i. 85–96.

Cato's activity at Naples as author and editor was rendered remarkable by his use of the printing press as a means of divulgation. He was one of the first to make use of the press which had only recently been introduced to Naples[1]; and his devotion to printing proved to be lifelong. Perhaps the most worthwhile benefit which he was later to confer on the church of Vienne, after he had become its archbishop, was to provide the diocesan clergy with a printed breviary.[2] Another small but significant fact is that the only surviving book, which is known through his autograph *ex-libris* to have belonged to Cato, contains a printed not a manuscript text.[3]

The dedicatory epistles with which he prefaced his Neapolitan publications indicate the range of advantages which he foresaw in the production of books from the printing press. In the first place there was his scholarly concern to eliminate misreadings in manuscripts and to establish a text on sound authority.[4] Cato regarded a pure text as indispensable to the advancement of scholarship; and on this point he is in alignment with the humanists with whom he had otherwise little in common. He did not shrink from republishing a book when in his estimation an earlier edition fell short of his requirements.[5] Secondly he was very aware of the

---

[1] After 1470: Fava and Bresciano, *La Stampa a Napoli nel xv secolo*, ii. 1–16.

[2] *Gesamtkatalog der Wiegendrucke*, no. 5507 see also below, p. 41.

[3] This is a copy of the work of Ariminensis to which reference was made above, p. 2. The example Paris B.N., Rés. D.54, carries the inscription 'Angeli Catonis: Archiepiscopi et comitis Vienensium et primi galliarum primatis et amicorum codex: parisii: MCCCC LXXXVI: prima: mai' in a fine humanist hand similar to the letter (see below, p. 39) which Cato wrote *manu sua* to Pope Sixtus IV.

[4] 'Ego quoque ut ingenio industriaque mea possim multis prodesse laborem suscepi non quidem condendi novi operis sed eius quod videbatur iam obliteratum conquirandi et emendandi ac dandi in lucem in communem usum'. Cato's edition of Silvaticus, f. 1vo printed in Fava and Bresciano, *op. cit.*, ii. 76. Elsewhere in the same preface he claimed no doubt rightly, that the MS of Silvaticus in the royal library at Naples contained the best text, but that it was so jealously guarded that it could never be easily transcribed and that in so far as this work had been copied it was 'magna tamen ex parte depravatum'.

[5] In the dedication of his edition of the *Tractatus de febribus* by Guainerius he speaks of an earlier edition presumably that printed by Conrad of Paderborn (Copinger, no. 2804) in the following terms: 'Fuerat quidem ante ab aliis nescio quibus artificiis impressus sed adeo inepte ut indignum iudicaverim permittere vulgari ulterius ... tam egregium utilemque libellum nisi diligentiore prius cura emendaretur', f. 2vo. The two editions may be compared in the British Museum. The one prepared by Cato IB. 29383 and the one printed by Conrad of Paderborn IB. 29887.

obstacle to the progress of learning, medical learning in his case, caused by the scarcity and costliness of manuscripts.[1] Thirdly he brought to his work of editing a sense of taste. He was proud that a book should be printed in fine characters[2]; and here again he is not so far removed from the aesthetics of humanist scholars. No doubt his good relations with the German printer, Bertold Rying, then established at Naples assisted Cato in assuring the quality of his publications.[3]

Between 1472 and 1475 Cato published four books at Naples. The first, of which he was also the author, was astrological while the other three, of which he was the editor, were medical. Of course, the two subjects were then combined.

His study of the comet that dismayed Europe in January 1472[4] was dated 1 March 1472 and printed by Sixtus Riessinger, the proto-typographer of Naples.[5] A small treatise, it was dedicated to John of Aragon, whose tutor, Pietro Ransano,[6] Dominican friar, classical scholar, and historian, had supplied corroborative data in support of Cato's own observations of the comet.[7] The book was a miscellany. Its theoretical contents were mainly concerned with the defence of astrology against the charge of impiety. The apology was based—as was common in the fifteenth century—on

---

[1] 'Quoniam vero permulti sunt adolescentes acutissimo ingenio qui se ad huiusmodi liberalia studia conferre quidem vellent, sed absterrentur penuria librorum pro quibus coemendis nequaquam eis suppetunt facultates, bono fortasse animo erunt nec referrent pedem si ea sit adhibita diligentia qua absque magno sumptu vulgo codices habeantur.' Silvaticus, *op. cit.*, f. 1ro. Fava and Bresciano, *op. cit.*, ii. 72. Cato did not exaggerate when he pleaded that the cost of manuscripts was a hindrance to students. Stephanus Illarius paid 22 gold ducats for a MS. of the *Expositio problematum Aristotelis* by Abano, which Illarius edited and had printed at Mantua in 1475. See f. 4vo of that edition (Hain, no. 16; Pellechet, no. 11).

[2] In the dedications of the *Tractatus de febribus* and of the *Practica de medicinis* both printed by Bertold Rying, Cato claims as follows: 'Curavi enim ut pulchris caracteribus ... opus imprimeretur.'

[3] In the dedication of *Tractatus de febribus*, the printer, Bertold Rying, is referred to by Cato as 'optimo artifice quo ego familiariter utor'.

[4] Seen in England Warkworth, *Chronicle*, p. 22. For the excitement which it evoked in Europe see Lynn Thorndike, *A History of Magic and Experimental Science*, iv (Columbia, 1934) 422–8.

[5] *Gesamtkatalog der Wiegendrucke*, no. 6385. Fava and Bresciano, *La Stampa a Napoli*, ii. 13.

[6] Quétif Echard, *Scriptores ordinis Praedicatorum*, 2 vols., Paris, 1719–21, i. 876–8. De Marinis, *La Biblioteca napolitana dei Re d'Aragona*, i. 85.

[7] *De Cometa*, f. 4ro. Cato acknowledged the help of Ransano in his, Cato's, edition of Silvaticus, *Liber Pandectarum*, f. 1ro.

a cautious interpretation of Acts, I:7. However, Cato's *De Cometa* was intended, among other things, as an astrological almanack setting out to show not only what the comet might portend, but also to bring its meaning into relation with world affairs. In this connexion the treatise provides evidence of its author's relatively early interest in the history of his own times. He was particularly struck by the expansion of Portugal; and, having identified the Canaries with the Fortunate Isles of the ancients, he went on to point out their value as a place of call for Portuguese navigators. He was even prepared to say that the capture of Tangiers by the king of Portugal was the most important single event of the year 1471.[1] At the other end of christendom he recorded the marriage of a Persian emir to a daughter of the emperor of Trebizond.[2] His interpretation of the portents offered by the comet were largely political in character: for example, baronial rebellions to which like earthquakes the kingdom of Naples was subject.[3]

No doubt Cato was busy at work in the royal library preparing his editions[4]; but his publications came in a sudden burst in 1474–1475 just as he was preparing to leave Naples. On 1 April 1474 he completed his edition of the *Liber cibalis et medicinalis pandectarum* of Matthew Silvaticus, who in the days of the gothic splendour of the Angevin kingdom of Naples had been physician to King Robert the Wise (1309–43). It was printed by Arnold of Brussels in a beautiful in-folio volume.[5] On 15 September 1474 Cato finished his edition of the *Tractatus de febribus* by Guainerius,[6] who had taught medicine at Pavia in the first half of the fifteenth century. Whereas he dedicated the Pandects of Silvaticus to King Ferrante, Cato offered the *Tractatus de febribus*, to one of his

---

[1] *De Cometa*, ff. 13ro, 15vo.
[2] *Ib.*, f. 12vo. Theodora, daughter of the emperor John IV and married to Usun Hassan (W. Miller, *Trebizond*, London, 1926, pp. 88–9).
[3] *De Cometa*, ff. 18ro, 26ro.
[4] As already stated (p. 32, n. 1 above) Cato based his edition of Silvaticus on the manuscript in this library. If the Aragonese library at Naples did possess a manuscript of Guainerius *Tractatus de febribus* it has not been traced. The present Paris B.N. MS, latin. 6947 of Mesue, did however belong to the Aragonese library and this is probably the text upon which Cato based his edition of Mesue's *Practica de medicinis*. De Marinis, *La Bibliotheca napoletana dei Re d'Aragona*, ii. 107–8.
[5] Hain, no. 15194. Osler, *Incunabula medica*, p. 24, no. 61.
[6] Fava and Bresciano, *op. cit.*, ii. 87–8. Osler, *op. cit.* p. 24, nos. 60, 65.

former pupils in dialectic, Antonello Bolumbrello, who now lectured on surgery at Naples and had become one of the king's physicians.[1] This spate of publication was abruptly cut short when on 26 October 1474 Cato quitted Naples with Federigo, prince of Taranto, en route for Burgundy. The dedication to his colleagues in the college of physicians at Naples of his edition of Mesue, *Practica de Medicinis*,[2] was dated 26 October 1474, the very day when the prince and his household departed from Naples.[3] The 'Valete' with which Cato closed the dedicatory epistle had an actual as well as a literary meaning. It was not until 12 January 1475, when Cato had left his native country, that the work was printed at Naples by his friend Bertold Rying.

Like many other European sovereigns, King Ferrante of Naples perceived an ideal daughter-in-law in the person of Mary, only child of Charles the Bold, duke of Burgundy. Her foreseeable dowry could be equalled by no other princess of the day. So then Ferrante sent his younger son Federigo on an extensive diplomatic mission through Italy, the ultimate objective of which was the court of Burgundy.[4]

Detained *en route* by diplomatic and military hazards Prince Federigo only met Charles, duke of Burgundy, on 26 September 1475 in Lorraine at Pont-à-Mousson; but from that day until 21 June 1476, the eve of the battle of Morat, when Federigo quitted the Burgundian camp, he was continuously in attendance on the duke. Of the numerous dynastic bidders for the hand of Mary, heiress of Burgundy, none were so completely fooled as the cunning Ferrante and his amiable son Federigo. It is strange that Federigo should have stayed so long in the Burgundian camp; and if Cato was really responsible for his departure on the day before the battle of Morat, he had at least one councillor who, whether from astrology or common sense, had accurately sized up the situation. As it was Federigo transferred too late from the Burgundian to the French court to receive more than a modest matrimonial reward from Louis XI of France, who married him

---

[1] Cannavale, *Lo Studio di Napoli*, document no. 568.
[2] Hain, no. 11117. Osler, *op. cit.*, p. 77, no. 90. Fava and Bresciano, *op. cit.*, ii. 88.
[3] Croce, *op. cit.*, p. 169.
[4] E. Pontieri, *Per la storia del regno di Ferrante I d'Aragona, Re di Napoli* (*Collana storica*, i. Naples, 1947) pp. 69–116.

in 1479 to Anne of Savoy[1] the far from wealthy niece of the queen of France, herself a daughter of Savoy.

Angelo Cato accompanied the prince of Taranto, as his physician, to the court of Burgundy and on to the court of France, where he, Cato, reaped a higher reward than his master. The list of the prince's household certifies Cato's status as the physician: 'Don Angelo de Supino, medico'.[2] His practice of his profession as physician raises a minor question on the reliability of Comines as a memoirist. The duke of Burgundy, as is known from other sources, fell ill[3] following his defeat by the Swiss on 2 March 1476 at Grandson and was, according to Comines, treated by Cato.[4] Having defected from Charles the Bold, Comines never loses an opportunity of portraying the duke as one on the verge of insanity.[5] In this case he invokes the authority of Cato, for whom

[1] Daughter of Amadeus IX, duke of Savoy (ob. 1472) and of Yolande daughter of Charles VII, king of France. Anne's aunt was Charlotte wife of Louis XI of France. For the marriage alliance with Federigo see Pontieri, *op. cit.*, pp. 113–14.
[2] Croce, *op. cit.*, p. 169.
[3] The battle was fought on 2 March but it was not until 13 April 1476 that the Milanese ambassadorial reports referred to Charles's illness (*Dépêches des ambassadeurs milanais sur les campagnes de Charles le Hardi de 1474–77*, ed. Baron Gingins-la-Sarra, Geneva and Paris, 2 vols., 1858, ii. 54). Between 13 April and 11 May 1476, by which date the duke was stated to have recovered, the reports regularly mention Charles's health (*ib.*, ii. 60, 105–7, 111, 118, 129, 147). See also Charles's letters to Dijon, *Correspondence de la mairie de Dijon*, ed. J. Garnier (*Analecta divionensia*) 3 vols., Dijon, 1868–70, i. 185, 188.
[4] *Mémoires*, ii. 117. 129.
[5] The allegations of Comines against the objects of his dislike are the more damaging for being almost invariably circumspect; but reading his account of Charles's illness after Grandson (*Mémoires*, ii. 117, 128–9) one is left with the distinct impression that he wished to convince his readers that the duke of Burgundy had grown mentally deranged. This is incompatible with the Milanese diplomatic reports which show the duke as perfectly *compos mentis* but as suffering from a disorder of the stomach (despatch of 15 April and of 1 May 1476, *Dépêches des ambassadeurs milanais*, ed. Gingins-la-Sarra, ii. 60, 105). Comines suggests that Duke Charles grew his beard as a result of sickness and mental disorder (*loc. cit.*), and, to prove his point, he proceeds to invoke the evidence of Cato, who, he alleges, persuaded the duke to shave. In the first place it appears that Comines has got the order of events wrong, since the duke grew his beard before falling ill. On 29 March 1476 the Milanese despatch reported that Duke Charles on a visit to the duchess of Savoy had told her that he would not shave until he had avenged himself on the Swiss (*Dépêches des ambassadeurs milanais*, ii. 9). On 16 May 1476 another Milanese report (*not* from the Burgundian camp) announced that the duke of Burgundy had had to shave before he could avenge himself on the Swiss because of his illness (*ib.*, ii. 183). Comines, whether from ignorance or design, omitted to record that Duke Charles had resolved not to shave in order to advertise his, Charles's, determination to avenge on the Swiss

he was by then ostensibly writing his *Mémoires*, to confirm his own interpretation that Charles was mentally deranged after the battle of Grandson. It has been held that by his appeal to Cato's own recollection of the events Comines furnishes the strongest proof of his own reliability.[1]

It must not, however, be overlooked that Comines and Cato had alike something to gain by representing Charles the Bold as one beside himself.[2] Comines had to justify his own desertion of the duke of Burgundy, which had taken place as long ago as 8 August 1472.[3] The case with Cato was far less serious; but nevertheless if Charles duke of Burgundy could be shown convincingly to have become mentally unsound after the engagement at Grandson no one could very well criticize Cato for having advised his master Prince Federigo to depart from the Burgundian camp on the eve of the battle of Morat. Comines is our sole authority for the report that Charles the Bold consulted Cato at this period, and this report is not corroborated by the Milanese ambassadorial despatches.[4] These despatches, which furnish an almost day to day account of Duke Charles's health and are careful to name those who had access to him between the battles of Grandson and

---

his defeat at Grandson. There is here a parallel between Charles the Bold and another militarist of slightly later date, Pope Julius II. On his ill-fated campaign of 1510–11 the pope grew his beard to exhibit his inflexible resolve to be avenged upon his foes, as appears in the Raffael portrait of the bearded Julius II (Florence, Uffizi, and Galleria Pitti) for the historiographical and iconographical bibliography of which see L. Dussler, *Raffael, kritisches Verzeichnis der Gemälde Wandbilder und Bildteppiche, Bruckmanns Beiträge zur Kunstwissenschaft*, Munich, 1966, pp. 32–4. The pope's master of ceremonies, Paris de Grassis, was however somewhat uncertain whether Julius II grew his beard because of a malady or in fulfilment of an oath: 'nam ex eo quo Bononiam ex Urbe ingressus est (22 September 1510), nunquam barbam totondit, causante tunc morbo qui tunc coepit ipsum molestare, et sic auto voto aut alia causa ut placet in similibus usque modo barbatus fuerit et est', *Documenti e studi pubblicati per cura della R. Deputazione di Storia patria per le provincie di Romagna*, Bologna, i (1886) 241.

[1] *Mémoires*, ii. 129, n. 3 by the editor J. Calmette.

[2] The extent to which the attitude of Comines towards Charles the Bold was influenced by a desire to justify his abandonment of the duke is one of the central themes considered by J. Dufournet, *La destruction des Mythes dans les Mémoires de Ph. de Commynes* (Publications romanes et françaises, lxxxix) Geneva, 1966 p. 123.

[3] *Mémoires*, i. vi.

[4] The question has been examined by Dufournet, *op. cit.*, p. 123.

Morat, do indeed name an Italian physician, magistro Bartolomeo[1] from Piedmont, as one of the duke's doctors, but they do not mention Cato.

There can be no doubt that Cato arrived at the French court in the household of Federigo. Symon de Pharès a fellow astrologer who talked, according to his own account, much with Cato, when the latter had become archbishop of Vienne, affirms positively that he, Cato, came to France with the prince of Taranto.[2] The absence of any information on this score in the *Mémoires* of Comines is not to be wondered at, for Comines did not offer his writings to Cato to inform him, the archbishop, about his previous movements.

Exactly when he became a physician to Louis XI, king of France, is uncertain; but it was Cato, who came to the aid of the king when in March 1479[3] he suffered some sort of stroke. The story is beautifully told by Comines. The lay courtiers restrained their stricken sovereign from seeking air at the window and not content with shutting the windows carried the king protesting to the fireside. At that moment Cato arrived, ordered the windows to be opened and with the conventional use of a clyster restored Louis XI to consciousness. No wonder Louis XI made the fortune of Cato for the king considered few rewards too high for those who could prolong life or predict the future.[4]

At all events he did not at this period remain continuously in France for in January 1480 he is found at Rome, where he carried out on behalf of the magistrates of Benevento a delicate mission to Sixtus IV.[5] By 1481, however, his position at the court of France as a royal physician and as a king's councillor was established.[6] Exactly how close Cato stood to the king of France we have few

---

[1] In the despatch of Antonius de Aplano, from Lausanne 1 May 1476 *Dépêches des ambassadeurs milanais sur les campagnes de Charles le Hardi de 1474 à 1477*, ed. Gingins-la-Sarra, ii. 105–7.

[2] *Recueil des plus célèbres astrologues*, ed. E. Wickersheimer, p. 265.

[3] The reasons given by Calmette (Comines, *Mémoires*, ii. 280, n. 2) for attributing the king's illness to 1479 rather than 1480 seem convincing.

[4] 'Car oncques homme (Louis XI) ne craignit tant la mort ny ne feït tant de choses pour y cuyder mectre remedde' Comines, *Mémoires*, ii. 316.

[5] Croce, *op. cit.*, p. 171, n. 2, quoting *Regestum Privilegiorum ab anno 1480* in the Biblioteca capitolare at Benevento, see also Borgia, *Memorie storiche di Benevento*, iii. 413.

[6] He was then receiving an annual salary as physician and councillor of 1925 livres tournois. Paris B.N. MS. français, nouvelle acquisition 7639, ff. 274–5ro.

means of telling save from the evidence of Comines, from the inventory of state-papers dating from the reign of Louis XI which remained in Cato's possession and lastly from the simple fact that Louis XI did promote him to the archbishopric of Vienne.

The evidence of Comines it must be conceded is equally flattering alike to himself and to Cato. It is contained in the well-known passage in which Comines describes the confidences that he himself received from the king and proceeds to invoke the recollections of Cato to confirm the king's habit of speaking secretly to those closest to him and of whispering in their ear.[1]

On Cato's death in 1496 an inventory was drawn up of the papers in his possession which concerned the crown of France.[2] None of the memoranda on the list are dated; and some of them from the names of the persons mentioned therein must be ascribed to the latter part of the reign of Charles VIII.[3] Others could equally well belong to the reign of Louis XI or to that of his son Charles VIII.[4] A few, however, certainly come from the reign of Louis XI.[5] Of these entries quite the most interesting is the notice of the ordonnances that the king had resolved to enact.[6] This memorandum of which Cato possessed a copy should be a register

---

[1] 'Car vous scavez, Monsieur de Vienne, nostre roy parloit fort privément et souvent à ceulx qui estoient plus prochains de luy ... et aymoit à parler en l'oreille', *Mémoires*, ii. 40.

[2] Paris B.N. MS. français 2896, f. 103 a list comprising 57 separate items, some of which were quite substantial, e.g. 'item, troys ou quatre cahiers faisans mencion du roy et du conté de Valentinoys'. Baron Kervyn de Lettenhoven in his *Lettres et négociations de Philippe de Commines* (i. 319 and note) printed the titles of 7 items with comments.

[3] For instance more than one entry refers to Pope Alexander VI (1492–1503): e.g. 'item, ung abrege des comptes d'Alexandre sextre'.

[4] For example: 'item ung livre deslyé qui contient la declaracion du different qui est entre le roy et le duc d'Austriche'; since Maximilian was known as the duke of Austria from his arrival in the Low Countries in 1477 until his assumption early in 1486 of the title King of the Romans.

[5] 'Item ung memoire de ce que Monseigneur de Lombez et maistre Martin Courtin ont besoigné avecques le roy et la royne d'Espaigne touchant le fait de Rousillon', referring to the negociations of 1481 undertaken by the bishop of Lombez and Martin Courtin, royal secretary, with the Catholic Kings (C. Samaran, *Jean de Bilhères-Lagraulas, cardinal de Saint-Denis*, Paris, 1921, pp. 31–3). Not a few of the pieces relating to the reign of Louis XI are to be found among the original documents contained in MS français 2896: e.g. the letter from Pons de Rivière and Pierre Landais, *ib.* f. 83 and the letter signed Beauharnoys at f. 100.

[6] 'Item ung memoire contenant les requestes et ordonnances que le roy avoit deliberé faire'.

of the reforming measures which at the end of his reign were contemplated by Louis XI. One of the most sincere and remarkable passages in the *Mémoires* of Comines[1] is that in which are described the projected measures of Louis XI for the reform of the judiciary and the royal administrations. According to Comines the king was only prevented by ill health and finally by death from carrying these measures into effect. Whatever view one takes of the several items listed in the inventory of state-papers in Cato's keeping at the time of his death it is hard to escape the conclusion that Cato had been entrusted during the reigns of Louis XI and of Charles VIII with a good deal of confidential business. The most convincing token of the king's esteem for Cato was his elevation to the archbishopric of Vienne. Cato was nominated by the king not to a paltry bishopric on the west coast such as Maillezais or to one of the innumerable bishoprics on the confines of Gascony and Languedoc but to an archbishopric that had pretensions on the Primacy of Gaul.

On 8 July 1482 Louis XI wrote to the chapter of Vienne recommending his physician as their next archbishop. The chapter of Vienne was unable to assemble immediately owing to plague; but as early as 12 July two of the canons wrote to assure the king that his candidate would be elected.[2] The letter, which Cato addressed in his own hand to Pope Sixtus IV, must date from this time, for it is clearly written to solicit the pope's goodwill. Writing from Notre-Dame-de-Cléry, where the king often stayed seeing to the construction of the Church intended for his mausoleum, Cato sought every means to ingratiate himself with Sixtus.[3] In doing

---

[1] ii. 278.
[2] *Lettres de Louis XI*, ix. 257–8. Charvet, *Supplément à l'histoire de l'Eglise de Vienne*, p. 23. Papal provision dated 25 July 1482, for which Cato proffered 1800 florins (Archivio segreto vaticano. Obl. C.A. p. 21). Visit *ad limina* by proxy 15 December 1484 (*Ib.*, Lib. 1. Min. Br. p. 52, no. 20). For Cato at Vienne see *Gallia christiana* xvi (1865) 118–9, 143.
[3] The original is in the Podocataro collection, Biblioteca Marciana, Venice, Cod. Lat. class x. cod. clxxiv. f. 151. See the notice by P. O. Kristeller, *Iter italicum: A finding list of uncatalogued or incompletely catalogued humanistic manuscripts of the Renaissance in Italian and other libraries*, London and Leiden, 1963–7, ii. 252. This letter was published in full in 1936 on pp. 58–60 of the first edition of this work and has since been printed by T. De Marinis 'Nota su Angelo Catone di Benevento' in *Miscellanea di scritti di bibliografia ed erudizione in memoria di Luigi Ferrari*, Florence, 1952, pp. 227–32. There seems then no point in printing the full text for a third time.

so he reveals some information about himself. He claims that the pope had formerly been his teacher and he assures his former tutor that he was putting forth a book on the immortality of the intellective soul in support of Sixtus's teaching.[1] If Cato ever did compose this work it does not seem to have survived. To show what a valuable friend he could be at the French court, where the papal wars particularly that against Florence following the conspiracy of the Pazzi (1478) were opposed, Cato claimed that he defended on historical grounds the wars of Sixtus in Tuscany and the Campagna and that he frequently spoke about the pope's patronage of arts and letters. Indeed, the most attractive section of the letter is that in which the writer shows something like genuine enthusiasm for the papal patronage. Cato enumerates the Sistine Chapel and the work that Sixtus had done at S. Maria del Popolo but above all he praises the pope's services to the learned world in creating such a splendid library.[2] Incidentally the letter also informs us that Cato was a papal protonotary and was, therefore, already creeping up the ecclesiastical ladder before he became an archbishop of Vienne with full papal and royal backing. On 4 October 1482 he entered Vienne to take possession of a church that was to bring him little but trouble. He early ran into difficulties with the canons and the dean of the cathedral and with the local inhabitants from whom he rigorously exacted the payment of rents, which he was accused of dispatching to his relatives in Italy. Nevertheless, he made some initial attempt, before retiring to Paris, to reside at Vienne where in June 1483 he acted as an arbitrator and celebrated on 26 September 1483 in the cathedral a requiem for Louis XI.[3]

Characteristically he, Cato, was not intellectually oblivious of his arch-diocese and he prepared for the press at his own expense

[1] 'Teneor enim sedem apostolicam defensare, cum sim illi subditus quia de Benevento, tum etiam quia prothonotarius, tum quia omne quod scio a sanctitate tua dum erat in minoribus habui atque didici, ita ut librum de anime intellective immortalitate tua doctrina nunc edam'.
[2] 'Sed quid dicemus de locupletissima biblioteca tua cui nunquam similis extitit in orbe terrarum? Admirantur veteres Ptholomei bibliotecam qui magno pondere auri librum Moysi et aliorum prophetarum libros emerit, tua, beatissime pater, hebraicis, grecis et latinis litteris splendore maximo fulget'.
[3] Charvet, *Histoire de l'Eglise de Vienne*, pp. 522, 524. Charvet, *Supplément à l'histoire de l'Eglise de Vienne*, pp. 23–4. N. Chorier, *Histoire générale du Dauphiné* 2 vols., Valence, 1868–9, ii. 482, 489.

and care a breviary of Vienne.¹ The book issued from the press of Johann Neumeister at Lyons on 23 January 1490. Once again Cato had chosen a master printer of some calibre.² Neumeister was from Mainz and had been apprenticed to Gutenberg as a young man.

In Paris Cato enjoyed the society of learned men such as Gaguin, general of the Trinitarians, and Gui de Rochefort brother of Guillaume de Rochefort, chancellor of France. They were wont to gather in the house of Jean Fernand to listen to a discourse from their host on Terence or some other literary subject. In this company Cato acquired the flattering title of *philosophorum amplissimus*;³ from which it is clear that he was not a poet or an orator but a scholastic philosopher.⁴ In fact he had a pronounced dislike for Plato.⁵

The tranquillity of Cato and his literary friends was disturbed by the arrival of a disreputable Venetian Hieronymus Balbus, who picked a quarrel with Guillaume Tardif, a French grammarian perhaps an indifferent classic but infinitely more respectable than Balbus. In a Paris, still unaccustomed to Italian literary quarrels, the affair was ill-received and the authority of the university was

---

[1] *Gesamtkatalog der Wiegendrucke*, no. 5507. M. Pellechet, *Catalogue des Incunables de la bibliothèque Sainte-Geneviève*, Paris, 1892, no. 537. The colophon states 'Quem Angelus Cato archiepiscopus et comes Vienne ... pro reipublice Viennensium et animarum commoditate et sue sancte ecclesie honore sua impensa et suis summis laboribus imprimendum curavit'.

[2] A Claudin, *Origines de l'imprimerie à Albi en Languedoc 1480–4: les pérégrinations de J. Neumeister*, Paris, 1880, pp. 76, 77, 95.

[3] Thuasne, *Gaguini Epistole*, i. 88. *Caroli Fernandi Epistole* [Paris, 1507] sig. civ.ᵛᵒ.

[4] In May 1486 he acquired the work of the schoolman Ariminensis. See above p. 31. n. 3.

[5] See the epigram of Balbus—'Ad Episcopum viennensem Angelum Catonem:

Mellifera hybleo volucris discedat ab agro
Et tarthesiacis sol oriatur aquis.
Iam mutent elementa fidem: iamque a resoluto
Luna per-vinosis precipitetur equis:
Cum canibus lepores ludant: cum tigride dame:
Nec timeat rapidos agna novella lupos.
Denique nature frangantur iura potentis,
Si Cato vaniloqui scripta Platonis amat.'

Epigrammata Balbi [Paris, G. Marchand, 1495] sig. a5ᵛᵒ. In the printed text the fourth line reads: 'Luna pruinosis precipitetur equis'; but it seems that *pruinosis* must be a misreading of *per-vinosis*! This is a rare edition of *Epigrammata Balbi* (Bodleian. Douce, O, 126) *Gesamtkatalog der Wiegendrucke*, no. 3179.

presently invoked.¹ Balbus found an easy way out by prevailing on Cato to act as peace-maker and appease Tardif. In the presence of witnesses he was compelled to swear in the hands of the archbishop never again to calumniate Tardif.² Most probably it was this face-saving intervention by Cato which evoked from Balbus a short piece of fulsome verse praising his knowledge of Greek and Latin and extolling his powers as a philosopher.³ Cato's part in this controversy, which produced an interesting crop of ephemeral publications, seems to have been wholly benevolent. But, needless to say, Balbus soon perjured himself and re-opened the attack on Tardif.

It would be interesting to know if Cato did anything to help Comines out of the political disgrace into which he had fallen with the royal government of the minority of Charles VIII for supporting Louis duke of Orleans in 'la Guerre folle'. Comines was only released from prison by the Parlement on 24 March 1489, and did not receive a pardon until December of that year.⁴ In effect he must have begun to write the *Mémoires*, at the request of Cato, almost as soon as he was free.⁵

On the one hand the archbishop of Vienne enjoyed some leisure, provided he did not visit his archdiocese, since the death of Louis XI; and no doubt he hoped to re-indulge in literary activity. Cato's history of Louis XI, for which the *Mémoires* of Comines were to provide material, was planned to be written in Latin,⁶ as indeed was only fitting for an academic and ecclesiastical author.⁷

¹ March 1486, *Auctarium Chartularii universitatis parisiensis, Liber procuratorum nationis alemanniae*, p. 602. The chronology and bibliography of the controversial exchanges between Balbus and Tardif were defined some time ago by P. S. Allen 'Hieronymus Balbus in Paris'. E.H.R. xvii (1902) 417–28. See also Thuasne, *Gaguini Epistole*, i.90.

² 'Ego Hieronymus Balbus confiteor mea manu subsignasse ... me nunquam posthac verbo scripto aut per alium Tardivi famam in quoquo ledere. Que inviolabiliter servare juravi in manibus reverendissimi in Christo patris domini Angeli Catonis, viennensis Archiepiscopi, Galliarum Primatis'. *Antibalbica seu antaccelina, Guillermi Tardivi Anicensis imo accelinum defensio* [Paris, G. Marchand 1488] sig. aii^vo–aiii. (B.M. I.A.39607) Copinger, no. 5702.

³ *Opera Balbi*, ed. Joseph de Retzer, 2 vols., Vienna, 1791–2, i. 180.

⁴ For the troubles of Comines at this period, see Kervyn de Lettenhoven, *op. cit.*, ii. 13, 60, sqq. *Mémoires*, ed. Dupont, iii. 128, 134, 138. *Mémoires*, ed. B. de Mandrot, i. p. xl. *Mémoires*, ed. Calmette, i. p. xiii.

⁵ *Mémoires*. ed. Calmette, i. pp. xii–xiv.

⁶ *Ib.* i. 2.

⁷ Cf. the work of Thomas Basin, bishop of Lisieux, *Historia Caroli VII et Ludovici XI*. Judging from the letter to Jacques de Langeac, viscount of Lamothe

What a pity that it could never be written for there is no reason to think that it like much humanist historiography would have been too subservient to neo-classical stylistic values.

On the other hand French involvement in Italy at first diplomatic and finally military drew Cato into the more arduous service of the crown; and a work on the Ethics of Aristotle which he began on 7 July 1487 at Paris he had to complete in August 1493 at Rome[1] whither he had gone to reside in the interests of the French king. It was inevitable that he should be used as an expert on Naples, a kingdom of which both Charles VIII of France and René II of Lorraine were anxious to undertake the conquest. In a letter Cato composed a circumstantial account of the well-known Revolt of the Barons of the kingdom in 1486 against his old master King Ferrante. Written in Paris on 6 September 1486 the letter was addressed to Jacques de Langeac, viscount of Lamothe, who had married a Neapolitan wife, a daughter of Tristram da Chiaramonte, count of Cupertino, a marriage which made him, Langeac, a brother-in-law of King Ferrante.[2] Cato's comments on the insurrection were not solely narrative for he saw the importance of the immediate claim of the duke of Lorraine on Naples and the growing likelihood of French intervention. Cato was particularly well informed on the secret reasons which had recently induced Pope Innocent VIII to come to terms with the king of Naples.[3] Throughout the letter he is at pains to represent himself as a loyal supporter of the Aragonese dynasty in Naples; and Cato evidently still kept in touch with Prince Federigo, for in advising Langeac to write and congratulate Ferrante on the suppression

---

below p. 44, n. 1. Cato could write perfectly good French as one would have supposed.

[1] *Commentaria super decem morales Aristotelis libros.* This work was never printed but was still extant in MS at the beginning of the eighteenth century. See Croce, *op. cit.*, p. 176, n. 3. quoting J. de Nicastro, *Beneventana Pinacotheca in tres libros digesta*, Benevento, 1720, pp. 502–3.

[2] *Dictionnaire de la Noblesse*, xi. 413.

[3] In September 1486 Cato from Paris wrote to Pope Innocent VIII announcing himself (Vatican, *Biblioteca apostolica*, MS. latin 5641, f. 123. P. O. Kristeller, *Iter italicum, a finding list ... humanistic manuscripts of the Renaissance in Italian and other Libraries*, ii (1967) 375) and on 7 December 1486 he applied to the university of Paris for letters under its seal recommending him to the pope (*Auctarium Chartularii universitatis parisiensis, Liber procuratorum nationis alemanniae*, p. 621). It is however most doubtful whether he ever did go to Rome at this date.

of the revolt, he offered the services of a messenger whom he was about to send to Federigo.[1]

Cato's departure for Italy may be placed somewhere at the end of the summer of 1490. On 22 July the king of France sent to the duke of Milan a letter of credence on behalf of the archbishop of Vienne, whom, the king declared, he was about to despatch to Rome.[2] The archbishop had instructions, so the royal letter stated, to pass by way of Milan in order to take up certain matters with the duke, more especially the dispute between France and Milan over Saluzzo.[3] Cato apparently did not start on his mission before 9 September 1490 for on that day the university of Paris formally took note of letters in which he once more petitioned for letters of recommendation addressed on his behalf to the pope to whom he was about to proceed as a royal ambassador.[4]

This visit to Rome was certainly not unconnected with the long-standing quarrel between the archbishop and his cathedral chapter of Vienne.[5] The royal letters of 22 July 1490 expressly state that the pope had summoned Cato to Rome,[6] and if the reason of the summons is not given it is not far to find.

As recently as 23 January 1490 the archbishop had had his breviary of Vienne printed at Lyons; and on the present journey he probably passed through Lyons, a normal stage on the route from Paris to Italy. His meeting with the astrologer, Symon de Pharès, is most likely to have taken place during a stay at Lyons on the way to Italy in 1490. He may even have been with the king when Charles VIII in November 1490 paid a visit to Symon de

---

[1] This letter has been frequently printed. See *Documents historiques inédits*, ed. Champollion-Figeac (C.D.I.H.F.) Paris, 1848, iv. 316–20. E. Cione, 'Una lettera poco nota di Angelo Catone sulla congiura dei Baroni', *Rivista storica italiana*, v (1940) 5.
[2] *Lettres de Charles VIII*, iii. 85–6.
[3] 'Du different de Saluces'.
[4] 'Cum mandato regio ad prefatum sanctissimum (Pope Innocent VIII) orator foret profecturus'. *Auctarium Chartularii universitatis parisiensis*, iii. 737–8.
[5] Cato's administration of his see and the quarrels in which it involved him have been purposely excluded from the present study. The subject is extensively documented judging by the fact that there are at least twenty documents relating to it inventoried in the Vatican Archives. See Archivio segreto vaticano, Indice, no. 510, f. 187ro. col. 1–187vo. col. 1.
[6] 'Pour ce que nostre saint père a mandé aller devers lui nostre amé et féal conseiller maistre Ange Caton de Benevent arcevesque de Vienne. . . .' *Lettres de Charles VIII*. iii. 85.

Pharès at Lyons.¹ This royal visit proved disastrous for Pharès since it heightened the notoriety of his skill as an astrologer and contributed to the envy and suspicion which shortly after, in 1491, culminated in a charge being brought against him of practising the 'black arts'.²

Following his condemnation, Symon de Pharès though he remained as self-confident as ever was put on the defensive. His appeal to the Parlement of Paris did him little good.³ He, therefore, tried a literary and historical justification rather than a legal apology and composed a collection of astrologers' lives, past and present, to vindicate the scholarship of astrologers and the truth of astrology.⁴ In this collection, Pharès included a notice of Cato based on his personal knowledge of the archbishop. The source is, then, slightly suspect since it is, apart from the anecdote, an *ex parte* statement on the author's behalf.

Symon had a high regard for the archbishop's wisdom ('subtil engin') though he naturally admired above all his astrological powers. During the archbishop's visit to Lyons he claimed to have been instrumental in saving his life from the murderous designs of the inhabitants of Dauphiné. By means of a strategem Cato was smuggled over the Alps on the road to Rome while his enemies believed that he was still in course of convalescence at the house of the Célestins of Lyons.⁵

¹ Symon de Pharès, *Recueil des plus célèbres astrologues*, pp. vii–viii.
² *Ib.*, pp. viii–x. Lynn Thorndike, *A History of Magic and Experimental Science*, iv. 547–8.   ³ *Ib.*, pp. 548–50.
⁴ The *Recueil des plus célèbres astrologues* was finished not later than 1498 the last year of the reign of Charles VIII. See the introduction by Wickersheimer to his edition, p. xi. H. C. Lea piously believed that Pharès perished as a martyr scientist at the hands of the Inquisition (*A History of the Inquisition of the Middle Ages*, 1887, iii. 445–6) but Lynn Thorndike has demonstrated that he ultimately got the better of his detractors presumably through being protected by the crown (*A History of Magic and Experimental Science*, iv. 550–2).
⁵ 'Aucuns dient qu'il [Cato] predist la prinse du duc de Gueldres. Quoy qu'il en soit, à cause de sa science le roy Loys le eut en moult bonne estime et lui donna ladite arceveschié de Vienne. Avecques cestui j'ay conversé souvent et ay veu par experience qu'il estoit bon astrologien et de subtil engin et lui feiz son partement pour soy retirer à Romme, pour les envies que aucuns du Daulphiné orent contre lui, qui plusieurs foiz faillirent à le tuer et le firent partir des Celestins de Lion et chacun pensoit qu'il eust pris medicine laxative et fut oultre les mons, avant que nul s'en apperceust'. Symon de Pharès, *Recueil des plus célèbres astrologues*, p. 265. The capture of the duke of Guelders referred to above relates to the taking prisoner of Charles of Egmond, hereditary duke of Guelders, at Béthune in August 1487 when the French routed the Austro-

The last phase of Cato's biography, in so far as we know it, centres around the papal court and the cities of Benevento and Naples. From this period dates the medal of the archbishop ascribed to Adriano Fiorentino[1]; but regarding Cato's public career scant evidence is at present available. Nevertheless the state-papers reclaimed by the French crown after his decease indicate that the archbishop of Vienne remained at the court of Rome an active representative of French diplomacy.[2] As late as 1495, Philippe de Comines was still writing for Cato the fifth chapter[3] of the book of his *Mémoires* on Charles VIII's expedition to Naples; and there is besides evidence which confirms that at this period Cato's learned interests were undiminished.

The actual dates and facts surrounding his existence in Italy are few and uninformative. Even the date of his arrival in Rome is uncertain; but in November 1491 he was at Benevento.[4] His son Lucrezio was playing a turbulent part in local affairs at Benevento opposing the interests of King Ferrante of Naples, whose chancellor Pontano visited Rome in 1492 and intimated in no uncertain terms to the archbishop that he should restrain Lucrezio. The archbishop was non-committal, but agreed to try and persuade his son to enter the church and accept a benefice that King Ferrante was ready to offer him.[5] Nothing came of this and in July 1493 Ferrante wrote again to his son Federigo, prince of Taranto, then resident in Rome, to expostulate in a friendly way with the archbishop and to remind him that the king had several times requested him to recall his son from Benevento.[6] Again the archbishop avoided taking action. However, his friendly relations with the house of Aragon at Naples appear undimmed in a letter addressed to him on 27 October 1493 by Ferrante thanking the archbishop for his letter of the 15th October containing news of Ciarletta the king's grand-daughter.[7]

Burgundian force under the leadership of Engelbert II count of Nassau (Molinet, *Chroniques*, ii. 576).
 [1] See below, p. 49, n. 6.   [2] See above, p. 38, n. 2.
 [3] *Mémoires*, i. xv; ii. 28, 35.
 [4] Letter of Cato to Joannes Laurentius. Vatican, Biblioteca apostolica, MS. latin 5641. f. 142. P. O. Kristeller, *Iter italicum*, ii. 375.
 [5] Trinchera, *Codice aragonese*, II, i. 215–17, 218–19. Letters of 11 and 15 December 1492.   [6] *Ib.*, Letter of 8 July 1493, p. 120.
 [7] *Ib.*, pp. 296–7. She was the daughter of Federigo, prince of Taranto, by his first wife Anne of Savoy.

Cato's residence in Rome during 1492–3 is confirmed by other evidence. For instance he was borrowing and returning books from the papal library between November 1492 and February 1493.[1] At the commemoration of St. Thomas Aquinas on 7 March 1493 he took his place in the pope's chapel beside the ambassador of the king of France.[2] During the month of August 1493 he terminated at Rome, as already mentioned, his work on Aristotle.[3] The following Ash-Wednesday, which fell on 12 February 1494, he preached before Pope Alexander VI.[4]

The invasion of Italy by Charles VIII of France to claim the crown of Naples must have confronted Cato with many problems. He evidently joined the king before Charles's entry into Rome (31 December 1494), since the archbishop of Vienne was one of the two French commissioners who received on 11 November 1494 the submission of Orvieto[5] pending the entry of the French into that town. He probably accompanied the French king onward to Naples. The following year 1495, he wrote on 24 June from Naples to the magistrates of Benevento about procuring for them a charter of privileges from Gilbert de Bourbon, count of Montpensier, the French viceroy of the kingdom.[6] Early in 1496 he died at Benevento. His will made provision for members of his family, including his children, and a bequest to the cathedral of Vienne.[7]

If Cato had the misfortune to witness the invasion of his country and the ruin of the Aragonese dynasty, which he had served, at least he was able during his time at Rome to enjoy the Vatican library. Some twenty years previous while he was teaching at Naples he had seized the opportunity which ready access to the

---

[1] See below, p. 48, n. 2.   [2] J. Burchard, *Diarium 1483–1506*, ii. 49.
[3] See above, p. 43, n. 1.   [4] J. Burchard, *Diarium*, ii. 89–90.

[5] *Diario di Ser Tommaso di Silvestro* in *Ephemerides urbevetanae*, ii. 31, 32 (*Rerum italicarum scriptores*, 1922). According to *Gallia christiana*, xvi (1865) 119, Cato rejoined the king in France and received Charles VIII at Vienne in July 1494. This is probable although I have not found sufficient evidence to confirm it. The king had his official residence at Vienne between 5 and 20 August 1494 (*Lettres de Charles VIII*, iv. 80–4).

[6] The letter is printed by Croce (*op. cit.*, p. 176, n. 4) from a copy in the archives of Benevento.

[7] Franciscus Marcus, *Decisiones aureae in sacro Delphinatus Senatu*, Lyons, 1600, questio, 1387; Charvet, *Histoire de l'Eglise de Vienne*, p. 525 and *Supplément à l'histoire de l'Eglise de Vienne*, p. 24. Père Anselme, *Histoire généalogique de la maison royale de France*, 9 vols., Paris, 1726–33, viii. 240. Croce, *op. cit.*, p. 177.

Aragonese library afforded to him. In writing to Sixtus IV he had congratulated that pope on his library foundation. There is then nothing surprising in the name of the archbishop of Vienne, once he was resident in Rome, appearing in the register of the early borrowers of books from the Biblioteca apostolica. On 27 November 1492 he took out a work of Eustratios, archbishop of Nicea, on the Ethics of Aristotle,[1] which he returned to the librarian on 9 January 1493. The day before, on 8 January, he had borrowed *Averroes contra Algazalem* (al-Ghazzālī) which in turn he brought back to the library on 20 February 1493.[2] These two works were required pretty certainly by Cato for his own book on Aristotle's Ethics, which he completed in the following month of August at Rome. Another treatise on ethics a manuscript of which is indirectly connected with Cato is the Isagogicon of Leonardo Bruni,[3] a copy of which was transcribed by Raphael de Peuchenat (*or* Penchenat) at Naples where he stayed for three months with the archbishop of Vienne who was at that time ambassador of the king of France.[4]

---

[1] First printed at Venice, Aldus, 1536, fol.

[2] M. Bertola. *I due primi Registri di Prestito della Biblioteca apostolica vaticana*, Città del Vaticano, 1942, p. 44.

[3] *Isagogicon moralis disciplinae ad Galeottum Ricasolanum*, for the text of which see H. Baron, *Leonardo Bruni Aretino, Humanistisch-philosophische Schriften mit einer Chronologie seiner Werken und Briefe* (*Quellen zur Geistesgeschichte des Mittelalters und der Renaissance*, ed. W. Goetz, i. Leipzig, 1928) pp. 20–41.

[4] Florence, Biblioteca laurenziana, Ashburnham MS. 1657. K. O. Kristeller, *Iter italicum*, i. 97, has published the colophon: 'ego Raphael Peuchenat Neapol: in domo illus: domini Salerni in qua cum Rmo: domino Archiepiscopo et Comite Viennensi Benventano [*corrected on erasure*] qui regis Christianissimi Francorum orator per trimestre vixi die xxiv Julii [?] 1490'. The year 1490 seems impossible as Charles VIII only wrote on 22 July 1490 to the duke of Milan that he was sending Cato to Rome *via* Milan (above p. 44). On the other hand Cato might well have been in Naples as the diplomatic representative of the French king in July of 1491, 1492, and 1493. The copyist, Peuchenat *or* Penchenat, may have been a notary in Cato's service, for when the archbishop in Paris had received the oath of Balbus to refrain from slandering Tardif (above, p. 42) the oath was witnessed by a notary whose name is given as Penchenat (*Antibalbica ... defensio*, sig. aii^{vo}.) The prince of Salerno at this time was Antonello, head of the house of San-Severino, who being implicated in the 1486 revolt of the barons went into exile rather than trust himself to King Ferrante and ultimately took refuge at the court of France, where he actively encouraged Charles VIII to claim and invade Naples. The prince of Salerno did not return to Naples until early in 1495 as a commander of the fleet supporting Charles's 1494–5 Italian campaign (Comines, *Mémoires*, iii. 10, 21, 32, 72, 96, 138).

The two books borrowed by the archbishop from the papal library are, like the copy of *Ariminensis* the only book that he is known to have owned, definitely medieval rather than classical in character. Throughout his career Cato's medical and philosophical interests were not greatly attracted to Antiquity. His own treatise on poisons relied extensively on the authority of the Islamic physicians.[1] Of the Pandects of Silvaticus and the *Practica* of Mesue it may be said that the former aimed chiefly at identifying the drugs employed by the Arab practitioners, and that the latter dealt with the use of drugs according to the methods of the Arab masters, of whom Mesue was one. For the period there was nothing unusual in this subservience to the Arabs and to their pharmacopoeia seeing that Greek theories of anatomy and surgery did not gain the upper hand until the sixteenth century.[2]

However Cato's intellectual preference was occasionally more pronouncedly in favour of mediaeval as against classical learning. It is remarkable that he rated Silvaticus well above many illustrious learned men of Antiquity,[3] whereas the typical Renaissance compliment would have been to liken Silvaticus to the physicians of the Ancients. He advertised his admiration for St. Thomas Aquinas[4]; and was said, at least by Balbus, to despise Plato.[5] If his unpublished study of Aristotle's Ethics were to be found, it might throw light on his real position.

In one respect Cato did conform to Renaissance aesthetics and to Renaissance ideas about self-commemoration for he was represented twice on a medal, as a man of less than middle age and again as an old man.[6] The earlier of the two medals shows him as a layman with his hair over his forehead in the fashion of the

---

[1] Vienna, Nationalbibliothek, Cod. 11245. ff. 28ro, 32ro, 35vo, 38vo.

[2] Osler, *Incunabula medica*, p. 17, seq.

[3] 'Qui (Silvaticus) in eo scribendi genere (*viz*. medicine) multis illustrium philosophorum veterum est iure optimo preferendus'. Cato's edition of Silvaticus f. 1ro printed by Fava and Bresciano, *op. cit.*, ii. 73.

[4] 'Nam quis Thoma aquinate doctior?' dedication to Ferrante of the Pandects of Silvaticus (f. 2vo) Fava and Bresciano, *op. cit.*, ii. 76.

[5] See above, p. 41.

[6] For the earlier medal see Hill, *Corpus of Italian Medals*, i. 14. no. 50, where the medal is ascribed to a date before 1470 on the mistaken assumption that by 1470 Cato was working for the Angevins at the court of Burgundy. The later medal is described *ib.*, i. 84; ii. no. 338. It is recognizably by Adriano Fiorentino who in 1493 was working for Ferdinand, prince of Capua in 1493 and was active in Naples in January 1494.

late 'sixties and early 'seventies of the fifteenth century; and the inscription around the obverse calls him 'phylosophus et medicus'. The later medal is larger and shows him as archbishop with the tonsure. The reverse exhibits in the centre a tree pollarded (? *Laurus nobilis*, Bay Laurel) beneath which to the left Apollo stands, at his feet a cartouche with his name. With his right hand he crowns himself, while his left holds a lyre. Above him from the tree hang bow and quiver. Opposite Apollo on the right hand side of the medal stands his bird, a swan, above which there is suspended from the tree a book with markers hanging from it. The inscription if pretentious is at least admissible: 'Exaltat virtus nobilitatque viros'.

The design of the obverse is successful. The head and features are clear and noble conveying to the onlooker an impression of dignity and composure. The reverse leaves much to be desired as regards the composition. Numerous details are juxtaposed within a narrow field, and, as in so many second rate Renaissance art objects, the iconography[1] wrecks the picture.

THE MANUSCRIPT AND ITS LANGUAGE

THE manuscript of the *De Occupatione Regni Anglie per Riccardum tercium* is preserved at the Bibliothèque municipale at Lille.[2] The measurements of the manuscript are 213 mm. × 146 mm. and it is bound in parchment, part of a sixteenth century notarial instrument. The manuscript is gathered in eights and it consists of two quires followed by one half-quire beside which a spare leaf is bound in at the end. The modern pagination in pencil begins on the second leaf of the first gathering and runs from 1 to 40.

[1] Iconographically everything that appears on the reverse can be related to Apollo. Book: attribute of Apollo (G. de Tervarent, *Attributs et symboles dans l'art profane, 1450–1600*, 2 vols., Geneva, 1958–9, ii. 250). Bow (*Ib.*, i. 32). Laurel (*Ib.*, ii. 231). Quiver (*Ib.*, i. 61). Swan (*Ib.*, i. 138). Nevertheless there are specific cross-references which relate to Cato personally. Book: the arms of the family Cato of Supino were a book or on a field azur (Croce, *op. cit.*, p. 164, n. 3). Swan: the prophetic bird appropriate to one, who like Cato was deemed capable of foretelling the future. 'Itaque commemorat, ut cygni, qui non sine causa Apollini dicati sint sed quod ab eo divinationem habere videantur. . . .' Cicero, *Tusc. Disp.* I. xxx, ed. J. E. King, Loeb Library, 1927, p. 27. Cicero has here in mind Plato, Phaedo, 84. E.

[2] *Catalogue général des manuscrits des bibliothèques publiques de France—Départements*, xxvi (1897) 581. Fonds Godefroy, MS. 129.

THE MANUSCRIPT AND ITS LANGUAGE 51

The watermark in the paper is made up of a crown surmounting a star, which is found on a document of Troyes dated 1489 and belongs to a type specially prevalent in Champagne. The single spare leaf at the end, containing no part of the text, has an ewer for watermark. This, one of the commonest watermarks after 1476, belongs to a group frequently met with in France and especially at Paris.[1] In view of the wide diffusion of paper containing this watermark it may be no more than coincidence that the paper of Cato's autograph letter to Sixtus IV[2] contains precisely the same watermark as this found in the last, the spare folio, of our manuscript.

The manuscript is not the holograph of Mancini, for a Latinist of his calibre, if he might inadvertently have written certain of the false constructions that occur up and down in the text[3] would assuredly have corrected such errors. In fact no corrections, save for a single correction written in over an erasure,[4] appear in the text.

The script is that of a French gothic hand, possibly of the late fifteenth century but more probably early sixteenth century. There is little evidence of Italian or classical taste in this handwriting save perhaps in the forms of capital letters.[5] The date of the manuscript can be roughly ascertained by the mark of ownership[6] entered on the spare leaf at the end of the text by Paulus Aemilius[7] Veronensis, who came to France about 1483 and died in 1529.

---

[1] C. M. Briquet, *Les filigranes: dictionnaire historique des marques du papier*, 4 vols., Geneva, 1907, ii. 349, 354. no. 6115; iv. 624, no. 12477.
[2] See above, p. 39, n. 3.
[3] E.g. p. 64, l. 26; p. 94, l. 4; p. 96, l. 18.   [4] P. 94, l. 11.
[5] E.g. the capital A in *Argumentum* on page ii of the manuscript and p. 58 below. It is noticeable that most of the capitals at the beginning of each of the eight chapters have been left blank in the manuscript. Presumably it was originally intended to add illuminated initials as was the usual practice when manuscripts were prepared for presentation to persons of importance.
[6] The handwriting of this inscription resembles that of another *ex libris* of Paul Aemilius in a Glasgow MS. *Catalogue of the MSS. in the Library of the Hunterian Museum in the University of Glasgow*, ed. John Young and P. Henderson Aitken, Glasgow, 1908, p. 15.
[7] For the historiographical activity of Aemilius in France see the lengthy notice on him by Thuasne, *Gaguini Epistole*, i. 151–3: Delisle, *Cabinet des MSS* i. 177. His history of France, *De rebus gestis Francorum*, books i–iv were published in 1517 and books v–ix, which brought French history down to the end of the fourteenth century, were printed during the lifetime of Aemilius, probably in 1520 (P. Renouard, *Bibliographie des impressions et des oeuvres de Josse Badius*

The manuscript bears no trace of any other sixteenth-century owner; but inside the binding it has the book-plate[1] of Denys Godefroy (1615–81), who succeeded his father Theodore as historiographer to the king of France, and who became on the conquest of French-speaking Flanders (Flandre gallicante) by Louis XIV the first director for the crown of the archives, which the Burgundian and Hapsburg rulers of the Low Countries had assembled at Lille.[2] Besides his book-plate Denys Godefroy left at the beginning of the text of our manuscript a note to the effect that Angelo Cato, to whom Mancini offered his work, was the person to whom Comines offered his memoirs.[3] Denys Godefroy produced an edition of Comines,[4] which provided the basic text until the nineteenth century edition of Mademoiselle Dupont. Moreover he and his successors published numerous and lengthy proofs corroborating or modifying major points in the memoirs. It may therefore appear remarkable that Denys Godefroy or his descendants, who for more than a century presided with distinction over the depot of archives at Lille, should have refrained from publishing the text of Mancini. However, the explanation is not far to seek: our manuscript did not directly concern France, nor did it furnish valuable precedents for the claims of the French crown against foreign dynasties, more especially the house of

---

ascensius, imprimeur et humaniste, 3 vols., Paris, 1908, ii. 2–3). In Sir Thomas More's open letter to Germain de Brie (Brixius) of 1520 (printed 1520 by Pynson, *Short Title Catalogue*, no. 18088, and published in *The Correspondence of Sir Thomas More*, ed. E. F. Rogers, Princeton, 1947, pp. 212–39) there occurs a well-known reference to Aemilius: 'simul sperantes fore ut Paulus Emilius, tam sanctus et incorruptus enarrator historiae, ut iureiurando putes obstrictum; tam elegans, ut nisi recentiora rescriberet videri possit haud infimus antiquorum, res utriusque [English and French] populi (quas quidem inter se gessere) syncera fide sit aliquando traditurus posteris' (Rogers, *op. cit.*, p. 223). The reference to Paulus Aemilius, as indeed is the rest of More's open letter to Brixius, must be considered sarcastic or at best ironic.

[1] The book-plate of Denys Godefroy is reproduced by J. Guigard, *Nouvel Armorial du bibliophile*, 2 vols., Paris, 1890, ii. 237.

[2] Lille was ceded to France by the treaty of Aix-la-Chapelle, May, 1668. Colbert instructed Godefroy on 30 September to proceed to Lille and the royal commission was issued to Godefroy 11 December 1668, Marquis de Godefroy-Ménilglaise, *Les savants Godefroy, mémoires d'une famille*, Paris, 1873, p. 162.

[3] See below, p. 56, n. a.

[4] In conjunction with his father Theodore: the folio edition in 1649 was published by the royal press at the Louvre. *Ib.*, p. 167.

Austria,[1] against which the Godefroy family used their pen as loyally as many more noble families served the Bourbons with their sword.

At the Revolution the greater part of the Godefroy papers were incorporated in the public library of Lille or in the departmental archives of the Nord. It was possibly at this period that two names,[2] which appear to be signatures, were added to the last leaf of our manuscript. With the establishment in 1801 of the Consulate the Godefroy family recovered much of their collection including the manuscript of *De Occupatione*, for in 1841 when Le Glay examined the library of Charles Godefroy he noticed the work of Mancini remarking that it did not feature in the catalogue of either the Harleian or Landsdowne manuscripts.[3]

By the will of Denis Charles Godefroy, marquis de Ménilglaise, our manuscript passed with the other contents of his library, to the city of Lille, at his death in 1878. The municipality showed admirable foresight in 1914, when faced with German invasion, by removing to the fifteenth century vaults of the Palais Rihour the finest part of their collection, so that our manuscript escaped the fire which on 23 April 1916 devastated the municipal library.[4]

There remain to be said a few words about the Latin of Mancini, which despite its superficial classicism retained some reminiscences of the vernacular: e.g. the references to the Flemings as *Flamingi*.[5] He had a general preference for latinizing English proper names: e.g. *Astinco* for Hastings or *Rhodera* for Rotherham. He could afford to do this since the individuals mentioned by name, with the exception of Argentine, would certainly have been known to the French court and recognizable therefore to Angelo Cato for whom Mancini was writing. In regard to geo-

---

[1] Following his research in the abbey of Engelberg Theodore Godefroy was able to prove that the house of Austria was descended from the counts of Hapsburg in Aargau and not from the Merovingian kings of Gaul, which would have conferred on the Austrian imperial house a dynastic claim to the throne of France older than that of the Bourbons. The evidence was published by Theodore Godefroy in *De la vraye origine de la maison d'Austriche contre l'opinion de ceux qui la font descendre des rois de France de la première race dicte des Mérovingiens* (s. l.) 1624, 4to.

[2] Pelloquin and Delaforestz.

[3] Godefroy-Ménilglaise, *op. cit.*, pp. 394–6. A. Le Glay, *Mémoires sur les bibliothèques publiques et les principales bibliothèques particulières du département du Nord*, Lille, 1841, pp. 367, 369.

[4] Max Bruchet, *Archives départementales du Nord, Répertoire numérique*, 2 vols. Lille, 1921, ii. ix.

[5] Below, p. 58, l. 20; p. 66, l. 14.

graphical names, it is noticeable that twice only is England referred to as *Anglia*. The first time when Richard III is correctly termed *rex Anglie*, while the second mention occurs shortly after in a similar allusion to the three kings who according to a prophecy were to reign within as many months.¹ Otherwise England appears as *Britannia*, a mere Roman province, and the English as *Britanni*. The king of France is quite properly called *Francorum rex*² and the French *Franci*³; but Mancini has to call the country itself *Gallia*.⁴ He did, however, take care to designate the inhabitants of the duchy of Brittany as *Armoricos*⁵ to avoid confusion with the *Britanni* or English.

The style of Mancini in his *De Occupatione*, and for that matter in his Latin verse published in his lifetime, has the merit of clarity and lack of ambiguity. As might be expected in an author of Latin verse, metre occasionally⁶ creeps into his prose construction. He also seems especially fond of using the subjunctive mood.⁷ The vocabulary which Mancini employed was never pedantic, even in the opening address to Angelo Cato, while it was sufficiently extensive to meet the needs of his subject matter. On the one hand it stretched to an obscure word from antiquity such as *leviusculus*⁸ to a word of popular origin like *dorsuarium*⁹ on the other extreme. However, it must be remembered that Latin prose was a very polished literary form in the hands of Italian authors of the late fifteenth century, so that while Mancini's style would have been advanced by fourteenth century standards it was not up to the highest standards of the neo-classical writers of his own day. According to Comines the history which Cato planned to write was to be written in Latin.¹⁰ Therefore, Mancini writing for the information of Cato could scarcely do less, but the historical usefulness of the *De Occupatione*, for us at least, might have been enhanced had it been composed in the vernacular.

¹ Below, p. 100, l. 14; p. 104, l. 8.
² E.g. *Ludovico Francorum rege*, p. 58, l. 10.   ³ E.g. p. 58, l. 21.
⁴ Below, p. 104, l. 12.   ⁵ P. 86, l. 33.
⁶ 'Purpureas sumens sepe per urbem mille stipatus comitibus equo vehitur'. P. 94, l. 6.
⁷ 'Fuere in concillio qui dicerent' p. 72, l. 25. 'Ille qui nobilissimus esset' p. 74, l. 8. 'Et quamvis id omnes populi maritimi facerent' p. 80, l. 11. 'In qua summi duces ... essent dispositi' p. 84, l. 27.
⁸ P. 58, l. 17.   ⁹ P. 100, l. 2.
¹⁰ '... en quelque oeuvre que vous avez intention de faire en langue latine' *Mémoires*, i. 2.

TEXT AND TRANSLATION

DOMINICI MANCINI, DE OCCVPATIONE REGNI ANGLIE PER RICCARDVM TERCIVM, AD ANGELVM CATONEM PRESVLEM VIENNENSIVM, LIBELLVS INCIPIT

SEPE a me efflagitasti Angele Cato,[a] antistes religiosissime, ut quibus artibus Riccardus tercius, qui nunc in Britannia regnat, ad corone fastigium pervenerit, ita litteris mandarem quemadmodum coram tibi sepe numero recensueram. Cum enim exemplum
10 relatu dignum existimares, putabas te rem non ingratam Federico principi Tarentino[1] esse facturum, si id quod libenter ipse audivisses, legendum ei exhibuisses. Ego vero, qui tua causa laborem non refugiebam, sed qui nomina describendorum, temporum intervalla, occultaque hominum consilia in tota re gesta, non satis explorata habebam, non putavi tam licenter in scriptis quam in dictis mihi esse versandum. Propterea cum diutius rem distulissem, sensi me negligentie simul et ingratitudinis tibi factum esse suspectum. Sed cum nihil a me magis alienum esse quam ingratitudinem semper voluerim, et suspitionem ipsam
20 altius tibi insedisse cognoscerem, statui hanc maculam hac forte mea temeritate esse abolendam, ut scilicet scribam quocumque modo potero, id quod sentio te cupere, quocumque modo potest fieri. Et cum tu modum cupiendi excedas, ut illustrissimo principi optime de te merito gratus videaris, ego quoque modestie limites excedam, ut ingrati nomen effugiam, magisque tue voluntatis rationem habebo, quam norme a scriptoribus retinende. Scribam ergo certe me legentium subiiciens censure, dum tue morem geram voluntati. Non expectes igitur a me singulorum hominum et locorum nomina, nec historiam ipsam omnibus suis partibus [p. ii]
30 absolutam, sed tanquam hominis simulacrum, cui aliqua membra desunt, et tamen hominem plane designat [spectator].[b] Ita ex

[a] Written in the m*r*gin against the name of Cato, 'le mesme à qui Philippe de Com[ines] adresse ses mémoires v.p. de cet autheur de l'impr [imerie] Royale'. This note is identical in handwriting with a note signed and dated by Denys Godefroy in 1644 (reproduced in *Album d'autographes de savants et érudits français et étrangers des xvi*[e], *xvii*[e] *et xviii*[e] *siècles*, ed. Henri Stein, Paris, 1907, plate xvi). The reference is to the edition of the memoirs of Comines prepared by Denys Godefroy, and printed in 1649 by the royal press at the Louvre.
[b] MS. *spectatur.*

DOMINIC MANCINI TO ANGELO CATO, ARCHBISHOP OF VIENNE, ON RICHARD THE THIRD'S USURPATION OF THE REALM OF ENGLAND

THE COMMENCEMENT

You have often besought me, Angelo Cato, most reverend father in God, to put in writing by what machinations Richard the Third, who is now reigning in England, attained the high degree of kingship, a story which I had repeatedly gone over in your presence. Since you thought the original account worth recording, you considered that you would be doing a pleasing service to Frederick prince of Taranto,[1] if you presented for him to read the story which you yourself gladly heard. I indeed decided that I ought not to expatiate so freely in writing as in talking, for, although on your account I did not shrink from pains, yet I had not sufficiently ascertained the names of those to be described, the intervals of time, and the secret designs of men in this whole affair. When for that reason I had deferred the composition over long, I saw myself rendered suspect of negligence and also ingratitude toward you. But as I have always desired that nothing should be more remote from me than ingratitude, when I learned that suspicion had penetrated you so deeply, I decided to remove this aspersion, though I were rash in doing so, consequently I shall write, that which I think you require, as best I can, and howsoever it may be done. Therefore, as you press me with unusual urgency in your desire to please the illustrious prince to whom you are so much indebted, so shall I exceed the bounds of modesty in avoiding the imputation of ingratitude, and shall be more concerned to please you, than to be remembered as a pattern for authors. As a result of my solicitude for your requirements I shall undoubtedly expose myself in writing to the criticism of my readers. Wherefore you should not expect from me the names of individual men and places, nor that this account should be complete in all details: rather shall it resemble the effigy of a man, which lacks some of the limbs, and yet a beholder delineates for himself a man's form. Thus by means

nostris scriptis rem gestam te noscit[at]urum[a] existimes, ut eam magis intelligas quam legas. Verum ut quecumque sum [scripturus][b] melius intelligantur, a morte Eduardi regis post quem Riccardus regnum occupavit repetere commodum duxi.

ARGVMENTVM

EDVARDVS igitur quartus, qui cum magna gloria in Britannia regnavit, Londoniis, que urbs regia et tam magnitudine quam opibus totius regni caput est, septimo Idus Aprilis moritur.[2] Ad causam eius mortis hec concurrisse dicunt: quod Flamingi, quorum partibus ipse latenter faverat, attriti longo bello a Ludovico Francorum rege, desperantes iam auxilium ab Eduardo, eo invito cum Ludovico federa pacis percusserunt. Destitutus igitur Eduardus a Flamingis, per quos sepe Francis formidolosus fuerat, in quibus palmarium glorie sue repostum iactabat, a Francis ludibrio haberi ceptus est: qui, sive quod ab Eduardo sepe antea iniuriis lacessiti fuerant, sive quod eius solius vires parvifacerent, pro natura eorum fera et bellicosa leviusculas nacti causas in mercatores et naves Britannicas predam exercere ceperunt. Ex qua re in maximam tristitiam Eduardus incidit, dolens quod sua lentitudine Flamingi amici veteres perpetuo [p. iii] a se alienati essent, Franci vero inimici facti essent potentiores, et propterea quod sui sibi infesti erant, existimantes propter avariciam Flamingos ab eo non fuisse adiutos.[3] Ad dolorem vero ipsum levandum vel dissimulandum etsi iis diebus Eduardus multos ludos cum scenicis et regiis apparatibus ediderit, nunquam tamen omnino occultare potuit.[4] Huic tristitie et illud adiungunt, quod homo procere stature, maximeque pinguis non tamen ad deformitatem, cum quadam die et ipse navicula vectus, cum iis quos piscari iusserat, avidius piscationem spectasset, humidum frigus ad medullas admisit. Unde eo morbo correptus est, a quo non convaluit, nec diu afflictus fuit.[5] Obiens Eduardus duos reliquit filios, Eduardum scilicet primogenitum, iam antea in consilio primorum totius regni principem Walicorum declaratum,[6] cui

[a] MS. *nosciturum*.   [b] MS. *lacuna*.

of our book you may expect so to comprehend the affair that you discern more of it than you read. In order that what I am to recount may be more intelligible, I thought it wise to glance back before the death of King Edward, after which Richard usurped the kingdom.

THE ARGUMENT

Now Edward IV, who ruled England with great renown, died on 7 April[2] [1483] in London, which is the royal city and capital of the whole kingdom both in size and wealth. Men say the following incidents contributed to cause his death. For the Flemings, whose cause he secretly promoted, against his will made peace with Louis [XI] king of France; as they had been exhausted by a long war with Louis, and now despaired of aid from Edward. When Edward was abandoned by the Flemings, he began to be regarded with scorn by the French, to whom he had often been dangerous by means of the Flemings, and he used to boast that the trophy of his victory was in their keeping. Whether because often exasperated by Edward's molestations in the past, or because they made light of his unaided forces, in accordance with their fierce and bellicose character the French seized trivial pretexts and began to plunder English traders and vessels. On this account Edward fell into the greatest melancholy, lamenting that by his inactivity the Flemings, ancient friends, had been permanently estranged from him, whereas his foes the French had been made the stronger, so that his own subjects were disaffected, supposing that it was owing to his meanness that the Flemings had received no help from him.[3] Albeit in these days Edward contrived many performances of actors amidst royal splendour, so as to mitigate or disguise this sorrow, yet was he never able altogether to hide it.[4] In addition to this sadness they say another reason for his death was, that he, being a tall man and very fat though not to the point of deformity, allowed the damp cold to strike his vitals, when one day he was taken in a small boat, with those whom he had bidden go fishing, and watched their sport too eagerly. He there contracted the illness from which he never recovered, though it did not long afflict him.[5] At his death Edward left two sons: he bequeathed the kingdom to Edward the eldest, who had already some time before been proclaimed prince of Wales at a council meeting of the magnates

regnum in testamento dedit; et alterum minorem natu, quem ducem Eboracensium appellatum in fraterno regno prefectura sua contentum esse voluit. Reliquit eciam filias; sed de iis nihil ad nos. Eodem testamento ut ferunt Riccardum fratrem, Closestriorum ducem, protectorem liberorum et regni fecit,[7] qui paulo post, Eduardi liberis oppressis, regnum sibi vindicavit.

CAPITVLVM PRIMVM
Quibus causis fertur Riccardus provocatus ut regnum fratris filiis auferret

VERVM quia non solum ambitione regnandique libidine Riccardus ad regnum sibi vindicandum videtur impulsus, sed etiam ex obscuro genere regine et iniuriis affinium Eduardi se predicabat lacessitum, de iis quantum ad hanc rem pertinet paucis ante absolvemus. Devicto igitur et e regno pulso Henrico, qui ante [p. iv] Eduardum regnavit, Eduardus regno potitus, aliquanto licentius omnia agere. Inter ea que licentie concessit, Helisabettam ex humili genere natam,[8] duxit uxorem; invitis quidem regni primoribus, qui mulieri non illustri ad tantum fastugium[a] evecte indignarentur regios honores exhibere. Hanc viduam et duorum filiorum ex prioribus nuptiis matrem[9] cum propter forme prestanciam et morum elegantiam amare cepisset, neque muneribus neque minis corrumpere potuit: fama est, pugione ab Eduardo eius iugulo admoto, ut in libidinem consentiret, imperterritam constitisse; morique potius statuisse, quam cum rege impudice vivere. Propterea Eduardus [in][b] eam multo magis exarsit, et que a furenti rege de pudicitia expugnari non potuit, marito rege dignam iudicavit.[10] Eam ob rem non solum principes sibi alienos reddidit,[11] cum quibus postea bellum gessit, sed etiam domesticos vehementissime offendit. Mater enim in tantam vesaniam prolapsa est, ut in publicam questionem se offerret, assereretque, Eduardum non ex

---

[a] Elsewhere spelt as *fastigium*, cf. p. 56.
[b] In classical Latin *exarsit* in this sense requires *in*.

of the entire realm.⁶ The king wished that his second son called the duke of York should be content with his apanage within his brother's realm. He also left behind daughters, but they do not concern us. Men say that in the same will he appointed as protector of his children and realm his brother Richard duke of Gloucester,⁷ who shortly after destroyed Edward's children and, then claimed for himself the throne.

CHAPTER ONE

The reasons alleged to have prompted Richard to snatch the kingdom from his nephews

FIRSTLY we shall say a few words about the queen's kindred in so far as they affect our narrative, because it seems that in claiming the throne Richard was actuated not only by ambition and lust for power, for he also proclaimed that he was harassed by the ignoble family of the queen and the affronts of Edward's relatives by marriage. Now when Henry [VI], who ruled before Edward, had been conquered and driven from the land, Edward on taking possession of the kingdom behaved for a while in all things too dissolutely. One of the ways he indulged his appetites was to marry a lady of humble origin,⁸ named Elizabeth, despite the antagonism of the magnates of the kingdom, who disdained to show royal honours towards an undistinguished woman promoted to such exalted rank. She was a widow and the mother of two sons by a former husband⁹: and when the king first fell in love with her beauty of person and charm of manner, he could not corrupt her virtue by gifts or menaces. The story runs that when Edward placed a dagger at her throat, to make her submit to his passion, she remained unperturbed and determined to die rather than live unchastely with the king. Whereupon Edward coveted her much the more, and he judged the lady worthy to be a royal spouse, who could not be overcome in her constancy even by an infatuated king.¹⁰ On that account not only did he alienate the nobles with whom he afterwards waged war,¹¹ but he also offended most bitterly the members of his own house. Even his mother fell into such a frenzy, that she offered to submit to a public inquiry, and asserted that Edward was not the offspring of her husband the

marito suo duce Eboracensium sibi conceptum sed adulterio quesitum, proptereaque regali culmine minime dignum.[12]

Fratres vero Eduardi, qui duo tunc vivebant, etsi graviter uterque eandem rem tulerunt; alter tamen, qui ab Eduardo secundo genitus erat et dux Clarentinorum, manifestius suum stomachum aperuit; dum in obscurum Helisabette genus acriter et palam inveheretur; dumque contra morem [maiorum][a] viduam a rege ductam predicaret, quem virginem uxorem ducere opportuisset.[13] Alter vero frater, Riccardus qui nunc regnat, tunc Closestriorum dux, tum quia ad dissimulandum aptior erat, tum quia minor natu, minus auctoritatis habebat, [p. v] nihil egit aut dixit quo argui posset.[14] Postquam igitur debellatis iis principibus qui propter huiusmodi nuptias bellum Eduardo renovaverant, et partes Henrici in spem regni reduxerant: postquam item Henrico ipso partibusque suis ad exitum perductis, Eduardus in regno confirmatus fuit: regina, memor contumeliarum in genus suum et criminum in seipsam obiectorum, quod scilicet more maiorum legitima regis uxor non esset, existimavit, nunquam prolem suam ex rege iam susceptam regnaturam, nisi dux Clarentie aufferretur: quod et ipsi regi facile persuasit.[15] Augebat hunc regine timorem, quod dux Clarentie elegantissime erat forme, ut dignus videretur imperio: preterea popularis eloquentie vero habebat tantum, ut nihil quod cuperet difficile ei factu visum esset.[16] Itaque sive conficto crimine, sive vero facinore delato, dux Clarentie reus est factus, quod in regis mortem cum magicis et maleficis aspirasset.[17] Quo iudicio agitato, condemnatus fuit: et ultimo supplicio affectus. Supplicii autem genus illud placuit, ut in dolium mollissimi falerni mersus vitam cum morte commutaret.[18] Eo tempore Riccardus dux Closestrius ex dolore fratris percitus, nequivit tantum simulare, quin auditus sit cum diceret, se aliquando fratris mortem esse vindicaturum.[19] Ex eo perraro in regiam veniebat. In provincia sua se continebat. Suos officiis et iusticia sibi devincire studebat. Alienos clara fama morum et studiorum suorum ad sui amorem non mediocriter alliciebat. In militia ita clarus erat,

[a] MS. *maiorem.*

duke of York, but was conceived in adultery, and therefore in no wise worthy of the honour of kingship.[12]

As for Edward's brothers, of whom two were then living, although both were sorely displeased at the marriage, yet one, who was next in age to Edward, and was called duke of Clarence, vented his wrath more conspicuously, by his bitter and public denunciation of Elizabeth's obscure family; and by proclaiming that the king, who ought to have married a virgin wife, had married a widow in violation of established custom.[13] But Richard, the other brother, who is now king but then was duke of Gloucester, being better at concealing his thoughts and besides younger and therefore less influential, neither did nor said anything that could be brought against him.[14] By reason of this marriage some of the nobility had renewed hostilities against Edward, and revived hope among King Henry's party of regaining the crown, but after their defeat and the complete overthrow likewise of Henry [VI] and his faction, Edward's power in the kingdom was reaffirmed. The queen then remembered the insults to her family and the calumnies with which she was reproached, namely that according to established usage she was not the legitimate wife of the king. Thus she concluded that her offspring by the king would never come to the throne, unless the duke of Clarence were removed; and of this she easily persuaded the king.[15] The queen's alarm was intensified by the comeliness of the duke of Clarence, which would make him appear worthy of the crown: besides he possessed such mastery of popular eloquence that nothing upon which he set his heart seemed difficult for him to achieve.[16] Accordingly whether the charge was fabricated, or a real plot revealed, the duke of Clarence was accused of conspiring the king's death by means of spells and magicians.[17] When the charge had been considered before a court, he was condemned and put to death. The mode of execution preferred in this case was, that he should die by being plunged into a jar of sweet wine.[18] At that time Richard duke of Gloucester was so overcome with grief for his brother, that he could not dissimulate so well, but that he was overheard to say that he would one day avenge his brother's death.[19] Thenceforth he came very rarely to court. He kept himself within his own lands and set out to acquire the loyalty of his people through favours and justice. The good reputation of his private life and public activities

ut quicquid arduum et cum periculo pro regno gerendum esset, eius consilio et ductui committeretur.[20] [p. vi] Iis artibus Riccardus populorum benivolentiam sibi quesivit: et regine invidiam, a qua procul vivebat, vitavit.

CAPITVLVM SECVNDVM
De moribus Eduardi regis et eorum qui apud ipsum intimi habebantur

SVPPLICIO igitur sumpto de duce Clarentie, et quemadmodum diximus, Riccardo in sua provincia se continente, regina multos de sua stirpe nobilitabat. Multos etiam alienos sibi asciscebat, in regiamque aulam ita insinuabat, ut publica et privata regis negocia illi soli obirent; regi assisterent; clientelas haberent; prefecturas donarent vel venderent; et denique regem ipsum regerent. Erant autem regine, ut supra memoravimus, duo filii ex priore matrimonio quorum alter Riccardus, alter marchio vulgo nuncupabatur; erant item duo fratres quorum alteri dominus de Rivera, alteri Eduardus nomen erat.[21] Postulare videtur hic locus ut regis mores et istorum, qui tunc in aula plurimum poterant, silentio non pretereantur. Fuit quidem Eduardus natura mitis, aspectu hilaris, ita tamen ut cum vultum torvum assumeret, aspicientibus esset maxime formidolosus. Et suis et alienis eciam minimis facile sui conveniendi copiam faciebat. Sepenumero ignotos ad se vocabat, si eos eo animo venisse putabat ut ipsum alloquerentur, vel ut propius intuerentur. Cupientibus se videre sese ostentabat, ex tempore causam capiens, quo diutius et manifestius illis, quantus erat, pateret.[22] In affando [p. vii] ita familiaris fuit,[a] ut si quem hominem novum conspectu suo splendoreque regio attonitum conspexisset, blanda manu super eius humeris apposita, animum ad loquendum ei prestaret. Conquerentibus et [iniurias][b] expostulantibus, faciles aures prebebat: querelisque de se aut excusatione satisfaciebat aut causam precidebat. Externis qui in suo regno aut negociabantur, aut alia causa erant, preter ceteros principes gratificabatur.[23] Munificentia perraro utebatur,

---

[a] MS. *erat* has been crossed out and *fuit* substituted in the same hand as that of the rest of the text.
[b] MS. *iniuriis*.

powerfully attracted the esteem of strangers. Such was his renown in warfare, that whenever a difficult and dangerous policy had to be undertaken, it would be entrusted to his discretion and his generalship.[20] By these arts Richard acquired the favour of the people, and avoided the jealousy of the queen, from whom he lived far separated.

CHAPTER TWO

Concerning the character of King Edward and of those who were accounted his intimates

AFTER the execution of the duke of Clarence, and while Richard, as we have said, kept himself to his own lands, the queen ennobled many of her family. Besides, she attracted to her party many strangers and introduced them to court, so that they alone should manage the public and private businesses of the crown, surround the king, and have bands of retainers, give or sell offices, and finally rule the very king himself. As we said before, the queen had two sons by a former marriage; one of them was called Richard and the other was popularly known as the marquess: she had also two brothers, the name of one being Lord Rivers and of the other Edward.[21] At this point it seems imperative to say something of the character of the king and of those who were then very powerful at court. Edward was of a gentle nature and cheerful aspect: nevertheless should he assume an angry countenance he could appear very terrible to beholders. He was easy of access to his friends and to others, even the least notable. Frequently he called to his side complete strangers, when he thought that they had come with the intention of addressing or beholding him more closely. He was wont to show himself to those who wished to watch him, and he seized any opportunity that the occasion offered of revealing his fine stature more protractedly and more evidently to on-lookers.[22] He was so genial in his greeting, that if he saw a newcomer bewildered at his appearance and royal magnificence, he would give him courage to speak by laying a kindly hand upon his shoulder. To plaintiffs and to those who complained of injustice he lent a willing ear; charges against himself he contented with an excuse if he did not remove the cause. He was more favourable than other princes to foreigners, who visited his realm for trade or any other reason.[23] He very seldom showed munificence, and

et cum utebatur ad mensuram: a quibus tamen beneficium acceperat pergratus. Alieni non rapax, pecunie tamen studiosus adeo, ut in querendo avaritie notaretur. Ad cumulandas pecunias ea arte utebatur, ut advocata concione ex toto regno, multas se fecisse impensas, multasque necessario parare tam mari quam terra pro regni tuitione, exponeret; quas equum esse dicebat sibi ab omnibus, in quorum usum redibant, restitui.[24] Itaque causis sive veris, sive veri non multum absimilibus, adductis; pecunias non videbatur extorquere sed propemodum supplex rogare. Idem cum privatis faciebat, sed cum iis aliquanto imperiosius.[25] Ita magnos thesauros composuerat, quorum copia non liberaliorem aut paratiorem ad solvendum reddiderat, quam cum pauper erat, sed multo duriorem ac dilatiorem; ut eius avaricia palam iam predicaretur.[26] Ea ex causa putatur Flamingos deseruisse: quia si illis contra Ludovicum regem Francorum suppetias tulisset, quinquaginta scutorum milia annuatim [p. viii] a Ludovico accipere desivisset. Tantum enim se ea accepturum sciebat, quantum ab ope Flamingis danda abstinuisset.[27]

Cibi et potus fuit intemperantissimus.[28] Vomitum provocare solitum accepi, ut voluptate edendi iterum stomachum referciret. Propter hoc et ocium, quod post confirmatum regnum valde ei amicum fuit, pinguis ad abdomen devenerat,[29] cum antea ut procerus ita submacer et laboriosus fuisset. Libidinis ut fuit intemperantissimus, ita in multas mulieres postquam eis potitus fuerat, fertur fuisse contumeliosus. Nam ut libidinis satietas eum cepisset, eas invitas aliis aulicis substernebat. Nuptas et innuptas: matronas atque humiles nullo discrimine egit, nullam tamen vi rapuit. Omnes pecunia aut promissis expugnabat: expugnatas dimittebat. Ministros vero ac socios suarum libidinum etsi plures haberet, illustriores tamen et precipui tres erant, ex supra memoratis regine coniunctis, duo filii, et alter ex fratibus.[30] Dominus vero de Rivera semper habitus est vir gratus, gravis, et iustus

then only in moderation, still he was very grateful to those from whom he received a favour. Though not rapacious for other men's goods, he was yet so eager for money, that in pursuing it he acquired a reputation for avarice. He adopted this artifice for piling up wealth: when an assembly from the whole kingdom was convened, he would set forth how he had incurred many expenses, and must unavoidably prepare for much further expenditure by land and sea for the defence of the realm. It was just, he said, that these sums should be repaid by the public in whose benefit they were spent.[24]

Thus, by appealing to causes, either true or at least with some semblance of truth, he did not appear to extort but almost to beg for subsidies. He behaved similarly with private individuals, but with them at times more imperiously[25]: and so he had gathered great treasures, whose size had not made him more generous or prompt in disbursement than when he was poor, but rather much more stringent and tardy, so that now his avarice was publicly proclaimed.[26] For the same reason he is believed to have abandoned the Flemings, for, had he given them succour against Louis [XI] the king of France, he would have ceased to receive from Louis fifty thousand scuts each year.[27] He knew that he would receive them just as long as he refrained from assisting the Flemings.

In food and drink he was most immoderate[28]: it was his habit, so I have learned, to take an emetic for the delight of gorging his stomach once more. For this reason and for the ease, which was especially dear to him after his recovery of the crown, he had grown fat in the loins,[29] whereas previously he had been not only tall but rather lean and very active. He was licentious in the extreme: moreover it was said that he had been most insolent to numerous women after he had seduced them, for, as soon as he grew weary of dalliance, he gave up the ladies much against their will to the other courtiers. He pursued with no discrimination the married and unmarried the noble and lowly: however he took none by force. He overcame all by money and promises, and having conquered them, he dismissed them. Although he had many promoters and companions of his vices, the more important and especial were three of the aforementioned relatives of the queen, her two sons and one of her brothers.[30] On the other hand, Lord Rivers was always considered a kind, serious, and just man, and

omnique vita probatus: qui nemini unquam in tanta fortuna obfuerit, pluribus profuerit: propterea primogeniti regis curam [et]ᵃ vite modum commissum habuit.³¹ Hi tres igitur non carebant odio populi, propter eorum mores, sed maxime propter quandam innatam invidiam inter eos qui sunt genere pares, ubi dispar fuerit [p. ix] condicio. Nobilibus vero invisi erant; quia ignobiles ipsi et novi homines longe nobilitate et sapientia prestantibus anteponerentur. De morte ducis Clarentie ab omnibus calumniam sustinebant.³² Erant eodem tempore tres alii apud regem non mediocris auctoritatis viri: quia cum et ipsi in hac regni mutatione secundas partes obtineant, non sunt in scribendo pretermittendi, Thomas scilicet Rhodera archiepiscopus Eboracensium, magnusque idem cancellarius; [alter]ᵇ episcopus Eliensium; tercius cubiculi regis prefectus, nomine Astinco. Hi, quemadmodum annis maturi et multarum rerum usu edocti, ita consilia regia preter ceteros adiuvabant et exequebantur. Astinco non solum publicorum consiliorum auctor, ut is qui omnibus discriminibus cum rege perfunctus esset, sed et privatarum voluptatum conscius ac particeps erat.³³ Dissidebat is odio capitali cum eo regine filio, quem diximus marchionem nuncupari, idque propter amores alteri ab altero ablatos, aut sollicitatos. Capitale iudicium inter eos per suppositos delatores fuerat intentatum.³⁴ Ab istorum dissidio non parva pars huius mutationis videtur originem habuisse. Et quamvis iussis ac precibus regis qui utrumque amabat, biduo antequam moreretur fuissent reconsiliata gratia,³⁵ tamen ut eventus postea docuit semper viguit latens invidia.

CAPITVLVM TERTIVM

[p. x] *De morte regis Eduardi, et consiliis eorum qui tunc erant Londoniis*

REBVS igitur sic sese habentibus Eduardus rex moritur, testamento condito, eoque modo, quo paulo ante diximus, rebus dispositis.

ᵃ MS. *at.*
ᵇ MS. The word *alter* is written in the margin by a hand different from that of the text, and apparently later.

one tested by every vicissitude of life. Whatever his prosperity he had injured nobody, though benefiting many; and therefore he had entrusted to him the care and direction of the king's eldest son.[31] The other three earned the hatred of the populace, on account of their morals, but mostly because of a certain inherent jealousy which arises between those who are equal by birth when there has been a change in their station. They were certainly detested by the nobles, because they, who were ignoble and newly made men, were advanced beyond those who far excelled them in breeding and wisdom. They had to endure the imputation brought against them by all, of causing the death of the duke of Clarence.[32] There were at the same time three others of no small influence with the king, and ones who must not be omitted from the narrative, because in this revolution they were to play the lesser parts. The first was Thomas Rotherham, archbishop of York, and at the same time lord chancellor; another was the bishop of Ely [John Morton], and the third was the king's chamberlain, by name Hastings. Now these men being in age mature, and instructed by long experience of public affairs, helped more than other councillors to form the king's policy, and besides carried it out. But Hastings was not only the author of the sovereign's public policy, as being one that had shared every peril with the king, but was also the accomplice and partner of his privy pleasures.[33] He maintained a deadly feud with the queen's son, whom we said was called the marquess, and that because of the mistresses whom they had abducted, or attempted to entice from one another. The suborned informers of each had threatened a capital charge against the other.[34] An important factor in this revolution appears to have originated in the dissension of these two: and although at the command and entreaty of the king, who loved each of them, they had been reconciled two days before he died,[35] yet, as the event showed, there still survived a latent jealousy.

CHAPTER THREE

Concerning King Edward's death, and the consultations of those who were then at London

IN the midst of these events King Edward died, having made a will and disposed of his affairs in the way we have related a little while

Verum cum is moreretur, Riccardus frater in Closestriis agebat,³⁶ procul ab urbe ducentis milibus passuum. Eduardus vero filius, qui regni successor erat, in provincia Walia, que semper primogenitis regum in sortem datur, et a qua principes cognominantur,ᵃ degebat, procul ab urbe itidem ducentis milibus passuum. Ibi equis et canibus aliisque iuvenilibus studiis ad corpus confirmandum indulgebat.³⁷ Regina cum altero filio, Eboracensium duce, et ceteris de stirpe sua Londonias tenebant:ᵇ ubi et Astinco cubicularius cum iis, quos amicos regis diximus, Eboracensium et Eliensium presulibus. Thesaurus regius, cuius ingens ferebatur pondus, in arce munitissima iuxta urbem in manu regine et suorum servabatur.³⁸ Peracto funere regio, et convenientibus in urbem nonnullis regni primoribus, qui viciniora sortiti erant, ante adventum Eduardi reguli et Riccardi ducis Closestrii consilium cogitur: in quo ad proceres refertur de regni administratione, quoad rex pervenerit in legitimam etatem. Due dicebantur sententie: altera quod dux Closestrius administraret, quia Eduardus ita testamento cavisset, et quia per leges ei administratio obveniret. Sed hec infirmior, altera validior erat: quod adminstratio per plures ageretur, [p. xi] a quorum numero dux non excluderetur, quinimmo princeps [ascriberetur]:ᶜ ita ut duci honor haberetur, et regia res magis in tuto locaretur; propterea quod compertum fuerat, nunquam unum administratorem deposuisse administrationis officium nisi invitum armisque cohactum, unde bella intestina sepe essent exorta. Propterea si ad unum tota adminstratio deferretur, facile eum posse sibi imperium usurpare. Sentiebant pro hac parte omnes qui favebant generi regine, timentes ne Riccardo regnum assumente vel solo administrante, ipsi qui sustinebant calumniam de morte ducis Clarentie aut penam capitis luerent, aut saltem a tanta fortuna deiicerentur.

Fama fuit, Astinconem cubicularium per litteras et nuncios hec omnia ad ducem Closestrium detulisse; propterea quod ei vetus amicitia cum duce fuerat, et quod toti generi regine propter

---

ᵃ At first written as *demoninantur*.
ᵇ *Tenebat* more grammatical. The use of the plural is probably an extension of the *constructio ad sensum*. Cf. p. 76, l. 2.
ᶜ MS. *ascribebatur*.

ago. At his death his brother Richard was living on the Gloucester estates, two hundred miles distant from the capital.[36] Edward, the king's son, who was heir to the throne, was also two hundred miles from the capital, for he was residing in the province of Wales, which always falls to the lot of the kings' eldest sons, and gives to these princes their appellation. In Wales he devoted himself to horses and dogs and other youthful exercises to invigorate his body.[37] The queen with her second son, the duke of York, and the rest of her family were in London, where was also the chamberlain Hastings with the bishops of York and Ely, whom we recently mentioned as friends of the king. The royal treasure, the weight of which was said to be immense, was kept in the hands of the queen and her people at an impregnable citadel beside the town.[38] On completion of the royal obsequies, and while many peers of the realm, who possessed neighbouring estates, were collecting in the city, a council assembled before the arrival of the young King Edward and Richard duke of Gloucester. In this meeting the problem of the government during the royal minority was referred to the consideration of the barons. Two opinions were propounded. One was that the duke of Gloucester should govern, because Edward in his will had so directed, and because by law the government ought to devolve on him. But this was the losing resolution; the winning was that the government should be carried on by many persons among whom the duke, far from being excluded, should be accounted the chief. By this means the duke would be given due honour, and the royal authority greater security; because it had been found that no regent ever laid down his office, save reluctantly, and from armed compulsion, whence civil wars had often arisen. Moreover, if the entire government were committed to one man he might easily usurp the sovereignty. All who favoured the queen's family voted for this proposal, as they were afraid that, if Richard took unto himself the crown or even governed alone, they, who bore the blame of Clarence's death, would suffer death or at least be ejected from their high estate.

According to common report, the chamberlain Hastings reported all these deliberations by letter and messengers to the duke of Gloucester, because he had a friendship of long standing with the duke, and was hostile to the entire kin of the queen on

marchionem infensus erat. Admonuisse insuper ducem ut cum forti manu ad urbem properaret, ut iniuriam sibi ab inimicis factam vindicaret. Vindicare autem facile posse, si antequam ad urbem veniret, Eduardum regulum in suam curam manumque reciperet: suos vero non sic opinantes inter oscitantes opprimeret. Se solum in urbe esse, nec sine magno periculo, vixque posse eorum insidias effugere, cum ad vetus odium accesserit amicitia que sibi est cum ipso duce.[39] Quibus rebus ille admonitus, ut commodius ea exequeretur, [p. xii] ad concilium litteras scripsit in hanc sententiam.[40] Se domi forisque, pace et bello, fidelem fuisse fratri suo Eduardo, eundem se fore fratris filio, si permittatur, et si quo casu, quod absit, is vita decedat pro omnibus qui sunt ex fratre orti, eciam mulieribus: se omnibus obiecturum caput periculis, ut illi in patrio regno consistant. Eos rogare, ut in hac administratione ex lege sibi debita et a fratre decreta sue dignitatis rationem haberent, idque statuerent, quod sua in fratrem merita et in totum regnum postularent: non posse quicquam contra leges et fratris voluntatem decerni, quod sit sine iniuria. Multum he littere moverunt popularium animos, qui cum antea ex qua[dam] integritatis opinione duci corde faverent, iam in aperto sermonibus favere ceperunt; ut vulgo omnes dicerent, duci administrationem deberi. Proceres tamen, qui consilium habebant, frequentiores in secundam sententiam iverunt, diemque imponende corone statuerunt, scribentes ad Eduardum regulum ut triduo ante diem corone statutum ad urbem veniat.[41] Fuere tamen in concilio qui dicerent, non esse ita omnia precipitanda, sed patruum reguli expectandum, ad quem res maxime pertineret; ut ipse tantis rebus tam decernendis quam perficiendis intersit; quia si secus fiat, egre esset accepturus, et forte omnia interturbaturus. Ad hec marchio

account of the marquess. Besides, it was reported that he had advised the duke to hasten to the capital with a strong force, and avenge the insult done him by his enemies. He might easily obtain his revenge if, before reaching the city, he took the young King Edward under his protection and authority, while seizing before they were alive to the danger those of the king's followers, who were not in agreement with this policy. Hastings added that he was alone in the capital and not without great danger, for he could scarcely escape the snares of his enemies since their old hatred was aggravated by his friendship for the duke of Gloucester.[39] The latter being advised of these things, and with a view to achieving them more easily, wrote to the council in this fashion.[40] He had been loyal to his brother Edward, at home and abroad, in peace and war, and would be, if only permitted, equally loyal to his brother's son, and to all his brother's issue, even female, if perchance, which God forbid, the youth should die. He would expose his life to every danger that the children might endure in their father's realm. He asked the councillors to take his deserts into consideration, when disposing of the government, to which he was entitled by law, and his brother's ordinance. Further, he asked them to reach that decision which his services to his brother and to the State alike demanded: and he reminded them that nothing contrary to law and his brother's desire could be decreed without harm. This letter had a great effect on the minds of the people, who, as they had previously favoured the duke in their hearts from a belief in his probity, now began to support him openly and aloud; so that it was commonly said by all that the duke deserved the government. However, the lords, who filled the council, voted in a majority for the alternative policy: and they fixed a day for the coronation, and wrote to the young King Edward that he should reach the capital three days before the date appointed for the coronation.[41] There were, however, in the council those who said that everything ought not thus to be hurried through; rather should they await the young king's uncle, whom this business greatly concerned, so that he might be present both at the making and execution of such important decisions. Because, should they act otherwise, the duke could only accede reluctantly, and perhaps might upset everything. To this the marquess is said to have

respondisse fertur: 'Nos tanti sumus momenti, ut etiam sine patruo possimus hec statuere, et statuta perficere.'[42]

CAPITVLVM QVARTVM

[p. xiii] *De coniunctione ducis Closestrii et ducis Buckingamie: de regulo ab ipsis capto sub pretextu administrationis et tutele*

Dvm ea Londoniis geruntur dux Closestrie cum duce Buckingamie in provincia se coniunxit.[43] Iniuriam sibi factam ab obscuro genere regine cum illo expostulat. Ille qui nobilissimus esset, facile alterius nobilis est commisertus: precipue quod regine genus ipse causa propria odio haberet; cum enim adolescentior esset, sororem regine uxorem ducere cohactus fuit, quam ipse propter generis humilitatem suo coniugio indignabatur. Communicatis igitur consiliis copiisque coniunctis, ambo ad regulum in Waliam scribunt; ut ab eo certiores fiant quo die quave via velit urbem intrare; ut ipsi ex provincia venientes ad eum iter inflecterent, et se ei coniungerent; ut ipsis comitibus honorificentior esset in urbem ingressus. Annuit iis regulus, et postulata facit.[44] Cum igitur ad duodecimum lapidem urbi appropinquasset, in quodam pago constitit, ut ibi patruum expectaret: patruo vero pago appropinquante, regulus omnes fere comites, quorum magnum numerum ex Walia duxerat,[45] in pagos urbi propinquiores procedere iubet; ut ad recipiendum patruum commodior pagus esset. Ipse cum paucis domesticis expectat. Quinetiam ut maiori pietate patruum demereretur, avunculum suum, quem dominum de Rivera diximus, illi obvium misit, qui ad ducem veniens, in oppido ipsius ducis quam munitissimo, benigne suscipitur: et nocte illa ex [p. xiv] magna parte convivio absumpta, ambo somnum petunt.[46] Postera die[47] cum dilucesceret, omnibus ad iter expeditis, paucutis verbis ad causam submissis, Riccardus illum cum suis comitibus opprimit custodieque in eo oppido commendat.

replied, 'We are so important, that even without the king's uncle we can make and enforce these decisions.'[42]

CHAPTER FOUR

Concerning the union of the dukes of Gloucester and Buckingham and their detention of the young king under pretext of forming a government and regency

WHILE in London these events were happening, in the country the duke of Gloucester allied himself with the duke of Buckingham,[43] complaining to the latter of the insult done him by the ignoble family of the queen. Buckingham, since he was of the highest nobility, was disposed to sympathize with another noble: more especially because he had his own reasons for detesting the queen's kin: for, when he was younger, he had been forced to marry the queen's sister, whom he scorned to wed on account of her humble origin. Therefore, having exchanged views and united their resources, both dukes wrote to the young king in Wales, to ascertain from him on what day and by what route he intended to enter the capital, so coming from the country they could alter their course and join him, that in their company his entry to the city might be more magnificent. The king assented to them, and did as they requested.[54] When therefore he had approached the twelfth milestone from the city, he halted at a certain village to await there his uncle. As his uncle drew near the spot, the young king ordered nearly all his attendants, of whom he had brought a large number from Wales,[45] to proceed to the hamlets closer to the city, so that the village might be more convenient to receive his uncle. The king awaited with a few of his household, and, to deserve well of his paternal uncle by extreme reverence, he even sent his maternal uncle, whom we said was called Lord Rivers, to meet him. Rivers on coming to Gloucester was graciously received in a very strong place belonging to the duke, and after passing a great part of the night in conviviality, they both retired to bed.[46] At dawn on the following day,[47] when everything was prepared for the journey, Richard, after secretly giving curt orders to this effect, seized Rivers and his companions and imprisoned them in that place. Then with a large body of soldiers, and in

Ipse cum magna manu militum, socio duce Buckingamie, concitatis equis, ad regulum [contendit];[a] et simul observatis viis cavent, ne quis ante eorum adventum hoc regulo nunciet. Ad regulum igitur rei ignarum, suisque militibus exutum perveniunt quem imprimis ut regem adorant.[48] Deinde de obitu patris in corde dolorem in vultu tristitiam ostendunt, cuius mortem eius administris imputant: quia qui parum eius honori consuluissent, cum libidinum socii et structores haberentur, eiusdem etiam salutem precipitassent. Qua re ne consimilem ludum in filium ludant, dicunt eos a suo latere amovendos; quia homini peradolescenti ad tantum regnum moderandum mediocribus viris deesset opus. Propterea dux ipse eos accusat, quod in suam mortem conspirassent, et insidias tam in urbe quam in via instruxissent, que a consciis essent ei patefacte. Illud vero palam omnibus esse dicit, quod administrationis honorem a fratre in se collatum illi eripere studuissent: et tandem, ut sibi cautum sit, ne in perditorum hominum manus incidat, qui ex preterita licentia omnia essent ausuri, illos procul habendos censet: seipsum, quem pater voluisset, cum peritia rerum tum gratia [p. xv] hominum omnia melius impleturum: nihil se preterire quod ad fidelissimi subditi et diligentissimi defensoris officium spectaret. Ad hec adolescens, ut erat magni ac paterni animi imago, indolisque et litterature spectate, respondit se eos habere administros, quos sibi pater dedisset, pro patris prudentia bonos et fidos sibi datos credere: se nihil mali in eis vidisse, velle eos habere nisi aliter mali demonstrarentur. Quod ad regni administrationem pertinet, se in principibus et regina maximam spem habere, ut ad ministros suos veteres parum hec cura pertineat. Audito nomine regine, tunc dux Buckingamie, qui eius genus invisum habebat, respondit, non esse officii mulierum regna administrare sed virorum; propterea

---

[a] MS. *contendunt*: another case of a plural verb with singular subject has already been noticed (cf. *supra*, p. 70, l. 4). But in this case there appears greater need for emendation as the verb is more directly governed by its subject.

company with the duke of Buckingham, he hastened at full gallop towards the young king. At the same time, by having the roads watched, the two dukes guarded against any one informing the young king of these happenings before their arrival.

Wherefore they reached the young king ignorant of the arrest and deprived of his soldiers, and immediately saluted him as their sovereign.[48] Then they exhibited a mournful countenance, while expressing profound grief at the death of the king's father whose demise they imputed to his ministers as being such that they had but little regard for his honour, since they were accounted the companions and servants of his vices, and had ruined his health. Wherefore, lest they should play the same old game with the son, the dukes said that these ministers should be removed from the king's side; because such a child would be incapable of governing so great a realm by means of puny men. Besides Gloucester himself accused them of conspiring his death and of preparing ambushes both in the capital and on the road, which had been revealed to him by their accomplices. Indeed he said it was common knowledge that they had attempted to deprive him of the office of regent conferred on him by his brother. Finally, he decided that these ministers should be utterly removed for the sake of his own security, lest he fell into the hands of desperate men, who from their previous licence would be ready to dare anything. He said that he himself, whom the king's father had approved, could better discharge all the duties of government, not only because of his experience of affairs, but also on account of his popularity. He would neglect nothing pertaining to the duty of a loyal subject and diligent protector. The youth, possessing the likeness of his father's noble spirit besides talent and remarkable learning, replied to this saying that he merely had those ministers whom his father had given him; and relying on his father's prudence, he believed that good and faithful ones had been given him. He had seen nothing evil in them and wished to keep them unless otherwise proved to be evil. As for the government of the kingdom, he had complete confidence in the peers of the realm and the queen, so that this care but little concerned his former ministers. On hearing the queen's name the duke of Buckingham, who loathed her race, then answered, it was not the business of women but of men to govern kingdoms, and so if he cherished

si quam spem in ea sitam habet, abiiciat. A suis principibus, qui nobilitate et potestate prestent, omnia speret. Tandem adolescens, cognito eorum animo, qui quamvis illum modestia inducerent, tamen se velle magis quam rogare ostendebant, se in curam patrui, quod necesse erat, tradidit. Eodem igitur die in illud oppidum,[49] in quo dominum de Rivera tenuerant, adolescens est deductus. Qui ei comites erant, aut obvii exierant, omnes fere ad propria redire iussi sunt.[50] In eodem pago simul cum regulo detentus est Riccardus alter regine filius, et ipse admodum adolescens, qui paulo ante ex urbe ad regulum venerat. In oppido simul cum fratre [custodibus][a] est traditus.

CAPITVLVM QVINTVM

[p. xvi] *De consiliis eorum qui erant in urbe, et fuga nonnullorum. De adventu ducis cum regulo in urbem, et eius apparatu ad regnum capessendum*

Cvm hec Londoniis nunciata essent[51], perculsit animos hominum rei novitas. Regina vero et marchio, qui regios thesauros habebant, exercitum comparare instituerunt: ut seipsos tuerentur, et regulum ab eorum manu in libertatem vendicarent.[b] Sed cum quosdam nobiles, qui ad urbem venerant, et alios ad capienda arma sollicitassent, senserunt omnium animos non solum infirmos sed a se penitus alienos. Nonnulli enim palam dicebant, equius et utilius esse adolescentem regulum cum patruo esse quam cum avunculis et fratribus uterinis. Qua re intellecta, regina et marchio in asylum Vesti monasterii, quod illi sanctuarium appellant, iuxta regias edes, se recipiunt. Ducem Eboracensium puerum octo annorum et filias iam adultas secum habent.[52] Antique observantie sunt asyla in Britannia: adeo ut usque ad ea tempora, sive metu religionis sive timore populi, nulli ausi fuerint violare. Ex quacumque causa quis reus aut inimicus esset, etiam a regibus invitum inde non fas est extrahi. In eodem asylo, cum rex Eduardus, occupato iam regno

[a] MS. *custoditus*.
[b] Hitherto written as *vindicare*; cf. *supra*, p. 62, l. 31; p. 72, l. 3.

any confidence in her he had better relinquish it. Let him place all his hope in his barons, who excelled in nobility and power. Finally, the youth, perceiving their intention, surrendered himself to the care of his uncle, which was inevitable, for although the dukes cajoled him by moderation, yet they clearly showed that they were demanding rather than supplicating. Therefore on that same day the youth was taken to the very town[49] where they had seized Lord Rivers. Of the king's attendants, or those who had come out to meet him, nearly all were ordered home.[50] Richard, the queen's other son, who was quite young, and but a little before had come from London to the king, was arrested with him in the same village, and with his brother, Richard was handed over to the care of guards in the same town.

CHAPTER FIVE

Concerning the consultations of those who were in the capital, and the flight of some. Concerning the entry of the duke with the young king into the city, and the duke's preparation for snatching the crown

WHEN this news was announced in London the unexpectedness of the event horrified every one. The queen and the marquess, who held the royal treasure, began collecting an army, to defend themselves, and to set free the young king from the clutches of the dukes.[51] But when they had exhorted certain nobles who had come to the city, and others, to take up arms, they perceived that men's minds were not only irresolute, but altogether hostile to themselves. Some even said openly that it was more just and profitable that the youthful sovereign should be with his paternal uncle than with his maternal uncles and uterine brothers. Comprehending this, the queen and marquess withdrew to the place of refuge at Westminster Abbey standing close to the royal palace, and called by the English a sanctuary. They had with them the duke of York, a boy of eight years, and the queen's already grown-up daughters.[52] In England these places of refuge are of ancient observance, so that up to those times, either from religious awe or from fear of the people, none had dared to violate them. For whatever reason a man may be accused or disliked, it is not lawful even for kings to drag him thence against his will. In the same sanctuary the

ab Henrico, qui cum eo contendebat, eiectus esset, regina Eduardum regulum pepererat: nec tamen ab Henrico qui tunc omnia in manu habebat, ulla vis ei facta est.[53] Postea vero, sive religione remissiore, sive populari potestate imminuta et regum longe aucta, asyla contra arma regia parum valent.[54] Eduardus vero, quem diximus alterum regine fratrem, pridie illius diei,[55] ex publico concilio prefectus classi xx^{ti} navium, mare intraverat. Ex quo enim mors Eduardi regis [p. xvii] cognita fuerat, Galli non solum maria infestabant, sed ab ipsis litoribus Britannicis predas avertebant.[56] Et quamvis id omnes populi maritimi facerent, qui pirate et studiosi sunt, auctores tamen predarum ferebantur milites domini de Cordis,[57] strenuissimi prefecti regis Francorum. Is sub nomine ulciscende private iniurie a Britannis ei facte, inter duas nationes inimicissimas belli inicium apperuisse putabatur: quod ii qui ab eo missi fuerant in Britanniam ad res repetendas, fuissent a Britannis contumeliosius tractati, aut saltem ludibrio habiti, nulla restitutione facta.[58] Ad imminens igitur bellum, consilium, absente duce Closestrie, Eduardum prefecerat. Regie pecunie per tot annos summo studio comparate inter reginam, marchionem et Eduardum creduntur distribute.[59] Inter hec dux Closestrie, quia sinistra fama de eo in urbe vagabatur, quod fratris filium non in curam sed in potestatem redegisset, ut ipse regno potiretur, ad concilium et prefectum urbis, quem illi maiorem appellant, epistolas scribit, quarum sententie inter se nec fuerunt[a] nec huic exemplo discrepantes. Se scilicet fratris filium et Britannie regem non detinuisse, sed potius ipsum cum regno a pernicie liberasse; cum in eorum iuvenis manum iturus [esset],[b] qui cum patris honori et vite non pepercissent, non poterant estimari adolescentie filii melius esse consulturi. Fuisse ita opus facto, ut sue consuleret saluti, et regi ac regno provideret. Nulli hominum tante cure esse

[a] The scribe has probably turned the original order, *nec inter se fuerunt* etc.
[b] MS. *erat*.

queen had given birth to the young Edward [V] when King Edward [IV] had been ejected following the occupation of the realm by Henry [VI], with whom he was contending for the crown. Nevertheless no violence was done to the queen by King Henry [VI], who at that time had everything under his control.[53] Since then, whether religion has declined, or the people's power diminished and that of the sovereigns vastly increased, sanctuaries are of little avail against the royal authority.[54] Edward, whom we spoke of as the queen's other brother, appointed by the council captain of a fleet of twenty ships, had put out to sea the day before.[55] For no sooner had the death of King Edward [IV] become known, than the French not only made the seas unsafe, but even bore off prizes from the English shores.[56] Although all seafaring people may behave thus, for they are pirates by profession and inclination, the originators of these raids were reported to be soldiers of the Lord Cordes,[57] the French king's extremely active commander. The latter, under colour of avenging a private wrong done him by the English, was supposed to have made the beginnings of a war between these two most unfriendly nations. The cause was, that those who had been sent by him to England in order to reclaim his goods had been insultingly treated by the English, or at least derided, while no restitution was made.[58] Therefore in the face of threatening hostilities a council, held in the absence of the duke of Gloucester, had appointed Edward [Woodville]: and it was commonly believed that the late king's treasure, which had taken such years and such pains to gather, was divided between the queen, the marquess, and Edward.[59] As there was current in the capital a sinister rumour that the duke had brought his nephew not under his care, but into his power, so as to gain for himself the crown, the duke of Gloucester amidst these doings wrote to the council and to the head of the city, whom they call mayor. The contents of both letters were something after this fashion. He had not confined his nephew the king of England, rather had he rescued him and the realm from perdition, since the young man would have fallen into the hands of those who, since they had not spared either the honour or life of the father, could not be expected to have more regard for the youthfulness of the son. The deed had been necessary for his own safety and to provide for that of the king and kingdom. No one save only

salutem Eduardi regis, et incolumitatem regni quante sibi uni. Se prope diem cum adolescente ad urbem affuturum, ut de eius corona et iis, que ad celebritatem pertinent, [p. xviii] honorificentius agatur. Denique in omnibus gratiam populi conciliare studet, sperans si eorum favore solus administrator [declararetur][a] facile postea etiam eis invitis imperium se adepturum.

His litteris in consilio et ad populum recitatis, omnes ducem Closestrium laudare, quod in fratris filios pius esset et ad inimicos ulciscendos consilio non careret. Nonnulli tamen qui eius ambicionem et artem non ignorarent, semper dubitarunt quorsum eius conatus evaderent. Paucis post diebus cum omnium animos explorasset, et in urbe per amicos omnia providisset, cum regulo in urbem venit, comitatus non pluribus quingentis militibus partim ex suis partim ex ducis Buckingamie pagis evocatis.[60] Is omni consilio et opibus semper presto aderat. Regulum invicem asservabant: timebant enim ne ab eorum manibus aufugeret, aut vi eriperetur; cum populi Walici iniquo ferrent animo ita per secordiam fuisse eis principem abductum.[61] Cum vero ii duo duces in omnibus invidiam facere regine generi studerent, ut animi popularium omnino ab eo alieni fierent; eo die quo urbe intrarunt, id maxime curaverunt. Nam quatuor currus armis oneratos ante omnem pompam premiserunt cum insignibus fratrum et filiorum regine et cum indicibus, qui passim per loca frequentiora quacumque transibant declararent: illa arma comparata ab inimicis esse, et in opportunis locis extra urbem disposita, ut ducem Clocestrie ex provincia venientem invaderent et interficerent. Que cum multi scirent falsa esse, quia arma illa multo ante regis mortem ad aliud opus, cum res adversus Scotos gereretur, ibi fuissent collocata, suspitio criminationis [p. xix] et affectati imperii vehementer fuit aucta.[62] In urbem ingressus, id primo curavit, ut auctoritate concilii et omnium procerum protector sive administrator regis

---

[a] MS. *declararatur*.

him had such solicitude for the welfare of King Edward and the preservation of the state. At an early date he and the boy would come to the city so that the coronation and all that pertained to the solemnity might be more splendidly performed. Thenceforward he sought in every way to procure the good will of the people: hoping that, if by their support he could be proclaimed the only ruler, he might subsequently possess himself of the sovereignty with ease even against their wishes.

After these letters had been read aloud in the council chamber and to the populace, all praised the duke of Gloucester for his dutifulness towards his nephews and for his intention to punish their enemies. Some, however, who understood his ambition and deceit, always suspected whither his enterprises would lead. After a few days when he had ascertained the attitude of every one, and with the help of friends in the capital had provided against all eventualities, he and the young king entered the city, accompanied by no more than five hundred soldiers drawn partly from his own and partly from the duke of Buckingham's estates.[60] The latter was always at hand ready to assist Gloucester with his advice and resources. By turns they guarded the king, for they were afraid lest he should escape or be forcibly delivered from their hands, since the Welsh could not bear to think that owing to their stupidity their prince had been carried off.[61] As these two dukes were seeking at every turn to arouse hatred against the queen's kin, and to estrange public opinion from her relatives, they took especial pains to do so on the day they entered the city. For ahead of the procession they sent four wagons loaded with weapons bearing the devices of the queen's brothers and sons, besides criers to make generally known throughout the crowded places by whatsoever way they passed, that these arms had been collected by the duke's enemies and stored at convenient spots outside the capital, so as to attack and slay the duke of Gloucester coming from the country. Since many knew these charges to be false, because the arms in question had been placed there long before the late king's death for an altogether different purpose, when war was being waged against the Scots, mistrust both of his accusation and designs upon the throne was exceedingly augmented.[62] Having entered the city the first thing he saw to was to have himself proclaimed, by authority of the council and all the lords, protector

et regni declararetur.[63] Deinde ad omnia, que sibi imperium capessenti obstare possent, amovenda aut debilitanda animum intendit. Et cum iam Thomam Rhoderam, quem Eduardi heredibus fidelem fore in omni fortuna putabat, et quem eorum propugnatorem olim in concilio intellexerat, ab officio cancellarii, antequam in urbem ingrederetur, amovisset,[64] suffecto in eius locum Johanne Grosello episcopo Lincolniensium, viro multe tum doctrine tum religionis,[65] ad alia impedimenta tollenda properavit. Tentavit ergo, ut decreto concilii in eos quos custodie commendaverat tanquam insidiatores immo maiestatis reos animadverteretur. Sed id minime impetravit: quia nec causa cognita de insidiis constaret, nec si constitisset crimen erat maiestatis; cum tempore delatarum insidiarum ipse nec administratorem nec alium gereret magistratum.[66]

Post hec ad classem Eduardo auferendam animum convertit, exsistimans multum roboris in ea suis inimicis esse situm. Itaque auctore concilio Eduardum classis [prefectum][a] hostem patrie iudicavit, si classem non dimitteret. Ducibus vero militum et magistris navium, qui eius imperio suberant, tempus ad redeundum vel ab eo deficiendum statuit: intra quod si neutrum fecissent, itidem patrie hostes habendos censuit, bonaque eorum publicanda denunciavit. Quinimo[b] premia certa et magna proposuit, si quis Eduardum captum aut interemptum [p. xx] curaret.[67] Qua re tota classis, duabus navibus demptis quibus ipse Eduardus imperitabat, brevi unde discesserat, reversa est. Non fuerit ab re, hic recensere qua arte quave industria tam cito tanta classis defecerit; in qua summi duces, et illis partibus deditissimi, essent dispositi. Inter alias igitur naves due erant et magnitudine molis et virtute militum potentissime, quas mercatores Ianuenses, qui Londoniis

---

[a] MS. *preffectum.*
[b] Elsewhere spelt with double *m*; cf. p. 70, l. 21; p. 92, l. 19.

or regent of the king and realm.⁶³ Then he set his thoughts on removing, or at least undermining, everything that might stand in the way of his mastering the throne. Before entering the capital he had removed from the office of chancellor Thomas Rotherham, who, he supposed, would be faithful to Edward's heirs come what might, and whom he learnt to have been their champion in the previous council meetings.⁶⁴ Having replaced Rotherham by John Russell, bishop of Lincoln, a man of equally great learning and piety,⁶⁵ he hastened to remove the other obstacles. Accordingly he attempted to bring about the condemnation of those [i.e. Rivers and associates] whom he had put into prison, by obtaining a decision of the council convicting them of preparing ambushes and of being guilty of treason itself. But this he was quite unable to achieve, because there appeared no certain case as regards the ambushes, and even had the crime been manifest, it would not have been treason, for at the time of the alleged ambushes he was neither regent nor did he hold any other public office.⁶⁶

After this failure he turned his attention to the problem of how to remove the fleet from the control of Edward [Woodville], as he considered that a great part of his adversaries' strength rested on the navy. Thus with the authority of the council he denounced the commander of the navy, Edward [Woodville], as an enemy of the state if he did not disband his fleet. The duke of Gloucester appointed a period of grace to allow for the return or desertion of officers of the soldiers and masters of the ships, who were under Edward's command. He decreed that, if they had done neither before the term elapsed, they in like manner should be regarded as outlaws, and he proclaimed that their goods were to be confiscated. On the other hand he offered specified and considerable rewards for any one taking Edward alive or dead⁶⁷; and as a result the entire fleet, excluding two ships that Edward personally commanded, returned in a short while to the port whence it had sailed. It would not be irrelevant to recapitulate the craft and ingenuity that caused such sudden desertion of so great a fleet, in which distinguished officers, and ones most devoted to that party [i.e. the Woodville], were commissioned. Now amongst the other ships, there were two particularly formidable because of their great size and the valour of the soldiers on board. For the purposes of that war the Genoese merchants trading in London had lent these

negociabantur, ad illud bellum ad tempus accommodaverant, nautasque et magistros Ianuenses preposuerant: qui, cum tam nautica re quam maritimis preliis ceteris gentibus excellant, et in eo periculo maxime declaraverunt.[68] Audito enim decreto Londoniis facto, quamvis iusta causa in bellum profecti essent, tamen intellexerunt iuste in bello remanere non posse, nec etiam sine damno bonorum, et periculo sociorum,[69] timebant tamen ne ab aliis ducibus, qui neutra harum rationum movebantur, vel cogerentur vel ut suspecti diriperentur; precipue cum in iis duabus navibus admixti essent milites lectissimi ex Britannis, et Eduardo prefecto omni genere necessitudinis coniunctissimi. In tam ancipiti igitur malo, magister alterius navis, qui peritia et virtute animi multum valebat, precipue ubi necessitas cogeret, appropinquante nocte uberiori modo quam solitus esset [mollissima][a] vina et epulas in cena apponit. Ad bibendum omnes hortatur, quia opporteat navis tedia bibendi hilaritate excludere. Postea vero quam cenati essent, ubi vidit milites somno nutantes [p. xxi] ipse altius tabulatum in [prora][b] ascendit, et astra ac celum contemplatus tanquam ex insperato secundi venti flare cepissent, acclamat nautas: eosque ut antennas, vela, rudentes, aliaque expediant, admonet: quia austri iam ad navigationem invitent. Milites vero, qui madidi hesterno mero iam per tabulata strati soporeque oppressi errant, rogat ne nautis impedimento sint, ut in alvum navis descendant, ubi molliter quiescent. Illi somno et vino oppleti obsequuntur. Paulo post e fundo navis singuli evocati, lino et vinculis a Ianuensibus sunt constricti. Idem admonet alterius navis magistrum facere: ubi vero ambe naves, eodem fere tempore communicato concilio, iisdem dolis experte essent: cum tubis et lituis canere ceperunt: erectisque vexillis regis, concilio et protectori se parituras declaraverunt.[70] Reliqua classis illas tanquam duces consequta est, preter duas naves que cum Eduardo in Galliam ad Armoricos profugerunt.[71]

[a] MS. *molissima*.   [b] MS. *proro*.

vessels for a fixed time, and manned them with Genoese sailors and captains. The latter surpass the other nations both in navigation and the conduct of naval warfare, as they very clearly showed in this dangerous predicament.[68] Although they had embarked on the war in a lawful cause, yet on hearing of the proclamation made in London they realized that they could not reasonably remain at war, not indeed without losing their wares and imperilling their fellow countrymen.[69] However, they were afraid of either being forced to remain or else of being plundered as suspects by the other leaders, who were not affected by either of these considerations. They had all the more reason for fear, since on these two ships had been put a sprinkling of picked English troops, and ones that by every kind of tie were most devoted to the commander Edward. But the captain of one of the two ships was a man excelling in wisdom and audacious resolution, especially where necessity compelled. Therefore in this twofold dilemma he prepared in the evening more lavishly than usual a dinner, with delicious wines and victuals. He exhorted them all to drink, for the tedium of navigation should be banished by joyous potations. After dinner, when he saw the soldiers falling asleep, he climbed aloft into the forecastle on the bow and observed the stars and sky. Then, just as though by unexpected chance favourable winds had begun to blow, he shouted to the sailors, and ordered them to make ready the yard-arms, the sails, the hawsers, and everything else, because now at last the south wind permitted navigation. As for the soldiers, they now lay upon the decks sodden with the wine of the previous night, or wandered about overcome with drowsiness. The captain asked them not to get in the way of the sailors, but to go below decks where they might rest agreeably. The soldiers, sleepy and replenished with wine, obeyed him; shortly after they were called up one by one from below the hatches and trussed up with ropes and chains by the Genoese. He told the captain of the other ship to do the same. When this stratagem had been executed aboard both vessels, that had simultaneously participated in a joint plot, the Genoese began to sound trumpets and horns, and hoisting the king's banners they announced that they would obey the protector and the council.[70] Save for two ships that fled with Edward to the Breton coasts of France, the rest of the fleet followed the lead of the Genoese.[71]

Reducta igitur aut discipata classe, dux Closestrie magna suspitione liberatus, audacius se ad alia accingit. Decrevit igitur ducem Eboracensium, quem diximus cum regina in sanctuarium confugisse, in suam manum redigere. Sentiebat enim illum, si eius frater sublatus esset, legitimo iure ad coronam vocari. Ad id perficiendum indixit diem coronationis,[72] quo appropinquante refert ad consilium, quod indignum videatur regem coronari absente fratre, qui sanguine et officio primas partes coronationis habet exercere. Qua re, cum is puer invitus a matre in asylo detineatur, dicit liberandum esse, quia asylum ad [p. xxii] refugium non ad carcerem a maioribus sit institutum; cupere autem puerum ipsum cum fratre esse. Concilio igitur consentiente asylum militibus obsedit. Regina ubi vidit se obsideri et vim parari, fidem dante cardinali Cantuariensi[73] de puero post coronationem restituendo, puerum tradidit: cardinalis enim nihil perfidie suspicans, et tam violationi asyli occurrere quam etiam sevam ducis voluntatem obsequio demulcere studens, id regine persuaserat.[74] Iisdem fere diebus filium alterius fratris ducis Clarentie puerum decem annos natum in urbem venire iubet,[75] et apud uxorem suam eandemque pueri materteram[76] custodiri mandat. Timebat enim ne et is qui e regio sanguine esset, si proles Eduardi tota defecisset, scrupulum sibi faceret.

Toto sanguine regio in suam potestatem redacto, cogitavit rem suam non satis esse in tuto, nisi illi qui fratri suo fuissent amici intimi, et eius proli existimabantur fore fidi, auferrentur aut detinerentur. Tales autem esse existimabat Astinconem cubiculariorum prefectum; Thomam Rhoderam, quem paulo ante officio amoverat; et episcopum Eliensium. Astinco enim ab ineunte etate Eduardi regis comes fidus et miles strenuus fuerat,[77]

Now that the ships, which had not been retrieved, had been put to flight, the duke of Gloucester was freed of a great apprehension and prepared himself to face other ventures more boldly. He therefore resolved to get into his power the duke of York, who, as we said, had fled with the queen to sanctuary. For Gloucester foresaw that the duke of York would by legal right succeed to the throne if his brother were removed. To carry through his plan he fixed the date of the coronation[72]; and, as the day drew near, he submitted to the council how improper it seemed that the king should be crowned in the absence of his brother, who on account of his nearness of kin and his station ought to play an important part in the ceremony. Wherefore, he said that, since this boy was held by his mother against his will in sanctuary, he should be liberated, because the sanctuary had been founded by their ancestors as a place of refuge, not of detention, and this boy wanted to be with his brother. Therefore with the consent of the council he surrounded the sanctuary with troops. When the queen saw herself besieged and preparation for violence, she surrendered her son, trusting in the word of the cardinal of Canterbury,[73] that the boy should be restored after the coronation. Indeed, the cardinal was suspecting no guile, and had persuaded the queen to do this, seeking as much to prevent a violation of the sanctuary as to mitigate by his good services the fierce resolve of the duke.[74] At about this time Gloucester gave orders that the son of the duke of Clarence, his other brother, then a boy of ten years old,[75] should come to the city: and commanded that the lad should be kept in confinement in the household of his wife, the child's maternal aunt.[76] For he feared that if the entire progeny of King Edward [IV] became extinct, yet this child, who was also of royal blood, would still embarrass him.

Having got into his power all the blood royal of the land, yet he considered that his prospects were not sufficiently secure, without the removal or imprisonment of those who had been the closest friends of his brother, and were expected to be loyal to his brother's offspring. In this class he thought to include Hastings, the king's chamberlain; Thomas Rotherham, whom shortly before he had relieved of his office: and the bishop of Ely. Now Hastings had been from an early age a loyal companion of Edward, and an active soldier,[77] while Thomas, though of humble origin, had

Thomas vero ex humili genere natus, sed suo ingenio clarus apud [Eduardum][a] factus, diu in cancellaria meruerat[78]; Eliensis vero, et temporibus Henrici regis in factionibus versatus, multi consilii et audacie erat; et post partes Henrici penitus deletas [p. xxiii] ab Eduardo in gratiam receptus, multum auctoritate poterat.[79] Ne igitur opes et auctoritas istorum sibi obessent, quorum fidem per ducem Buckingamie exploraverat, et quos in eorum domos convenire aliquando intelligebat,[80] ad facinus maturavit. Cum enim ii tres et complures alii quadam die[81] pro eorum consuetudine ad salutandum protectorem, horam circiter decimam, ad turrim Londoniarum venissent, et in penitissimas edes admissi essent: ex composito acclamat protector insidias sibi instructas esse, eosque cum armis latentibus venisse ut primi vim facere inciperent. Tunc milites, qui per dominum dispositi erant, et dux Buckingamie accurrentes, sub falso proditionis nomine Astinconem gladio obtruncant. Ceteros detinent, quibus religionis et sacerdotii reverentiam vite causam fuisse arbitrantur.[82] Cecidit ergo Astinco non ab inimicis, quos semper cavit, sed ab amico de quo nunquam dubitavit. Sed quibus parcet vesana regnandi libido, si iura sanguinis et amicitie audet violare?[b] Cum ea cedes in arce patrata esset, oppidani, qui tumultum acceperant, incerti quid cause esset, trepidare: quisque arma capere. Sed dum dux ad sedandum vulgus statim per preconem facit denuntiari, insidias in arce detectas esse, et de insidiarum auctore Astincone penas sumptas. Qua re iubet omnes quieto animo esse. Credidit ab initio imperitum vulgus, quamquam multis in ore esset ipsa veritas, simulatas scilicet a duce esse insidias, ut invidiam effugeret tanti facinoris.[83] Eodem tempore marchionem asylum exisse per exploratores dux [p. xxiv] cognovit, quem dum vicinioribus locis latitare existimat, adultas iam circum fruges et consita ac nemorosa loca militibus simul et canibus cingit; exactissimaque indagine venatorum more perquirit, sed nusquam inventus est.[84] Ceterum ut nihil sibi

[a] MS. *Eduardus*.
[b] A finger in the margin of the manuscript draws attention to this passage.

become, thanks to his talent, a man of note with King Edward, and had worked for many years in the chancery.[78] As for the bishop of Ely, he was of great resource and daring, for he had been trained in party intrigue since King Henry's [VI] time; and being taken into Edward's favour after the annihilation of King Henry's party, he enjoyed great influence.[79] Therefore the protector rushed headlong into crime, for fear that the ability and authority of these men might be detrimental to him: for he had sounded their loyalty through the duke of Buckingham, and learnt that sometimes they forgathered in each other's houses.[80] One day these three and several others came to the Tower about ten o'clock to salute the protector, as was their custom.[81] When they had been admitted to the innermost quarters, the protector, as prearranged, cried out that an ambush had been prepared for him, and they had come with hidden arms, that they might be first to open the attack. Thereupon the soldiers, who had been stationed there by their lord, rushed in with the duke of Buckingham, and cut down Hastings on the false pretext of treason; they arrested the others, whose life, it was presumed, was spared out of respect for religion and holy orders.[82] Thus fell Hastings, killed not by those enemies he had always feared, but by a friend whom he had never doubted. But whom will insane lust for power spare, if it dares violate the ties of kin and friendship? After this execution had been done in the citadel, the townsmen, who had heard the uproar but were uncertain of the cause, became panic-stricken, and each one seized his weapons. But, to calm the multitude, the duke instantly sent a herald to proclaim that a plot had been detected in the citadel, and Hastings, the originator of the plot, had paid the penalty; wherefore he bade them all be reassured. At first the ignorant crowd believed, although the real truth was on the lips of many, namely that the plot had been feigned by the duke so as to escape the odium of such a crime.[83] At this same time the duke learned from his spies that the marquess had left the sanctuary, and, supposing that he was hiding in the adjacent neighbourhood, he surrounded with troops and dogs the already grown crops and the cultivated and woody places, and sought for him, after the manner of huntsmen, by a very close encirclement: but he was never found.[84] For the rest, so as to leave no source of danger to himself

suspectum (ubique locorum)[a] relinqueret, dominum de Rivera et Riccardum, quos in oppido detentos diximus, cum a concilio id non impetrasset, propria auctoritate tanquam protector per certos questores ultimo supplicio affici iussit.[85]

Hucusque quamvis affectari regnum omnia argumenta conspicerentur, attamen aliquid spei relinquebatur, quod sibi regnum non astrueret, cum tanquam iniuriarum et proditionis vindicem hec omnia se facere iactaret: cumque omnia privata monumenta et rescripta publica titulis et nomine Eduardi quinti notarentur.[86] Sed postquam Astinco amotus est, omnes familiares qui regulo inservierant ab eius accessu prohibiti sunt.[87] Ipse cum fratre in penitiores ipsius turris edes reducti, rarius per cancellos et fenestras in dies conspici ceperunt; usque adeo ut penitus desierint apparere.[88] Referebat Argentinus medicus, quo ultimo ex suis regulus usus fuit, regulum tanquam victimam sacrificio paratam singulis diebus confessione et penitentia suas noxas diluere, quod mortem sibi instare putaret.[89] Postulare videtur hic locus ut adolescentis indolem silentio non preteream. Sed cum tam multa sint, que ab eo liberaliter humane quinimmo sapienter dicta et facta preterquam illi convenerat etati, memorantur: [p. xxv] ut multo indigeant labore, laborem ipsum meo iure excusabo. Illud tamen non preteribo, quod apprime litteris eruditus fuit, ut loqui eleganter posset, et quicquid ad manus veniret, sive carmen sive prosa, nisi ex difficilioribus auctoribus esset, plane intelligeret et optime enuntiaret. Dignitatis habebat tantum in toto corpore et in vultu gratie, ut intuentium oculos, etsi multum pasceret, nunquam tamen satiaret.[90] Non paucos homines in lacrymas et fletus [prorupisse][b] vidi, cum eius memoria fieret postquam a conspectibus hominum est amotus, et jam suspitio foret esse sublatum.[91] An autem sublatus sit, et quo genere mortis nihil adhuc compertum habeo.

---

[a] These two words have been added in the margin of the manuscript but are by the same hand as the rest of the text.
[b] MS. *prorupsisse*.

from any quarter, when by means of the council the duke could not compass the execution of Lord Rivers and Richard [Grey], who, as we have said, were confined at a place in the country, of his own authority as protector he ordered dependable officers to put them to death.[85]

Thus far, though all the evidence looked as if he coveted the crown, yet there remained some hope, because he was not yet claiming the throne, inasmuch as he still professed to do all these things as an avenger of treason and old wrongs, and because all private deeds and official documents bore the titles and name of King Edward V.[86] But after Hastings was removed, all the attendants who had waited upon the king were debarred access to him.[87] He and his brother were withdrawn into the inner apartments of the Tower proper, and day by day began to be seen more rarely behind the bars and windows, till at length they ceased to appear altogether.[88] The physician Argentine, the last of his attendants whose services the king enjoyed, reported that the young king, like a victim prepared for sacrifice, sought remission of his sins by daily confession and penance, because he believed that death was facing him.[89] This context seems to require that I should not pass over in silence the talent of the youth. In word and deed he gave so many proofs of his liberal education, of polite, nay rather scholarly, attainments far beyond his age; all of these should be recounted, but require such labour, that I shall lawfully excuse myself the effort. There is one thing I shall not omit, and that is, his special knowledge of literature, which enabled him to discourse elegantly, to understand fully, and to declaim most excellently from any work whether in verse or prose that came into his hands, unless it were from among the more abstruse authors. He had such dignity in his whole person, and in his face such charm, that however much they might gaze he never wearied the eyes of beholders.[90] I have seen many men burst forth into tears and lamentations when mention was made of him after his removal from men's sight; and already there was a suspicion that he had been done away with.[91] Whether, however, he has been done away with, and by what manner of death, so far I have not at all discovered.

CAPITVLVM SEXTVM

De declaratione animi ducis, et regni occupatione, auctore duce Buckingamie, et de causis quibus dicit sibi regnum competere

SECVRVS igitur Riccardus omnium que ab inicio [timenda]ᵃ putavit, iam pullas vestes ponit, quas post mortem fratris semper induerat. Purpureas sumens sepe per urbem mille stipatus comitibus equo vehitur. Visendum ac salutandum populo adhuc protectoris nomine se exhibet. In dies maiorem numerum hominum in suis privatis edibus pascit.⁹² Dum se per urbem ostentat a nullo fere spectatur: quin dignum [ei exitum imprecantur]ᵇ cum nullus iam dubitet quorsum tendat. [Precipuam occasionem]ᶜ sui animi omnibus declarandi [p. xxvi] inde cepit. Nam predicatores divini verbi ita corrupit, ut in sacris ad populum concionibus dicere non erubescerent⁹³ contra fas [et] omnem religionem Eduardi prolem protinus esse extirpandam; quia nec ille fuisset legitimus rex nec eius proles esset futura. Per adulterium enim conceptus Eduardus omnibus absimilis erat duci Eboracensium defuncto, cuius falso dicebatur filius: Riccardus vero dux Closestriorum patri quam simillimus legitimus successor ad regnum vocatur. Interea dux omnes regni principes Londonias convocat.⁹⁴ Putabant ii vocari tum ut necis Astinconis causas intelligerent, tum ut de coronando Eduardo iterum ageretur; quia tanta novitate sequta, coronatio in alium diem differenda videretur. Quisque venit cum eo comitatu quem sua dignitas et ordo postulabat. Sed dux eos admonet, ut paucis comitibus retentis, qui ad corporis curam magis necessarii erant, reliquos ad proprias domos remittant. Formidare enim cives Londonienses causatur, ne tantus hominum conventus in urbe opulenta ipsis dominis invitis ad predas se convertant: memorat id alias accidisse.⁹⁵ Parent illi monitis. Ubi omnia dux constare vidit, ducem Buckingamie ad

---

ᵃ MS. *timida.*   ᵇ MS. *ei exitui imprecetur.*
ᶜ Written over an erasure.

CHAPTER SIX

How the duke of Gloucester showed his hand, and how he took possession of the realm at the instigation of the duke of Buckingham, and on what grounds he claimed to deserve the crown

WHEN Richard felt secure from all those dangers that at first he feared, he took off the mourning clothes that he had always worn since his brother's death, and putting on purple raiment he often rode through the capital surrounded by a thousand attendants. He publicly showed himself so as to receive the attention and applause of the people as yet under the name of protector; but each day he entertained to dinner at his private dwellings an increasingly large number of men.[92] When he exhibited himself through the streets of the city he was scarcely watched by anybody, rather did they curse him with a fate worthy of his crimes, since no one now doubted at what he was aiming. After that he took a special opportunity of publicly showing his hand; since he so corrupted preachers of the divine word,[93] that in their sermons to the people they did not blush to say, in the face of decency and all religion, that the progeny of King Edward should be instantly eradicated, for neither had he been a legitimate king, nor could his issue be so. Edward, said they, was conceived in adultery and in every way was unlike the late duke of York, whose son he was falsely said to be, but Richard, duke of Gloucester, who altogether resembled his father, was to come to the throne as the legitimate successor. In the meantime the duke summoned to London all the peers of the realm:[94] the latter supposed they were called both to hear the reason for Hastings's execution, and to decide again about the coronation of Edward, for it seemed after such an unprecedented alarm that the coronation must be deferred. Each came with the retinue that his title and station demanded: but the duke advised them to retain a few attendants, who were indispensable for their personal service, and to send back the others to their own homes. As a pretext for this he alleged the fear of the London citizens, lest so great a concourse of men in a wealthy city might turn to plundering against the will of their masters: and he reminded them that it had happened before.[95] They obeyed his instructions, and when the duke saw that all was ready, as though he knew nothing

principes submittit, tanquam ipse nihil intelligeret, ad quos referri facit, quid de regno faciendum sit.[96] Videri enim iniquum quod is puer corone munus suscipiat, qui spurius sit: spurius autem ideo, quia Eduardus pater cum Helisabettam duceret, aliam uxorem [p. xxvii] omni iure pactam haberet, quam dux Berbiciensium ei copulasset: dux enim, Eduardi mandato, ultra mare per verba, ut dicunt, deputati antea aliam pepigerat.[97] Preterea Helisabettam ipsam alii viro coniugatam fuisse, et ab Eduardo potius ereptam quam ductam esse.[98] Quo fit ut omnis eorum proles regno sit indigna. Filium vero ducis Clarentie propter crimen patris expertem diadematis factum; damnatus enim pater maiestatis non solum sibi ipsi, sed et filiis omnem honoris successionem ademerat.[99] Nullum superesse e regio genere preter Riccardum ducem Closestrie, qui per leges mereatur, et per virtutem possit corone onera sustinere. Anteactam eius vitam moresque integros certissimum esse pignus rei bene administrande: eum vero, etsi huiusmodi onus recuset, posse tamen animum flectere, si a principibus rogetur. His auditis, [principes],[a] exemplo Astinconis admoniti, et videntes duos duces convenire, quorum viribus propter militum multitudinem resistere difficile et periculosum esset, se vero quasi circumventos eorum manibus teneri, proprie saluti consuluerunt; et Riccardum regem declarandum rogandumque ut onus suscipiat, censuerunt. [Postridie][b] in domum matris ad quam consulto se contulerat Riccardus, ne in turri ubi regulus detinebatur ea fierent, omnes principes convenerunt, ubi omnia transacta sunt;[100] iuramenta enim fidelitatis prestita et cetera, que exiguntur, ordine perfecta; idem fecerunt duobus proximis diebus populus Londoniensis [p. xxviii] et sacrorum [antistites][c].[101] Ab iis enim tribus ordinibus hominum, quos tres status appellant, omnia ardua consultantur et decreta rata habentur.[102] Iis ita perfectis, dies coronationis indicitur. Gesta vero nomine Eduardi quinti post mortem patris rescinduntur aut suspenduntur. Signa et tituli mutantur. Omnia nomine Riccardi tercii confirmantur et geruntur.[103]

[a] MS. *princeps*.   [b] MS. *postridio*.   [c] MS. *antistes*.

USURPATION OF RICHARD III 97

of the affair, he secretly dispatched the duke of Buckingham to the lords with orders to submit to their decision the disposal of the throne.[96] He argued that it would be unjust to crown this lad, who was illegitimate, because his father King Edward [IV] on marrying Elizabeth was legally contracted to another wife to whom the [earl] of Warwick had joined him. Indeed on Edward's authority the [earl] had espoused the other lady by proxy—as it is called—on the continent.[97] Besides, Elizabeth herself had been married to another, and had been ravished rather than espoused by Edward,[98] with the result that their entire offspring was unworthy of the kingship. As for the son of the duke of Clarence, he had been rendered ineligible for the crown by the felony of his father: since his father after conviction for treason had forfeited not only his own but also his sons' right of succession.[99] The only survivor of the royal stock was Richard, duke of Gloucester, who was legally entitled to the crown, and could bear its responsibilities thanks to his proficiency. His previous career and blameless morals would be a sure guarantee of his good government. Although he would refuse such a burden, he might yet change his mind if he were asked by the peers. On hearing this the lords consulted their own safety, warned by the example of Hastings, and perceiving the alliance of the two dukes, whose power, supported by a multitude of troops, would be difficult and hazardous to resist. Whereas they saw themselves surrounded and in the hands of the dukes, and therefore they determined to declare Richard their king and ask him to undertake the burden of office. On the following day[100] all the lords forgathered at the house of Richard's mother, whither he had purposely betaken himself, that these events might not take place in the Tower where the young king was confined. There the whole business was transacted, the oaths of allegiance given, and other indispensable acts duly performed. On the two following days the people of London and the higher clergy[101] did likewise. All important matters are deliberated, and decrees made law by these three orders, whom they call the three estates.[102] This being accomplished, a date was fixed for the coronation: while acts in the name of Edward V since the death of his father were repealed or suspended, seals and titles changed, and everything confirmed and carried on in the name of Richard III.[103]

CAPITVLVM SEPTIMVM

De militibus in urbem evocatis et eorum armatura: et de regis coronatione

INTEREA dum dies coronationi dictus adveniret, ex provincie sue Closestrie et Buckingamie pagis milites in urbem evocat ad numerum sex milium. Timebat enim ne in coronatione, in qua conventus maximus erat futurus, aliquis tumultus contra se excitaretur. Militibus antequam in urbem ingrederentur ipse obviam exit: illisque tum campo maximo per circuitum dispositis, aperto capite circumeundo acies, gratias agit. Inde illis comitantibus in urbem revertitur.[104] Admonet me res ipsa que agitur, ut de Britannorum militum armatura pauca referam. Nullus fere est sine galea, nullus sine arcu et sagictis. Arcus vero et sagicte solidiores ac longiores sunt quam cetere gentes utantur, quemadmodum et ipsi corpore robustiores: ferreas videantur habere manus et brachia. Non minoris iacture eorum sunt arcus quam nostre [p. xxix] sint [balliste]:[a] unicuique preterea ad latus pendet ensis etsi non minus longus, gravis tamen ac solidus. Ensi semper iunctus est ferreus umbo: hec enim precipua studia illius gentis, ut passim per vicos festis diebus iuniores certent umbonibus obtunsis gladiis crepitantibus vel loco gladiorum solidioribus baculis. Ubi vero adulti sunt, in campis cum arcubus et sagittis.[b][105] Nec ipse quidem mulieres in venando huiusmodi armorum sunt ignare. In pectore et reliqua parte corporis nil habent ferri pro munimento preterquam nobiliores, qui toracibus utuntur et [cataphractis].[c] Vulgus vero militum tunicas habet aptiores, infra inguen demissas, stupa sive alia molli materia referctas. Ictus sagictarum et gladiorum tanto melius sustinere eas dicunt, quanto molliores sunt, preterea estate minus graves quam ferrum, et hyeme utiliores.[106] Huiusmodi igitur armatura evocati milites veneruntg muniti,[107] et preterea equites: non quod ex equo consueverint pugnare, sed quia illis utantur, ut portentur ad locum pugne, ut ibi sint recen-

[a] MS. *babliste.*   [b] Elsewhere spelt with a *c.*   [c] MS. *catapultis.*

CHAPTER SEVEN

Concerning the soldiers summoned to the capital, and of their equipment, and the king's coronation

MEANWHILE as the day appointed for the coronation approached, Richard summoned troops to the number of six thousand into the city from his own estates and from those of the duke of Buckingham. He was afraid lest any uproar should be fomented against him at his coronation, when there would be a very great concourse of people. He himself went out to meet the soldiers before they entered the city; and, when they were drawn up in a circle on a very great field, he passed with bared head around their ranks and thanked them; then accompanied by the troops he returned to the city.[104] The matter in hand prompts me to say a few words about the equipment of the English soldiery. There is hardly any without a helmet, and none without bows and arrows: their bows and arrows are thicker and longer than those used by other nations, just as their bodies are stronger than other peoples', for they seem to have hands and arms of iron. The range of their bows is no less than that of our arbalests; there hangs by the side of each a sword no less long than ours, but heavy and thick as well. The sword is always accompanied by an iron shield; it is the particular delight of this race that on holidays their youths should fight up and down the streets clashing on their shields with blunted swords or stout staves in place of swords. When they are older they go out into the fields with bows and arrows, and even the women are not inexperienced at hunting with these weapons.[105] They do not wear any metal armour on their breast or any other part of the body, except for the better sort who have breastplates and suits of armour. Indeed the common soldiery have more comfortable tunics that reach down below the loins and are stuffed with tow or some other soft material. They say that the softer the tunics the better do they withstand the blows of arrows and swords, and besides that in summer they are lighter and in winter more serviceable than iron.[106] The soldiers who had been sent for arrived equipped with this sort of armour,[107] and in addition there were horsemen among them. Not that they are accustomed to fight from horseback, but because they use horses to carry them to the

tiores neque fessi labore vie, ideo quibuscumque equis insident etiam dorsuariis. Ubi ad locum pugne ventum fuerit, omnes, relictis equis, equo marte pugnant, ut nulli sit spes fuge[108]: sed hiis satis. Dispositis igitur militibus in locis opportunis, dies, qui coronationem [p. xxx] precessit, advenit. Eo die,[109] ut moris est apud illos, rex discedens a turri Londoniarum, que est in extrema parte urbis ad orientem, et per mediam transiens urbem cum tota nobilitate et regio apparatu capite aperto omnes per vicos ad spectaculum stantes salutando, et ab eis salutes accipiendo, equo portatur usque ad edem, quam dicunt Vestum monasterium, in altera urbis parte ad occidentem, itinere fere duorum milium passuum.[110] In ea enim ede consueverunt Britanni suos reges diademate insignire. Die vero sequenti a cardinali Cantuariensi quamvis invito[111] rex Anglie inunctus fuit et coronatus.[112]

CAPITVLVM OCTAVVM

De situ urbis Londoniarum

SED neque a materia nostra alienum fuerit, cum de urbe Londoniarum tociens mentionem fecerimus, ut de eius situ et opibus aliquid referamus. Iure enim de nobis ipsa queri posset, cum sit toto orbe terrarum celeberrima et de nobis benemerita, quod eam preteriverimus: iure etiam non legentes accusent quod eius cognoscende desiderium ingeramus, sitim autem non extinguamus.

Iuxta fluvium Themisem ad sinistram, que septentrionem spectat, urbs sita est: Themises autem ab occidente orientem versus in oceanum fluit, fluvius quidem navigabilis a mari usque Londonias non solum triremibus sed maioribus navigiis. Non solum enim propriis aquis fecundus est, sed a marinis adiuvatur ubi ex alto fluxus in terras sese reiecerit, id quod bis in die in illo oceano perpetuo fieri solet. Ad dexteram vero fluminis, que meridiem aspicit, suburbanum est multis vicis et [p. xxxi] edificiis conspicuum, quod, si menibus cinctum foret, altera urbs dici posset.

scene of the engagement, so as to arrive fresher and not tired by the fatigue of the journey: therefore they will ride any sort of horse, even pack-horses. On reaching the field of battle the horses are abandoned, they all fight under the same conditions so that no one should retain any hope of fleeing,[108] but enough of this matter. The troops being stationed at suitable points, the day arrived preceding the coronation. As is customary with the English, the king on that day left the Tower of London, which stands at the eastern extremity of the town.[109] Passing through the midst of the city attended by the entire nobility and a display of royal honours, with bared head he greeted all onlookers, who stood along the streets, and himself received their acclamations. He rode a distance of approximately two thousand paces,[110] as far as a church called by them Westminster, which stands at the other end of the town towards the west. In that church the English have been accustomed to crown their sovereigns. On the following day, the cardinal of Canterbury, albeit unwillingly,[111] anointed and crowned him king of England.[112]

CHAPTER EIGHT

Concerning the situation of the town of London

NOR, since we have mentioned London so frequently, will it be incompatible with our subject to speak somewhat of its position and wealth. Indeed, London herself might justly complain of us for ignoring her, as she is so famous throughout the world, and has deserved well of us: and our readers also, finding no description, might with justice reproach us with arousing but failing to satisfy their curiosity to know her. The town lies upon the left bank of the Thames on the north side of the river: the Thames flows from west to east into the ocean. Up to London the river is navigable not only for rowing-boats but for larger vessels. For it does not only abound in its own water, but is replenished by the sea, when the incoming tide has set, an event that always happens twice a day on the shores of that ocean. On the right bank, which is on the south side, is a suburb remarkable for its streets and buildings, which, if it were surrounded by walls, might be called a second city. The latter is joined to the metropolis by a very famous bridge built partly of wood and partly of stone. On it

Illud cum urbe celeberrimo ponte partim ligneo et partim lapideo coniungitur, in quo habitationes et porte cum cataractis crebre, habitationes vero cum subiectis officinis sunt diversorum generum opificum.[113] Et quemadmodum suburbanum in loco equo et plano in orbem fere a tergo colligitur, ita urbs ei adversa iuxta fluvium in longum distenta partim in plano partim in clivo est posita. A ripis enim Themiseis assurgere incipiens molli ac facili clivo usque ad medium prona est. Reliquum dimidium planum est et equabile, campos habens ad septentrionem patentes tum in alia suburbana diffusos. Ab oriente terminatur arce munitissima fluvio imminente, quam turrim Londoniarum appellant. A turri ad Vestum monasterium, quod occidentem versus eciam flumini imminet, iter est duorum milium passuum. Sed id quod interiacet, non est totum urbe comprehensum, cum preter mille passus reliquum sit suburbanum cum urbe continuatum parumque discrepans ab urbis imagine. Super Themisis ripis ingentia sunt edificia delatarum mercium receptacula, machine vero frequentes et molis eximie ad naves mercibus exonerandas.[114] Ab ea parte, que est ad orientem et turrim, ducuntur tres vie strate usque ad alteram in moenia, que sunt occidentis, in tota urbe celebriores, et tote fere recte, quarum ea que fluvio propinquior est, et ceteris depressior, mercibus liquidis et gravibus referta est; ibi metalla omnia, vina, mella, pix, cera, lina, funes, tele, frumenta, pisces, et cetera sordentia.[115] In ea vero, que inter utramque media est, [p. xxxii] nihil fere venale reperies preter pannos.[116] In tertia, que medium urbis attingens in plano sita est, merces tractantur preciosiores: quemadmodum vasa aurea argenteaque, purpura, et omnia sericea, aulea, tapetes, multaque alia peregrina.[117] Quamvis enim ubique nihil desit, tamen hec loca memoratis mercibus sunt magis propria. Multi preterea sunt alii urbani vici celebres et artibus frequentibus. Quicquid enim in urbe est id totum artificum et mercatorum est. Domus vero eorum non, ut in plerisque solet, in primo aditu tantum mercibus extructe. Sed in penitissimis edibus[118] spaciosa receptacula, in quibus merces cumulate congesteque et stipate sunt, ut mella in cellis apium cernuntur. Sed de urbe hactenus: si enim

there are houses and several gates with portcullises: the dwelling houses are built above workshops and belong to diverse sorts of craftsmen.[113] Just as the suburb lies on flat and low land and is gathered into a circle from behind, so the city opposite it is stretched out lengthwise beside the river, and lies partly on a level and partly on a slope. Beginning to rise from the banks of the Thames with a gentle and easy incline as much as half the town is slanting towards the river. The remaining half is flat and uniform and has on the north open fields stretching out towards other suburbs. On the east it is bounded by a very strong citadel overlooking the river, they call it the Tower of London. From the Tower to Westminster, which is on the western side and also overlooking the river, is a journey of two thousand paces. But the intervening space is not all included in the city, as, save for a thousand paces, the rest is a suburb continuing uninterruptedly from the metropolis and differing in appearance very slightly from it. On the banks of the Thames are enormous warehouses for imported goods: also numerous cranes of remarkable size to unload merchandise from ships.[114] From the district on the east, adjacent to the Tower three paved streets lead towards the other quarter in the direction of the walls on the west, these are the busiest in the whole city and almost straight. Of these three, the one closer to the river and lower than the rest, is occupied by liquid and weighty commodities: there are to be found all manner of minerals, wines, honey, pitch, wax, flax, ropes, thread, grain, fish, and other distasteful goods.[115] In the one that lies between the other two you will find hardly anything for sale but cloths.[116] In the third street, which touches the centre of the town and runs on the level, there is traffic in more precious wares such as gold and silver cups, dyed stuffs, various silks, carpets, tapestry, and much other exotic merchandise.[117] Though there is nowhere a lack of anything, yet these places are better adapted to the aforementioned wares. Besides there are in the town many other populous quarters with numerous trades, for whatever there is in the city it all belongs to craftsmen and merchants. Yet their houses are not, as is the case with most, encumbered with merchandise just at the entrance: but in the inmost quarters[118] there are spacious depositories, where the goods are heaped up, stowed and packed away as honey may be seen in cells. But so much for London; did I intend to

et de hominum cultu, conviviorum magnificentia, et sacrorum ritu, templorumque ornatu et opulentia, persequi vellem, maius opus quam instituerim aggrederer. Iam canam igitur receptui, si prius, quanto tempore hec que modo memoravi gesta sunt, expressero. Ab obitu Eduardi ad regnum Riccardi non plures tribus mensibus intercesserunt. Vaticinium fuerat, nescio cuius vatis, sed tamen ore totius vulgi circumlatum, tres reges tribus mensibus Angliam esse habituros.[119] Cuius eventus tunc demum fuit intellectus, cum tercius ab Eduardo Riccardus fuit coronatus.
10 Hec sunt que ad mutationem regni spectent. Quomodo autem postea regnaverit, et nunc regnet, mihi satis compertum non est, qui statim post huiusmodi successus a Britannia in Galliam, te revocante Angele Cato, decessi. Tu vero vale, [p. xxxiii] et huic labori nostro saltem blandire, cum qualiscumque sit, pro te libenter est susceptus. Iterum vale. Date apud Bugiantias[a] in agro Aurelianensi. Calendis Decembribus 1483.

FINIS

---

[a] The accepted and most usual Latin forms of Beaugency are Balgentiacum, Belgentiacum (*Orbis latinus*, Graesse-Benedict, ed. 1922, pp. 36, 41), Balgeniacum (*Essais historiques sur la ville et canton de Beaugency par M. Pellieux*, ed. Lorin de Chaffin, 2 vols., Beaugency, i. 2–3), Baugentiacum (*Mémoires de la Société archéologique et historique de l'Orléanais*, vol xvi [1879], fasciculus i, p. xxi). A letter of Charles VIII written in November 1483 has Balgensium (*Lettres de Charles VIII*, i. 26). Bugiantiae is probably derived from the vernacular, of which it is merely a Latinized form. For literary purposes it seems as if the Latin name of Beaugency was falling out of use at the end of the fifteenth century. Thomas Basin, the contemporary French historian, while retaining the Latin names of places such as Orleans, gives the vernacular form to Beaugency (Basin, *Historia Caroli VII et Ludovici XI*, i. 61, 73).

enlarge on the refinements of the inhabitants, the magnificence of the banquets, the ecclesiastical ceremonial, the adornment and opulence of the churches, I should embark on a larger work than I intended. To finish my work I need only now relate the duration of events here recounted: between the death of Edward [IV] and the accession of Richard no more than three months intervened. There had been a prediction, by I know not what prophet, yet circulating on the lips of all the crowd, that three kings in three months should possess England.[119] The fulfilment of this was at last recognized when Richard was crowned the third king after Edward [IV]. These are the facts relating to the upheaval in this kingdom; but how he may afterwards have ruled, and yet rules, I have not sufficiently learnt because directly after these his triumphs I left England for France, as you Angelo Cato recalled me. Therefore, farewell, and please show some mark of favour to our work, for whatever its quality, it has been willingly undertaken on your account. Once more farewell. Concluded at Beaugency in the County of Orleans. 1 December 1483.

THE END

HISTORICAL NOTES TO THE TEXT

1. See above, p. 34. Succeeded to the Neapolitan throne in 1496, dispossessed by the French and Spaniards in 1501 (L. Volpicella, *Federico d'Aragona e la fine del regno di Napoli*, Naples, 1908). Retired with his library to Tours where he died in 1504 (Delisle, *Cabinet des MSS.*, i. 233 seq. 238 seq.). For a study of his learned and literary interests see De Marinis, *La Biblioteca napolitana dei Re d'Aragona*, i (1952) 118–22, and additionally Hill, *Corpus of Italian Medals*, i. nos. 312, 315.

2. Edward IV died 9 April 1483 at Westminster. The deputy at Calais received the news on 10 April; but Edward V at Ludlow only heard of his father's death on 14 April. C. A. J. Armstrong, 'Some examples of the distribution and speed of news in England at the time of the Wars of the Roses'. *Studies in Medieval History presented to F. M. Powicke*, Oxford, 1948, p. 450. A premature report of the king's death was current at York 6 April (*York civic Records*, p. 71). See below, n. 44.

3. It is true that Edward IV gave little military support to Mary of Burgundy and her husband Maximilian duke of Austria against the attacks of Louis XI on the Austro-Burgundian Netherlands. After the death of Mary (March 1482) the estates of Brabant and Flanders compelled Maximilian to conclude with France the peace of Arras (23 December 1482, best text in Molinet, *Chroniques*, i. 378–406), the provisions of which were humiliating to Edward IV. Not only was England excluded from the peace of Arras; but under the terms of the treaty the Dauphin Charles [later Charles VIII] was betrothed to Margaret of Austria, daughter of Mary and Maximilian. In concluding this marriage alliance Louis XI repudiated the marriage treaty of 1475 between England and France, which had provided for the betrothal of the Dauphin to Elizabeth, eldest daughter of Edward IV. The undertaking of Louis XI dating from 1475 to marry his son, the Dauphin, to Elizabeth of England was recapitulated in the *Promise of Matrimony*, printed without date or place by William de Machlinia (B.M., IB. 55451). The *Promise of Matrimony* was assigned to a date 'after March 1486' (R. Proctor, *An index to early printed books in the British Museum*, London, 1898–1903, no. 9678; E. Gordon Duff, *Fifteenth Century English Books*, London, Bibliographical Society, 1917, no. 351). In fact the *Promise of Matrimony* represents the reply of Edward IV to the peace of Arras and should, therefore, be dated between the end of 1482 and the king's death in April 1483. It is an unusually early example of a

publication, official or semi-official, produced by a diplomatic controversy between sovereigns. Dr. D. E. Rhodes, Department of Printed Books, British Museum, has been kind enough to confirm that the forthcoming *British Museum Catalogue of Incunabula* attributes the *Promise of Matrimony* to the early months of 1483, not to 1486.

4. *Historia croylandensis*, p. 563 and *Household Book of John duke of Norfolk 1481–90*, p. 149, report the magnificence of the Christmas revels in 1482.

5. There is nothing inherently improbable about the story of a chill caught on the river since the king seems to have been residing at Westminster for some time before his fatal illness (P.R.O. Chancery, Writs and Bills of Privy Seal, 22 and 23. Edw. iv. C.81/1326). Comines attributed the death to apoplexy following a surfeit (*Mémoires*, ii. 334), Jean de Roye to over indulging in the wine of Chaillot, a growth of Paris (*Journal*, ii. 130–1) and Basin (*Historia*, ed. Quicherat, iii. 133–4) to an excess of vegetables on Good Friday [28 March 1483] cf. Molinet (*Chroniques*, i. 414). Not till the sixteenth century do English sources refer to the causes of death. Polydore Vergil records the suspicion of poison (*Anglica Historia*, p. 683–4), but by this date sudden death in noble or princely families usually aroused such suspicion. According to Hall (*Chronicle*, p. 338) Edward IV brought back from the French expedition of 1475 an ague which 'turned to an incurable quarten'.

6. Two days after his father's death Edward V was proclaimed in London on 11 April 1483 (*Great Chronicle*, p. 230). He had been created prince of Wales 26 June 1471, his uncle the duke of Gloucester being a witness to the charter (*Rotuli Parliamentorum*, vi. 9. *Calendar of Charter Rolls 1427–1516*, p. 239). The following 3 July forty-seven lords spiritual and temporal, among them the dukes of Gloucester and Buckingham, took the oath to him as heir to the crown (*Calendar of Close Rolls 1468–76*, p. 229–30). The oath in an expanded form was also administered at Coventry, a borough on the prince's estates (*Coventry Leet Book*, pp. 393–4).

7. The duke of Gloucester was not constituted protector under the will Edward IV made before his expedition to France in 1475 (*Excerpta historica*, pp. 366–79). As the executors who met in 1483 to prove the late king's will (*Registrum Thome Bourgchier*, pp. 52, 54) were not the same as those named in the will of 1475 it appears that either Edward IV made another will after 1475 or that he substantially modified his 1475 will. Possibly Gloucester was designated protector in the codicils, which Edward IV on his death-bed added to his will: 'in morte codicillos nonnullos adjecit: cujus omnis tam sagax dispositio quam miserum et infelicem exitum sortita fuit, sequens tragoedia declarabit', *Historia*

croylandensis, p. 564. Mancini, it should be noted, qualifies his assertion with an *ut ferunt*; but two other foreigners, Bernard André and Polydore Vergil, who wrote in England for Henry VII and Henry VIII respectively, had no hesitation in affirming that Edward IV committed his kingdom and children to the duke of Gloucester (André, *Vita Henrici VII*, p. 23; Polydore Vergil, *Anglica Historia*, p. 685). See below, n. 63.

8. Her father, Sir Richard Woodville, created in 1448 (*Complete Peerage*, xi. 19–22) Lord Rivers, was of relatively humble origin. He had married Jacquetta of Luxembourg, widow of John duke of Bedford, to whom Sir Richard Woodville's father had been chamberlain. On her mother's side Elizabeth Woodville belonged to one of the great houses of Europe since Jacquetta of Luxembourg, her mother, belonged to the cadet branch of the Luxemburg family, the elder line of which had in the fourteenth and fifteenth centuries provided emperors of Germany and kings of Bohemia (W. K. Prinz von Isenburg and F. Baron Freytag von Loringhoven. *Europäische Stammtafeln*, 2nd edn., Marburg 1958–61, iii. no. 109 and *corrigenda* at end of the volume). Anxious to emphasize his wife's Luxembourg connexion, Edward IV invited members of that family to attend her coronation as queen (Du Clercq, *Mémoires*, iv. 88) which took place 26 May 1465 at Westminster (*The Coronation of Elizabeth Wydeville*, ed. George Smith, London (Ellis) 1935; A. R. Wagner *Heralds and Heraldry in the Middle Ages*, Oxford, 1939, p. 108). Some years later the queen's illustrious ancestry was introduced into a pageant given at Coventry (*Coventry Leet Book*, p. 393).

9. She was the widow of Sir John Grey, died of wounds after the second battle of St. Albans 17 February 1461, and their sons were Thomas (afterwards marquess of Dorset) and (Lord) Richard Grey (*Complete Peerage*, v. 361–2).

10. The marriage took place secretly at Grafton Regis, Northants, on 1 May 1464 (*Great Chronicle of London*, p. 202; Fabyan, *Chronicles*, p. 654) and was not made public until 29 September 1464 at a great council in Reading (William Worcester, *Annales*, p. 783). Elizabeth's refusal of any but marital relations with the king does not appear in English sources before the sixteenth century (More, *Richard III*, pp. 60–1; Hall, *Chronicle*, p. 264; Grafton, *Chronicle of England*, ii. 7) unless the view is accepted that the fragment commonly called *Hearne's Fragment* (*A Fragment relating to King Edward IV*, in *Thomae Sprotti Chronica*, ed. T. Hearne, Oxford, 1719, p. 293), although written not before 1516 embodies a much earlier account of Edward IV's court (Kingsford, *English historical Literature in the Fifteenth Century*, p. 177). None the less a story of Elizabeth's refusal to become yet another royal mistress

may have been current soon after 1464. Its absence from English fifteenth century historiography could be accounted for by the paucity of contemporary English sources, seeing that Dr. Conor Fahy has brought to light impressive new evidence proving that the story was known at an early date in North Italy ('The Marriage of Edward IV and Elizabeth Woodville: A new Italian source', E.H.R., lxxvi (1961) 660–72). The *De mulieribus admirandis*, which Antonio Cornazzano began at Milan early in 1466 and gave up probably in 1468 at Venice, provides with certain variations (e.g. regarding the dagger) a narrative close to that of Mancini. The possibility can not then be excluded that Mancini had heard the story on the continent: the more so since Dr. Fahy points out that Cornazzano admits his source to have been an oral one. The difference between Cornazzano and Mancini is that the former was concerned with the literary value of the subject and the latter with its historical interest. Continental sources such as *Dépêches des ambassadeurs milanais*, ii. 304; Du Clercq, *Mémoires*, iv. 87; Caspar Weinreich, *Danziger Chronik*, 728–9, and Comines, *Mémoires*, ii. 232; are only of interest in recording some of the gossip circulating abroad.

11. On state occasions such as the churching of Elizabeth after the birth of her eldest child in 1466 Edward IV surrounded his queen with exceptional pomp (Rozmital. *Ritter- Hof- und Pilger-Reise*, [the account in German by Gabriel Tetzel of Nuremberg] pp. 155–7). Otherwise Edward IV seems to have taken precautions that she should not give unnecessary offence by too lavish spending. At the start her household was by no means overgrown or extravagant, certainly not compared with that of Margaret of Anjou. See A. R. Myers, 'Household of Queen Elizabeth 1466–7', *Bulletin of the John Rylands Library*, l (1967) 207–35.

12. One result of the xenophobia prevalent in England during the later middle ages was that a member of the royal house born abroad was liable to be called a changeling or a bastard by his enemies. John of Gaunt born in Flanders was slandered both as the son of a Flemish butcher and as an illegitimate child (*Anonimalle Chronicle 1333–1381*, ed. V. H. Galbraith, Manchester, 1927, p. 104; *Chronicon Angliae*, ed. E. M. Thompson [Rolls Series, 1874] p. 107). His grandson Henry V prudently conducted Queen Catherine of France to England to give birth at Windsor, 6 December 1421, to his heir the future Henry VI (J. H. Wylie and W. T. Waugh, *The Reign of Henry the Fifth*, Cambridge, 1929, iii. 393). Edward IV was born at Rouen, 28 April 1442, (C. Scofield, *Life and reign of Edward the Fourth*, London, 1923, i. 1). Richard III was born at Fotheringay, 2 October 1452 (J. Gairdner, *Life of Richard III*, 2nd edn., 1898, p. 4); and when Parliament peti-

tioned him to assume the crown the fact that he was born in England was stressed: 'Ye be born withyn this lande, by reson wherof... all the thre estatis of the lande have, and may have, more certayn knowlage of your byrth and filiation' (*Rotuli Parliamentorum*, vi. 241). Richard Neville, earl of Warwick, as early as 1469, employed the same imputation to discredit Edward IV (Calmette and Perinelle, *Louis XI et l'Angleterre*, pièce justificative, no. 30).

13. Apart from More (*Richard III*, p. 62) native sources are silent about any tradition forbidding English kings to marry widows; but abroad, Basin (*Historia*, ed. Quicherat, iii. 135) and Caspar Weinreich (*Danziger Chronik*, p. 729) reported that Richard III appealed to this English custom as one of the reasons justifying his claim to the crown. As recently as 1403 Henry IV had married the dowager of Brittany, but only after his first wife had borne him six children of whom four were sons.

14. At Michaelmas 1464 when the marriage of Edward IV to Elizabeth Woodville was announced Richard of Gloucester was less than twelve years old (William Worcester, *Annales*, p. 771), but see Wavrin, ed. Dupont, ii. 333 and Wavrin, ed. Hardy, v. 459.

15. For the condemnation of Clarence, see Lander, (*Treason... of the duke of Clarence*, pp. 9–22) who gives a very full review of the sources native and foreign. Unlike other authorities Mancini directly blames the Woodvilles for the fall of Clarence (see above, p. 62, l. 19), More (*Richard III*, p. 7) is cautious on the subject, but he was up to a point writing in defence of the Woodvilles. Buchon's publication of Molinet, used in the first edition of this work (1936) states: 'le duc de Clarence querella contre *sa marâtre* et fut vaincu par procés et jugé à mourir' (*Chroniques*, ii. 377); although Elizabeth Woodville was not Clarence's step-mother the use of the word 'marâtre' might seem to point to her. The modern critical edition of Molinet's chronicle (ed. Doutrepont and Jodogne) gives a more intelligible reading as follows: 'le duc de Clarence querella contre *sa majesté* (*viz.* Edward IV) et fut vaincu par prochèz....' (i. 415).

16. The eloquence and handsome appearance of Clarence are confirmed by native sources close to these events: *Historie of the Arrivall of Edward IV*, p. 11; *Historia croylandensis*, p. 557; John Ross of Warwick, *Rows Roll*, no. 59.

17. Clarence himself was not charged with sorcery against the king in the text of the official indictment (*Rotuli Parliamentorum*, vi. 193–5). It was a member of his household Thomas Burdett who was executed at Tyburn 20 May 1477 for treason and necromancy against the king (Lander, *Treason... of the duke of Clarence*, p. 8).

18. This story of Clarence's end was reported by the contemporary Parisian annalist, Jean de Roye (*Journal*, ii. 64) and the same was accepted essentially by Comines (*Mémoires*, i. 53), La Marche (*Mémoires*, iii. 70) and Molinet (*Chroniques*, i. 415) also the Neapolitan diarist Notar Giacomo (*Cronica di Napoli*, p. 141). In England the story only appears at the end of the century (*Great Chronicle*, p. 226; Fabyan, *Chronicles*, p. 666; Polydore Vergil, *Anglica historia*, p. 681; More, *Richard III*, p. 7).

19. Owing to the lack of sources this statement can not be controlled by reference to other contemporary authorities; but for a different view see More (*Richard III*, p. 8).

20. The duke of Gloucester's efficient rule in the West Marches against Scotland was remembered long into the Tudor period (J. S. Brewer, *Letters and Papers Foreign and Domestic of Henry VIII* (ed. 1920), i. pt. 2, nos. 2382, 2913; iv. pt. 1, no. 133). The success, for what it was worth, of the aggressive policy in 1481–2 against the Scots was attributable to the financial, military and naval organization of Edward IV, his councillors and various commanders; but Gloucester's reputation benefited the more since he was identified with military victory in the north while keeping clear of the inglorious continental policy of the same years.

21. For the rise of the queen's relatives to power and wealth, particularly through judicious marriages, see J. R. Lander, 'Marriage and Politics in the Fifteenth Century: The Nevilles and the Wydvilles', B.I.H.R., xxxvi (1963) 120–52. Their prosperity brought on the Woodvilles considerable envy: but Mr. Lander wisely warns (*op. cit.*, p. 143 and *passim*) against supposing that the ruling class was excessively concerned at their prosperity. This point is exemplified by the University of Oxford, which in addressing Lionel Woodville in 1478, when he was dean of Exeter, drew a direct comparison between his exalted station and the status of his ancestry: 'Nos igitur, quoniam certo scimus ea te nobilitate pollere ad quam nulli tuorum maiorum propemodum aspirare poterant. . . .' (*Epistolae academicae*, ed. H. Anstey (Oxford Historical Society, xxxvi. 1898) ii. 448), but elected him the following year chancellor of the University (A. B. Emden, *Biographical Register of the University of Oxford to 1500*, Oxford, 1959, iii, 2083). See n. 32 below.

22. Confirmed by other evidence. The king walked through Croyland commenting on the pleasant situation of the village (*Historia croylandensis*, p. 542) and during his few months exile at Bruges (1470–1) his readiness to walk about through crowds aroused interest among a people accustomed to the remoter magnificance of Charles the Bold

(*Dits die excellentie Cronike van Vlaenderen*, Antwerp, Vorsterman, 1531, fol. f. cliii^{vo}).

23. Coming from an Italian visitor this is an interesting remark, but in its general application not so easy to verify or reject. The relations between the Yorkist crown and the Hanseatic merchants were unfriendly from 1461 to 1471 and did not become normal until 1475 (*Studies in English Trade in the Fifteenth Century*, ed. E. Power and M. M. Postan, London, 1933, pp. 132–7). Relations with merchants of the Italian powers were harmonious. In the first place the royal government prevented the recrudescence of anti-Italian violence, which had disturbed London in 1456–7 (A. A. Ruddock, *Italian Merchants and Shipping in Southampton 1270–1600*, Southampton, 1951, pp. 163–7); and in May 1463 the king ordered the removal from office of John Payne, mayor of Southampton, a professed enemy of the Italians, who had seized and sold goods of Venetian merchants (*ib.*, pp. 179–80). In the last parliament of the reign (January–February 1483), when Mancini was perhaps in England, the king exempted the various colonies of Italian merchants from the alien subsidy granted by Parliament on aliens resident in the country (*Rotuli Parliamentorum*, vi. 198a). It would be possible to cite numerous instances of royal favour shown to influential Italians; for example the king granted an audience to Ludovico Acciaiuoli, captain of the Florentine galleys to England and Flanders 1466–7 (M. E. Mallett, *Florentine Galleys in the Fifteenth Century*, Oxford, 1967, p. 51). These considerations were largely dictated by Edward's financial requirements: the payment of the dowry of his sister the duchess of Burgundy was made possible through Tommaso Portinari, factor of the Medici Bank in Bruges (C. A. J. Armstrong, 'La politique matrimoniale des ducs Valois de Bourgogne', *Annales de Bourgogne*, xl (1968) 47–8. R. de Roover, *Rise and Decline of the Medici Bank 1397–1494*, Cambridge, Mass., 1963, pp. 329–32) see also below, n. 27.

24. This is the first of two disappointingly vague references to the English parliament; but it is fairly descriptive of the king's attitude, for instance in his speech to the 1467 parliament (*Rotuli Parliamentorum*, v. 572; and see below, p. 96, l. 29).

25. Cf. the report on the king's methods for collecting the 1474–5 benevolence (*Calendar of State Papers, Milan*, pp. 193–4).

26. Corroborated by Polydore Vergil (*Anglica Historia*, pp. 684).

27. Louis XI undertook to pay 25,000 écus at Easter and Michaelmas annually during his life and that of Edward IV (Rymer, *Foedera*, xii, 14). The instalments were transmitted through the Medici bank (*Archaeologia*, xxxii (1847) 328).

28. The king's diet and menus were controlled by a physician of Edward IV's household. *The Household of Edward IV*, ed. A. R. Myers, p. 123.

29. More, *Richard III*, p. 4.

30. Thomas, marquess of Dorset, Lord Richard Grey and Sir Edward Woodville; Grey did not survive king Richard's accession, but in two proclamations directed against Dorset and Sir Edward Richard III denounced them as libertines (Rymer, *Foedera*, xii. 204-5; *Paston Letters*, vi. 81).

31. More (*Richard III*, p. 14) also admires the courage and political sense of Rivers. For details of Rivers's authorization as governor of the prince see Ives 'Andrew Dymmock and the papers of Antony earl Rivers 1482-3', B.I.H.R., xli (1968) 223, n. 5.

32. From the death of Clarence the Woodvilles did not derive great material profit. The marquess of Dorset received the custody and marriage of Clarence's infant son (*Calendar of Patent Rolls, 1476-85*, pp. 212, 283-4) and a grant for life of the office of master of the game in certain forests (*ib.*, p. 139). Rivers was granted the usufruct of various estates for six years in satisfaction of 1000 marks owed him by Clarence (Rymer, *Foedera*, xii. 95). Richard duke of Gloucester also made inconsiderable gains out of the death of his brother Clarence (P. M. Kendall, *Richard III*, p. 127). The real gainer was the king, who took into his hands, on pretext of wardship of the heir, not by virtue of escheat, the best placed and richest estates of the late duke (B. P. Wolffe, 'Management of English royal estates under the Yorkist kings', E.H.R., lxi (1956) 7; *Ministers' Accounts of the Warwickshire estates of the duke of Clarence 1479-80*, ed. R. H. Hilton, *Dugdale Society*, xxi (publication for the year 1944) printed Oxford, 1952).

33. Cf. the remarks of Comines (*Mémoires*, i. 78-9) and of More (*Richard III*, pp. 10-11).

34. See Ives 'Andrew Dymmock and the papers of Antony earl Rivers 1482-3', B.I.H.R., xli (1968) 221 and K. B. McFarlane 'Wars of the Roses' *Proceedings of the British Academy*, l (1964), 117, n. 3.

35. See the death-bed speech which More (*Richard III*, p. 11) puts into the mouth of Edward IV. The quarrel was continued by a son of the marquess of Dorset, George Grey, dean of Newarke College, Leicester, 1517-30, and Mary, Lady Hungerford, whose first husband had been Sir Edward Hastings, son of William, Lord Hastings (*Lincoln Record Society*, xxxiii (1940) pp. xci-xcii).

36. The duke of Gloucester was then residing on his Yorkshire estates (Polydore Vergil, *Anglica Historia*, p. 685). Mancini mistakenly supposed that in England appanages were granted to members of the

royal house on the same terms as in France, where the recipients held their land and usually resided in the places providing their titles. Polydore Vergil in his discussion of the origins of the dukedom of Clarence was the first historian to explain this form of English landtenure (*ib.*, p. 501). See above p. 98, l. 5.

37. See *Collection of Ordinances... for the Government of the Royal Household*, pp. 27*–33* for the regulations concerning the health and safety of the prince and his education. For further details and a correction of date see *The Household of Edward IV*, ed. A. R. Myers, p. 11, n. 7.

38. Keeping the dead king's treasure in custody at the Tower of London was in accordance with precedent, e.g. on the death of Henry V in 1422 his treasure and jewels were immediately sent from France for safe keeping in the Tower. (Thomas Walsingham, *Historia anglicana*, ed. H. T. Riley [Rolls Series, 1864] ii. 345.)

39. The Croyland Chronicle also implies that at this time Lord Hastings was in communication with the dukes of Gloucester and Buckingham, and further that Hastings felt so insecure in London that he talked of withdrawing to Calais, where he was lieutenant, if the council were to accept unconditionally all the demands of the Woodville faction (*Historia croylandensis*, pp. 564–5 confirmed by Polydore Vergil, *Anglica Historia*, p. 685).

40. The duke of Gloucester wrote to queen Elizabeth Woodville professing his allegiance to Edward V (*Historia croylandensis*, p. 565; Polydore Vergil, *Anglica Historia*, p. 685).

41. For the membership of the council see J. R. Lander, 'Council, Administration and Councillors 1461–85'. B.I.H.R. xxxii (1959) 166, sqq. The day fixed for the coronation was Sunday 4 May 1483 (*Historia croylandensis*, p. 565). Had everything gone according to plan Edward V might have reached London just in time to be crowned on that day, seeing that early on 30 April he was preparing to leave Stony-Stratford (Bucks.) about fifty miles from London when overtaken by the dukes of Gloucester and Buckingham (see below, n. 44). For the subsequent procrastination of the coronation see below n. 72 and 94.

42. The aim of the Woodville party was probably to form a regency resembling the government established by Edward IV during his absence on the French expedition of 1475. The prince of Wales was then created Keeper of the Realm, brought to London and installed in the household of his mother the queen, Elizabeth Woodville (*Calendar of Patent Rolls 1467-77*, pp. 534–5. Rymer, *Foedera*, xii. 13; B.M., Cotton MS., Vespasian C. xiv. f. 272vo).

43. For Henry Stafford, second duke of Buckingham, see *Complete*

HISTORICAL NOTES TO THE TEXT 115

Peerage, ii. 389 and *Dictionary of National Biography*. The date of his birth is uncertain. His father died in the autumn of 1458 (not killed at the battle of St. Albans, May 1455, see C. A. J. Armstrong, 'Politics and the battle of St. Albans 1455' B.I.H.R., xxxiii (1960) 69, n. 1) and Henry and his brother were for many years royal wards (*Calendar Patent Rolls 1461–7*, pp. 324, 463; P.R.O. Exchequer Treasury of Receipt Miscellaneous Books. no. 207, p. 32, E36/207). In February 1466 he married Catherine sister of Elizabeth Woodville, queen of Edward IV (William Worcester, *Annales*, p. 785). The duke of Buckingham according to Grafton's Continuation of Hardyng's Chronicle (Hardyng, *Chronicle*, p. 475) was the first person to communicate with the duke of Gloucester following the death of Edward IV. Buckingham sent his servant Persivall who met the duke of Gloucester at York. This meeting was prior to 23 April 1483 before which date Gloucester had left York (*York civic Records*, p. 71). Bringing instructions from the duke of Gloucester, Persivall then returned to the duke of Buckingham, who was in the Welsh Marches. His master sent him back with further instructions to Richard duke of Gloucester, who in the meanwhile had moved as far south as Nottingham, from the records of which it appears that the duke of Gloucester was approaching Nottingham by 26 April (W. H. Stevenson, *Records of Nottingham*, London, 1883, ii. 394). Persivall carried out his mission so quickly that the duke of Buckingham was able to meet the duke of Gloucester close to Northampton which the dukes entered together on 29 April (*Historia croylandensis*, p. 565; *Great Chronicle*, p. 230). See below, n. 44.

44. Cf. More (*Richard III*, p. 17) and n. 2 above. Edward V left, on 24 April 1483, Ludlow for London (Ross, *Historia regum Anglie*, p. 212). His advisers adapted his itinerary so as to effect a junction with the duke of Gloucester at some distance outside London in order that the king and his uncle might make a joint entry into the capital. The fact that the king was overtaken by the duke of Gloucester in the morning of 30 April at Stony-Stratford (Bucks) on Watling Street indicates just how far out of the direct route Ludlow–London the councillors of Edward V had taken him in order to suit the convenience of the duke of Gloucester who was approaching London on a more or less straight course from York (see above, n. 36 and 92 below).

45. On 8 March 1483 Rivers wrote to his attorney, Dymmock, 'Send me by som sure man ... a patent that the kyng gave me towchyng pouer to rayse peple if need be in the marche of Welles'; Ives, *op. cit.*, B.I.H.R., xli (1968) 229. Since the size of the force that should accompany Edward V to London was one of the main subjects of dispute between the Hastings and Woodville faction, the queen, by way of

compromise, wrote bidding him bring no more than 2000 men (*Historia croylandensis*, pp. 564-5).

46. Edward V was not twelve miles from London when overtaken by the dukes of Gloucester and Buckingham but at Stony-Stratford fifty-two miles from London along Watling Street. The earl of Rivers was not arrested by the duke of Gloucester 'in oppido ipsius ducis quam munitissimo'. However when the dukes subsequently took Edward V on to London the earl of Rivers, and the king's half brother, Lord Richard Grey, besides other attendants of the king not mentioned by Mancini such as Vaughan and Haute were sent to the Yorkshire castles in the possession of Gloucester. Clearly Mancini had heard that Rivers, Grey, and the others were finally imprisoned in one of Gloucester's strongholds; but his ignorance of English topography outside London led him to confuse localities. The *Great Chronicle* (p. 230); John Ross (*Historia regum Anglie*, p. 212); Polydore Vergil (*Anglica Historia*, p. 686) describe briefly the seizure of the king and the arrest of his councillors, and Fabyan (*Chronicles*, p. 668) is both brief and inaccurate. The account given by Mancini does not agree altogether with that of Croyland chronicle (*Historia croylandensis*, p. 565) according to which Rivers and Lord Richard Grey were sent by the king to Northampton for the purpose of associating Gloucester with their policy. The arrest of Rivers and Grey took place according to this source as they, accompanied by the two dukes of Gloucester and Buckingham, were returning to the king and were about to enter Stony-Stratford. Mancini agrees with More's account (*Richard III*, pp. 17-19) on three points: (i) Rivers being arrested at dawn before the dukes set out to salute the king, (ii) guards posted along the road by the dukes to prevent the news of their arrest of Rivers reaching the king, and (iii) the arrest of Richard Grey in the king's presence.

47. Wednesday 30 April 1483 (*Historia croylandensis*, p. 565).

48. 'Dux ille Glocestriae ... nihil reverentiae quod capitis nudatio, genuflectio, aliusve quilibet corporis habitus in subdito exigit, dicto nepoti suo regi facere distulit aut recusavit' (*ib.* cf. Ross. *Historia regum Anglie*, p. 212; More, *Richard III*, p. 19).

49. Northampton was the town to which the king was taken and from which he wrote on 2 May 1483 to the archbishop of Canterbury. See below n. 59.

50. '... fecit (duke of Gloucester) publice proclamari, ut omnes familiares regis sese incontinenter a villa (Stony-Stratford) subtraherent, et quod non accedant prope loca ad quae rex se diverteret, sub poena mortis' (*Historia croylandensis*, p. 565).

51. The news reached London during the night 30 April-1 May

HISTORICAL NOTES TO THE TEXT 117

shortly before midnight (*Ib.*, p. 565; More, *Richard III*, p. 20). 'Vidisses eo mane fautores unius et alterius partis alios vere alios dissimulanter, propter eventus dubios, his aut illis partibus adhaerentes. Nam aliqui apud Westmonasterium sub titulo reginae alii apud Londonias sub umbra domini de Hastyngs, societates suas congregaverunt' (*Historia croylandensis*, pp. 565–6). According to Polydore Vergil (*Anglica Historia*, pp. 686–7) Lord Hastings was also dismayed and now regretted his support previously given to Gloucester. All whom he knew to be concerned for Edward V's safety he, Hastings, summoned to a council at St. Paul's. At this meeting some proposed to liberate the king by force while others considered that the use of arms would not improve the situation; the latter opinion prevailed. More on the other hand attributed the defeat of the queen's party in London to Hastings who persuaded the Lords in council that Gloucester's action would prove to be justifiable when legally examined (*Richard III*, p. 23). Vergil's account seems more likely to be true.

52. According to Mancini the queen and the marquess of Dorset did not take sanctuary until the failure of their efforts to raise an army. This implies that they did not go into sanctuary for at least a day after hearing of the king's detention by Gloucester, *viz.* on the evening of 1 May. Other authorities are unanimous in stating that the queen taking her children with her accompanied by the marquess entered sanctuary at night immediately on receipt of the news from Stony-Stratford (*Historia croylandensis*, p. 565; Ross, *Historia regum Anglie*, p. 213; *Great Chronicle*, p. 230; Fabyan, *Chronicles*, p. 668; More, *Richard III*, p. 20; Polydore Vergil, *Anglica Historia*, p. 686). For the date of the birth of Richard, duke of York, the queen's other son, whom she took into sanctuary, see *Archaeologia*, lxxxiv (1934) 4–5.

53. During the restoration of Henry VI 1470–1 a proclamation was issued in his name forbidding any infringement of sanctuary or injury to those who had taken refuge there (B.M., Harl. MS. 543. f. 172ro, a transcript by Stow).

54. This is an interesting reflection on the increase of royal power following Edward IV's recovery of the throne in 1471. The most famous incident had occurred following the battle of Tewkesbury; but the king's apologist declared that Tewkesbury Abbey possessed no franchise for the protection of traitors (Warkworth, *Chronicle*, pp. 18–19; *Historie of the Arrivall of Edward IV*, pp. 30–1). There is also evidence suggesting that in 1472 the duke of Exeter was taken out of Westminster sanctuary and kept in honorary confinement at the Tower (Warkworth, *Chronicle*, pp. 16–17; P.R.O., Issue Roll, Easter, 11 Edw. IV, m. 8, E403/844; Tellers Roll, Michaelmas, 11 Edw. IV, m. 6, E405/54;

Rymer, *Foedera*, xi, 713-14). On the other hand the brother of the bastard of Fauconberg took sanctuary and was later granted a pardon (*Paston Letters*, v. 113; *Calendar of Patent Rolls, 1476-85*, p. 57). It is striking that in the pre-Tudor period a visiting foreigner such as Mancini should have been so concerned with the rights of sanctuary. Foreigners occasionally found sanctuary useful as in 1468 when all the Hansards in] London were arrested save those who could reach Westminster sanctuary (*Hanserecesse*, Abtheilung II. Bd. vi. Leipzig, 1890, pp. 90-1).

55. Either 30 April or 1 May. The latter date would be consistent with the narrative seeing that Mancini puts the queen's flight to sanctuary a day later than other sources.

56. The treaty of 1482 concluded between Edward IV and Louis XI (printed by J. Gairdner, E.H.R., xii (1897) 522-3) had nevertheless provided for the continuance of peace between the two powers during the year following the death of either sovereign. Between 1450 and 1483 it was not unknown for the French to harry the coasts and at times to seize individuals and hold them to ransom (*Paston Letters*, ii. 135; iv. 68; v. 177-8). In his unpublished Oxford D.Phil. thesis (1962) Dr. C. F. Richmond taking piracy cases recorded on the Patent and Close Rolls has shown by means of a graph that after the outburst of piracy accompanying the re-adeption of Henry VI (1470) a decline set in after 1471. According to this source some of the lowest figures for piracy since 1399 were recorded before the rise of incidents in 1482-3 which again dropped after Richard III had re-established the royal keeping of the sea.

57. Philippe de Crèvecoeur, sire d'Esquerdes (*Dictionnaire de la Noblesse*, ed. De la Chenaye-Desbois, vi (1865) 505) known in England as Lord Cordis (*Great Chronicle*, p. 243). After 1477 champion of French expansion to north and east ('which so sore longed for Caleys that he would commonly saye that he would gladly lye vii yeres in hell, so that Caleys were in possession of the Frenchmen'. Hall, *Chronicle*, p. 447). Died in 1494 near Lyons during preparation for Charles VIII's expedition to Italy insisting on burial at Boulogne-sur-Mer against the frontier that he had for so long sought to extend (Molinet, *Chronique*, ii. 389 and *passim*).

58. On 11 May less than a week after the entry into London of the duke of Gloucester an envoy was sent to France to negotiate an exchange of naval prizes (Nichols, *Grants of Edward V*, p. 2). At about this time, or earlier, a servant of the duke was arrested at Tours (Calmette and Perinelle, *Louis XI et l'Angleterre*, p. 254). The instructions given to an embassy sent in July 1483 by Richard III to Philippe de Crèvecoeur for

the 'restitution of two ships pertaining to the Lord Cordes' sufficiently elucidate the circumstances referred to by Mancini (*Letters and Papers of Richard III and Henry VII*, i. 18, sqq.).

59. Seeing that Edward IV had died in the midst of preparation for war with France and in view of England's lack of allies it is difficult to see what other course the council in London could have taken. However, it is not easy to tell what the real motives were. No sooner was Edward IV dead than the council ordered the embarkation of 300 men at arms for the defence of Calais (P.R.O., Tellers Rolls, Michaelmas, 22 Edw. IV, m. 2, dorse E405/71). Was this a genuine measure to defend Calais (of which 80 per cent of the land frontier had become since 1477 contiguous with France) or was it a means to prevent Hastings lieutenant of Calais (see above n. 39) from setting himself up there as an independent power imitating the earl of Warwick in 1459? According to More (*Richard III*, p. 19) the dukes of Gloucester and Buckingham told Edward V on 30 April at Stony-Stratford that the incursion upon the treasure and the naval expedition were part of a plot to bring the realm under the control of the queen's relatives. If however Edward Woodville's expedition sailed on 30 April or 1 May 1483, the dukes at Stony-Stratford could have had no knowledge of its departure. There is even reason to believe that on 2 May the dukes though anxious about the treasure were unaware that the Woodvilles had disposed of it. On that date the king who had been brought back to Northampton by Gloucester and Buckingham wrote to Thomas Bourchier, archbishop of Canterbury, as follows:

'by the king'

R.E. 'Most reverend ffader in God and right entirely beloved cousyn. We grete you hertely wele and desire and pray you to see for the saufegarde and sure keping of the gret seale of this our realme unto our comyng to our cite of London. Where by your good advice and others of our counsaill the same ferther may be demeanded for the weele of us and our said realme; and that it woll like you to call unto you the lords there and provide for the suerte and saufegarde of our toure of London and the treasure beyng in the same in all diligence, and our faithfull trust is in you. Geven under our signet at our towne of Northampton, the second day of May'

[signed] Edward.

(P.R.O., Ancient Correspondence, xlv, no. 236, exhibited in P.R.O. Museum Pedestal 21.)

Mancini is unique in recording the partition of Edward IV's treasure by the queen, the marquess, and Sir Edward. This is damaging evidence

against the Woodvilles. Why should Sir Edward embark with a third of the treasure if it was not desired to place this sum beyond the reach of the rivals of the Woodville family? The partition probably resulted in considerable loss to Richard duke of Gloucester and affords further explanation for his rapid impoverishment after his accession, which the *Great Chronicle of London* (p. 234) attributes to his reckless purchase of friends. Sir Edward's share of the treasure was presumably taken to Brittany where he took refuge. It seems that the duke of Gloucester endeavoured to trace that portion of the treasure taken by the marquess of Dorset. Simon Stallworth wrote 9 June 1483 'Wher so evyr kanne be founde any godyse of my lord Markues it is tayne. The Prior of Westminster wasse and yet is in a gret trobyll for certeyne godys delyvered to hyme by my lord Markues' (*Stonor Letters*, ii. 159–60).

60. The king entered London 4 May 1483 (*Great Chronicle*, p. 230; Fabyan, *Chronicles*, p. 668; *Chronicles of London*, p. 190; More, *Richard III*, p. 24). He was lodged at the bishop's palace beside St. Paul's which was the usual residence of English kings within the city (Stow, *Survey of London*, ii. 20; *Chronicles of London*, 165, 172, 182).

61. Molinet also identifies the Welsh as the special supporters of the young king (*Chroniques*, i. 431). Many prominent Welshmen had prospered in the service of Edward IV, one of whom, Sir Thomas Vaughan, not mentioned by Mancini, was treasurer of the king's chamber and chamberlain to the Prince of Wales. He was arrested like Rivers on 30 April by the duke of Gloucester, and, like Rivers, suffered at Pontefract 25 June 1483 (*Historia croylandensis*, p. 565).

62. More, *Richard III*, p. 24; *Cely Papers*, p. 87.

63. Whether or not Gloucester was designated protector under the will of Edward IV (see above n. 7) the duke does not appear to have assumed office until chosen and appointed by the council after his arrival in London with Edward V. Gloucester at this time was studiously observing legality and it would have been in keeping with the precedents of 1422 and 1454 to have awaited appointment by the council before assuming office (J. S. Roskell, 'The office and dignity of Protector of England with special reference to its origins' E.H.R., lxviii (1953) 193–233, *esp.* 227; J. R. Lander; 'Henry VI and the duke of York's second protectorate'. *Bulletin John Rylands Library*. xliii (1960) 46–69, *esp.* 48). Other evidence supports the statement of Mancini. It is significant that the bidding prayer prepared for a convocation convened for 18 April 1483 made no mention of Gloucester either as protector or individual, the only persons publicly prayed for being Edward V and Elizabeth the queen-mother (Nichols, *Grants of Edward V*, p. xxxviii). After relating the duke's entry into the city and other events in London

the Croyland Chronicle states 'accepit dictus Richardus dux Glocestriae illum solennem magistratum qui duci Humfrido Glocestriae, stante minore aetate regis Henrici, ut regni Protector appellaretur, olim contingebat.' *Historia croylandensis*, p. 566. Similarly the *Great Chronicle of London* (p. 230) says that Gloucester was proclaimed protector shortly after his entry into London, while according to More (*Richard III*, p. 24) he was made protector at the first council meeting held after his arrival. This view, however, was not shared by Gairdner, who drew attention to a couple of documents on the Patent Roll, dated respectively 21 April and 2 May 1483 in which the duke of Gloucester is styled 'Protector of England' (J. Gairdner, *Life of Richard III*, ed. 1898, p. 55). The probable explanation is that these documents were not enrolled until after Gloucester had become protector. See above p. 70, l. 15.

64. Thomas Rotherham, archbishop of York, was still in office as chancellor 22 April 1483 (R. L. Storey, 'English officers of state 1399–1485', B.I.H.R., xxxi (1958) 85). More (*Richard III*, p. 22) is unique in reporting that the archbishop of York, Edward IV's chancellor, surrendered the seal to the queen on the same night as she took sanctuary at Westminster, but that on second thoughts he subsequently recovered it from her. According to More (*ib.*, p. 25) Thomas Rotherham was not removed from office till Russell was made chancellor at the first council held in London after the arrival of the duke of Gloucester. It is clear, however, that when Edward V wrote on 2 May from Northampton to the archbishop of Canterbury, he, Edward V, or rather his captors the dukes of Gloucester and Buckingham, supposed that Thomas Bourchier, archbishop of Canterbury, was in possession of the great seal (see above, n. 59). Actually the archbishop of Canterbury would appear not to have taken possession of the great seal until 7 May. On that date the executors of Edward IV assembled at Baynard's Castle, the London house of Cicely, duchess of York, mother of the late king, and the archbishop then and there took over all Edward IV's seals, Great, Privy, and Signet (*Registrum Thome Bourgchier*, pp. 52–3).

65. John Russell, bishop of Lincoln, was appointed chancellor 10 May 1483 (R. L. Storey, *op. cit.*, p. 86). He was appointed much against his own wish according to John Ross (*Historia regum Angliae*, p. 213). For his career see A. B. Emden, *Oxford*, iii. 1609. He was the only official of Richard III to receive unqualified recommendation from More (*Richard III*, p. 25).

66. The council, therefore, was not yet subservient to the Protector and adhered to the strict interpretation of the Statute of Treason.

67. On 10 May 1483 orders were given to Sir Thomas Fulford and

Halwelle 'to rigge them to see in al hast and to goo to the Dounes among Ser Eduard [Woodville] and his company in that they may' (Nichols, *Grants of Edward V*, p. 2). For John Halwell or Holwell see *passim* in *Calendar of Patent Rolls 1467–77* and *Calendar Patent Rolls 1476–85*. This was almost certainly an attempt to entice the fleet away from its commander Sir Edward Woodville. On 14 May more explicit orders were issued to Edward Brampton, John Wellis, and Thomas Grey 'to go to the see with shippes to take Ser Edward Wodevile' (*Grants of Edward V*, p. 3) 'with a clause to receyve all that wolle come except the Marquys, Ser Edward Wodevile and Robert Ratclyff'. At about this time Lord Cobham and other gentlemen passed through Canterbury toward Dover and Sandwich under orders from the Protector. At Canterbury it was so uncertain whom they were to resist that the name of the enemy was left blank in the city record (H.M.C., *Ninth Report* (1883), *Canterbury City muniments*, pt. i, p. 145). On 21 May further orders to the captains of the Carvel of Eu and the Elizabeth to take soldiers to sea (B.M. Harl. MS. 433, f. 225vo).

68. At times of crisis throughout this period the crown could not do without foreign ships hired or seized from their owners in order to supplement available English vessels both royal and private. In 1460 the Lancastrian government employed four carracks of Venice and Genoa to combat the Yorkist lords, whose ships held the Channel (*Letters and Papers illustrative of the Wars of the English in France*, ii. pt. 2, 516–17; J. Heers, *Les Génois en Angleterre: la crise de 1458–60*, in *Studi in Onore di Armando Sapori*, Milan, 1957, ii. 809–32). In 1461 the Milanese envoy in France advised the duke of Milan to hire some large ships from Genoa to serve the English for four months if he wished to see the English government secure at home (*Calendar of State Papers, Milan*, p. 88). In 1468 the Yorkist government alarmed by a threatened invasion from France by Margaret of Anjou, queen of Henry VI, unloaded and armed four Genoese galleys, while the Genoese brought other ships to England to furnish Edward IV with a fleet (William Worcester, *Annales*, p. 792; *Calendar of State Papers, Milan*, pp. 126–7). On 14 January 1485 Richard III faced with the threatened invasion of Henry Tudor, ordered a Genoese carrack bound for Flanders, lying at Southampton, to be commandeered for royal service and its cargo discharged. A few days later he acquired by forced purchase a ship of Lübeck driven by storm into Dartmouth (B.M., Harl. MS. 433, ff. 202ro, 203ro). For 1458 and for 1465–6 there is evidence of some very large Genoese ships of which some traded to England and Flanders (J. Heers, *Gênes au XVe siècle* [*Centre de Recherches historiques: Affaires et gens d'affaires*, xxiv, 1961] p. 269,

app. xii). During the period 1400–51 English ships hired by the crown compared for size not unfavourably with those of other European countries (D. Burwash, *English Merchant Shipping 1460–1540*, Toronto, 1947. app. ii, tables A–B); but during the reign of Edward IV the average size of English ships may have begun to decline (G. V. Scammell, 'English Merchant Shipping at the end of the Middle Ages: some east coast evidence', *Economic History Review*, xiii [1961–2] 332–4). It was characteristic of the haphazard but not altogether unsuccessful administration of Edward IV that his brother Richard, duke of Gloucester, was appointed at the age of ten Admiral of England in 1462 (*Calendar of Patent Rolls 1461–7*, p. 214), but that nevertheless twenty years later the king disposed of a formidable fleet with which to prosecute the war against Scotland (C. F. Richmond, 'English naval power in the fifteenth century', *History*, lii [1967] 10).

69. Failure to obey would have exposed the Genoese in England to retaliation. After the commanders of the Venetian fleet had ignored similar orders of the council in 1460 Venetian merchants and their goods were seized in London and caution money of 36000 ducats extorted (*Calendar of State Papers, Venice*, i, 88).

70. One of the vessels may have belonged to Johannes Ambrosius de Nigrono, a Genoese merchant who came to England in February 1481 (P.R.O., French Rolls, 20 Edw. IV, m. 1, C.76/164). He was rewarded for unspecified services by a grant dated 4 June 1483 of £384. 7s. 6d. on the customs (Nichols, *Grants of Edward V*, p. 54), subsequently he received from Richard III two further grants (*Calendar of Patent Rolls 1476–85*, p. 467).

71. The two royal ships that Sir Edward Woodville carried off were probably the Falcon and the Trinity neither of which appear in crown records during the reign of Richard III, but re-appear once again in royal service as from the beginning of Henry VII's reign (C. F. Richmond, 'English naval power in the fifteenth century', *History*, lii (1967) 11, n. 53).

72. The first date for the coronation Sunday 4 May 1483 had of necessity to be abandoned (see above n. 41 and 60); and the next date to be chosen appears to have been the Nativity of St. John Baptist Tuesday 24 June (*Historia croylandensis*, p. 566). This date was probably decided upon before 13 May since writs bearing that date were issued convening the first parliament of the reign for the following 25 June (see below n. 94), and on 20 May letters were addressed to sheriffs with orders that all those eligible for knighthood should present themselves in London by 18 June so as to receive that dignity at the coronation (Rymer, *Foedera*, xii. 181). In the second week of June

there was still some uncertainty among the public: Simon Stallworth, writing on 9 June, believed that the coronation would take place on 23 June as was commonly reported (*Stonor Letters*, ii. 160). The councillors, who met on 13 June at Westminster, had received orders from the Protector to announce the precise date (Polydore Vergil, *Anglica Historia*, p. 689); but this proclamation, if ever made, must have been quickly superseded because of the execution of Hastings, which occurred on the very same day and gave the Protector an excuse for deferring the coronation, according to Grafton (*Chronicles*, ii. 102) until Sunday 2 November.

73. For the career of Thomas Bourchier, archbishop of Canterbury, see the introduction in *Registrum Thome Bourgchier* of F. R. H. du Boulay, pp. vii–xlvi and R. J. Knecht, 'The episcopate and the wars of the Roses', *University of Birmingham Historical Journal*, vi (1957–8) 111, 123. The author of the *Great Chronicle* (p. 231), like Mancini, is at pains to exonerate the septuagenarian archbishop from abetting the designs of the duke of Gloucester. During the critical period at the end of May 1483 Bourchier probably withdrew to the manor of Knole (*Registrum Thome Bourgchier*, p. 55). See below, n. 111.

74. The delivery of the duke of York is here described prior to the execution of Hastings; and later sources give the same order to these two events as does Mancini (*Great Chronicle*, p. 231; Fabyan, *Chronicles*, p. 668; *Chronicles of London*, p. 190; More, *Richard III*, pp. 41, 49–50; Polydore Vergil, *Anglica Historia*, pp. 688–9). However, the Croyland chronicle and a letter written from London by Simon Stallworth, the latter within a week of the events, point to Monday 16 June as having been the date on which the duke of York was given up by his mother from sanctuary (*Historia croylandensis*, p. 566; *Stonor Letters*, ii. 161). There is no doubt that Hastings was executed the previous Friday, 13 June. The date 16 June for the surrender of the duke of York is also indicated by a significant entry in the household accounts of John Howard, duke of Norfolk, who according to a late source was one of the Protector's envoys to the queen in Westminster sanctuary (Grafton's addition to Hardyng's chronicle in Hardyng, *Chronicle*, p. 488): under 16 June Howard's clerk accounted for '8 botes uppe and down from Westminster' (*Household Books of John duke of Norfolk, 1481–90*, p. 402). The minutes of the City Council of London for 23 May 1483 show that the Protector and the lords of the king's council in London were then trying to induce the queen to leave Westminster sanctuary peaceably: 'Isto die lectum fuit iuramentum Richardi ducis Gloucestriae protectoris Anglie, Thomae archiepiscopi Cantuariensis, Thomae archiepiscopi Eboracensis, Henrici ducis Buckinghamiae et

dominorum nuper factum domino nostro Regi. Item iuramentum quod dicti domini facere voluissent domine Elizabethae regine Anglie modo existenti in sanctuario Sancti Petri Westminster, si eadem domina privilegium eiusdem loci relinquere voluerit' (London, Guildhall, MS., Journal 9, f. 23vo). By the second week of June relations between the queen and the royal council had so far deteriorated that none of the councillors spoke to her when a meeting was held at Westminster (*Stonor Letters*, ii, 159–60).

75. Edward earl of Warwick born 21 February 1475 at Warwick perished on the scaffold in 1499, a conspicuous victim of Henry VII (*Complete Peerage*, xii, 394–7).

76. Anne duchess of Gloucester, younger daughter and co-heiress of Richard Neville, earl of Warwick, was a uterine aunt of Edward earl of Warwick since her sister Isabelle had married his father George duke of Clarence. She arrived in London Thursday 5 June 1483 (*Stonor Letters*, ii. 160). She died, queen of England, 16 March 1485 leaving a reputation of 'a woman of gracious fame' (*Great Chronicle*, p. 234).

77. At p. 68, l. 16 and p. 70, l. 8 William lord Hastings is referred to merely as a courtier. In this passage Mancini seizes something of his importance as the life-long servant of the Yorkist dynasty. For the political and social significance of his career see W. H. Dunham jr. 'Lord Hastings' indentured retainers 1461–83', *Transactions of the Connecticut Academy of Arts and Sciences*, xxxix. (1955) 1–175.

78. A. B. Emden, *Oxford*, iii. 1593, and *Cambridge*, p. 489. The son of a Yorkshire knight Sir John Rotherham.

79. Emden, *Oxford*, ii. 1318; Emden, *Cambridge*, p. 412.

80. More relates that Gloucester sounded the opinions of William lord Hastings through William Catesby, esquire (More, *Richard III*, p. 45). Catesby was closely associated with Hastings and the duke of Buckingham as their estate agent (J. S. Roskell, 'William Catesby counsellor to Richard III', *Bulletin John Rylands Library, Manchester*, xlii (1959–60) 145–74). The Protector contrived that the council should meet in two parts. One section comprising Hastings, Rotherham, Morton, and others noted for their devotion to Edward V, assembling at Baynard's Castle, while the Protector and the duke of Buckingham gathered their adherents at Crosby Place, where Gloucester was lodging (*Great Chronicle*, p. 230; More, *Richard III*, p. 44; Graftons' Continuation to Hardyng's Chronicle, Hardyng, *Chronicle*, p. 492). From what Mancini says it seems that the friends of the young king preferred to hold their deliberations at home altogether outside the council.

81. Friday 13 June 1483 council meeting in the Tower, perhaps the best recorded event of Edward V's reign (*Historia croylandensis*,

p. 566; *Great Chronicle*, p. 231; Fabyan, *Chronicles*, p. 668; *Chronicles of London*, p. 190; More, *Richard III*, p. 48–9; Polydore Vergil, *Anglica Historia*, p. 689–90). Mancini thought that Hastings and his companions had come not to a council but to make a customary call upon the Protector. On this particular day the more official part of the council was assembled under the chancellor, John Russell, at Westminster (*Historia croylandensis*, p. 566). Mancini is mistaken in supposing that Hastings was murdered immediately the armed men intruded. Such procedure was un-English and reminiscent of Italian practice; e.g. the conspiracy of the Pazzi (1478) at Florence or the assassination of the duke of Milan (1476).

82. The university of Cambridge interceded on behalf of Rotherham, archbishop of York, while that of Oxford intervened for Morton, bishop of Ely (Emden, *Cambridge*, pp. 413, 490). The former was released on 4 July, just before the coronation of Richard III (Grafton's Continuation of Hardyng's Chronicle, Hardyng, *Chronicle*, p. 516); but Morton had to make good his own escape during the reign of Richard III under circumstances which are insufficiently known (More, *Richard III*, pp. 91, 269).

83. Cf. More, *Richard III*, p. 53; Polydore Virgil, *Anglica Historia*, p. 690.

84. None of the sources give a date for the marquess's evasion. The reference to the grown crops presupposes some time in the month of June. Cf. *Great Chronicle*, p. 232; Fabyan, *Chronicles*, p. 670; *Chronicles of London*, p. 191.

85. Rivers was detained at Sheriff Hutton (Yorks.) where he made a will on 23 June 1483 (*Excerpta historica*, p. 246–8) and Lord Richard Grey at Middleham (Yorks.) (B.M., Harl. MS., 433, f. 118ro). They were taken to Pontefract (*Great Chronicle*, p. 232) and there beheaded on 25 June 1483. The date of Earl Rivers's death is precisely recorded by the obituary of St. Stephen's chapel Westminster (B.M., Cotton MS., Faustina B., viii, f. 4vo). According to the Croyland chronicle, they and the other victims of Richard duke of Gloucester were not accorded the form of a trial (*Historia croylandensis*, p. 567). Possibly they underwent some summary form of justice since John Ross (*Historia regum Anglie*, p. 213–14) refers to Henry earl of Northumberland as 'eorum principalis iudex'. Rivers and Richard Grey were long remembered by the old Yorkists who survived into the Tudor Age: e.g. the will of Sir Richard Sutton dated 16 March 1524 (R. Churton, *Lives of William Smyth, bishop of Lincoln, and Sir Richard Sutton knt. Founders of Brasen Nose College*, Oxford, 1800, p. 540).

86. Cf. the remarks of Ross, *Historia regum Anglie*, p. 213. For the

coinage of Edward V see G. C. Brooke, *English Coins from the seventh Century to the Present Day*, 3rd ed., London, 1955, p. 160.

87. 'And afftyr this [Hastings' death] were the prince and the duke of York holdyn more streygth and than was pryvy talkyng in London that the lord protectour shuld be kyng' (*Great Chronicle*, p. 231). The date is uncertain when Edward V was removed from the bishop's palace (see above n. 60) to the Tower. Probably the king was taken there on or soon after 16 June 1483, the date when the Protector got into his hands the king's brother Richard, duke of York (see above, n. 74, and p. 88, l. 5). There would appear nothing sinister at such a time in the transfer of the king and his brother to the Tower in preparation for the forthcoming coronation (see above, n. 72) since the ceremony was traditionally preceded by a royal procession from the Tower to Westminster (see above, p. 100, l. 6).

88. 'During this mayris yere. The childyr of kyng Edward were seen shotyng and playyng in the gardyn of the Towyr by sundry tymys' (*Great Chronicle*, p. 234). The mayor alluded to is Edmund Shaw, who held office from 29 October 1482 until 28 October 1483. (For the chronology of mayoral years and its effect on city historiography, see Kingsford, *English historical literature*, p. 73 and *Great Chronicle*, pp. xlvi, lix-lx.)

89. John Argentine, 1443–1508, physician to Edward, prince of Wales, and afterwards to the son of Henry VII, Arthur, prince of Wales. In the first edition (1936) of the *De occupatione* I failed to identify *Argentinus medicus* with John Argentine. The identification was first set out in my paper 'An Italian astrologer at the court of Henry VII' published in *Italian Renaissance Studies. A tribute to the late Cecilia M. Ady*, ed. E. F. Jacob (Faber and Faber) London, 1960, p. 449. Subsequently Dr. D. E. Rhodes, 'The Princes in the Tower and their Doctor', E.H.R. lxxvii (1962) 304–6, 624, independently reached the same conclusion. The extensive bibliography in manuscript and print relating to Argentine's academic career and to his activity as a book collector is to be found in the biographical notice by A. B. Emden, *Cambridge* (1962), pp. 15–16 and the book by D. E. Rhodes, *John Argentine, Provost of King's, his life and library*, Amsterdam, 1967. See above, p. 20 and n. 2.

90. John Alcock, bishop of Worcester 1476 translated 1486 to Ely, was tutor to the prince of Wales, of whom John Ross wrote 'virtuose a virtuosis erat nutritus mirabilis ingenii et in literatura optime expeditus' (Ross, *Historia regum Angliae*, p. 212).

91. Mancini left for France shortly after King Richard's coronation, which took place on 6 July (see above, p. 104, l. 12) and his reference

therefore to rumours current in England that Edward V was by then already dead is in point of time the earliest report of such suspicions, if we exclude the cryptic note, probably written between 13 and 26 June 1483, forming part of the Cely correspondence, and also expressing fears for the lives of the king and of the duke of York his brother (*Cely Papers*, pp. 132–3). It has been suggested that the king's brother, Richard duke of York, was dead by 28 June 1483 (M. J. Tucker, *Life of Thomas Howard, earl of Surrey, second duke of Norfolk*, The Hague, 1964, pp. 38–9, 42–3). This suggestion is based on the fact that Richard III granted, 28 June 1483, to John Howard the dukedom of Norfolk, which had been held since 1482 by Richard duke of York. He as a child had married another child Anne daughter of the last Mowbray duke of Norfolk. Their marriage settlement of 1478 reserved the dukedom to him together with the Mowbray estates in the event of her predeceasing him without leaving children of their marriage. She died in 1482 without children, when the conditions of the marriage contract became operative. Of course from the moment on 26 June 1483 when Richard III seated himself on the throne, the two sons of Edward IV were *legally* dead in the sense of being incapacitated from holding any honours from the crown downward, but this need not imply that either of them was then *physically* dead. It would be here out of place to recapitulate conflicting views about the disappearance of Edward IV's sons. But in any review of the question the following studies should not be overlooked:

L. E. Tanner and W. Wright, 'Recent investigations regarding the fate of the Princes in the Tower', *Archaeologia*, lxxxiv (1934) 1–26.
A. R. Myers, 'The Character of Richard III', *History Today*, iv (1954) 511–21; 'Richard III and historical Tradition', *History*, liii (1968) 181–202. P. M. Kendall, *Richard III*, London, 1955, appendix i, 'Who murdered the Little Princes?', pp. 393–418. The work of Tanner and Wright is especially interesting since the remains which they inspected are unlikely to become available for re-examination without a major change in Church and State.

92. At York on his first public appearance after the death of his brother Edward IV the duke of Gloucester assumed mourning (*Historia croylandensis*, p. 565); and, although the king entered London in blue velvet, the duke accompanied him 'in blak cloth like a mourner' (*Chronicles of London*, p. 190; *Great Chronicle*, p. 230). Richard Neville, earl of Warwick, had already demonstrated the political advantages to be gained from a liberal feeding of the London populace (*ib.* 207).

93. Mancini refers to preachers and sermons as though more than

HISTORICAL NOTES TO THE TEXT 129

one preacher was induced to advocate the claims of Richard III. On Sunday 22 June Dr. Ralph Shaw (Emden, *Cambridge*, 519) preached at Paul's Cross, declaring the duke of Gloucester's right to the crown on account of the illegitimacy of Edward IV and his children (*Great Chronicle*, pp. 231-2; Fabyan, *Chronicles*, p. 669; *Chronicles of London*, p. 190; More, *Richard III*, pp. 58-9, 66; Polydore Vergil, *Anglica Historia*, p. 691). These sources give the wrong date, *viz* the Sunday following the death of lord Hastings; but the true date is to be ascertained by counting the days backward from Richard III's accession 26 June 1483. More records a sermon preached on behalf of Richard III by Thomas Penketh, an Augustinian hermit (Emden, *Cambridge*, p. 448), but this was apparently not before Easter 1484 (More, *Richard III*, p. 58).

94. Writs dated 13 May 1483 were issued for a parliament to meet 25 June at Westminster (*Seventh Report of the Deputy Keeper of the Public Records*, 1846, Appendix ii, p. 212; *Registrum Thome Bourgchier*, p. 53). This parliament was doubtless intended to coincide approximately with the coronation of Edward V (see above, n. 72). At New Romney (Kent) a messenger coming from Dover castle brought, at an unspecified date, news of the cancellation both of the coronation and of the parliament (H.M.C., v. (1876), 547). The summons to parliament was cancelled by writ of *supersedeas* received 21 June at York (*York civic Records*, i. 75; see below, n. 102).

95. In 1450 see Fabyan, *Chronicles*, p. 626; *Chronicles of London*, p. 162.

96. Unlike other sources (*Great Chronicle*, p. 232; Fabyan, *Chronicles*, p. 669; *Chronicles of London*, p. 190; More, *Richard III*, p. 69; Polydore Vergil, *Anglica Historia*, p. 692) Mancini does not report a speech delivered at the Guildhall to the assembled mayor, aldermen and citizens of London by the duke of Buckingham, but gives instead a speech made by Buckingham to the lords ('*ad principes*', p. 96, l. 27) who had been summoned to London. It should be noted that Mancini dates Buckingham's address to the lords as 24 June 1483, the day preceding that on which a general deputation waited on the Protector and petitioned him to take the crown (see above, p. 96, l. 24 and n. 100 below). Other sources mentioned above assign Buckingham's speech before the Londoners in the Guildhall to the same date, *viz.* 24 June. Therefore, Mancini could be merely reporting Buckingham's well authenticated Guildhall oration. Buckingham, however, is unlikely to have harangued the Londoners and the lords together; and Mancini may be preserving an account of an assembly of lords concerning which other sources are silent. How many lords were in London on 24 June is

uncertain; but a large number attended Richard III's coronation on 6 July 1483. See below, n. 112.

97. *Per verba deputati*.... Mancini evidently believed a report that the earl, whom he calls duke, of Warwick had as the king's proxy contracted Edward IV to another woman *per verba de presenti* or *per verba de futuro*. The first constituted a binding declaration of marriage and the second a binding declaration of betrothal: see G. Le Bras in *Dictionnaire de théologie catholique*, ix. pt. 2 (1927) col. 2153 sqq. In 1463–4 Louis XI was soliciting the help of Warwick in bringing about a marriage of Bona of Savoy, sister-in-law of the French king, to Edward IV (Calmette and Perinelle, *Louis XI et l'Angleterre*, pp. 41–61). Evidence is not forthcoming to show that prior to 1 May 1464 (the date of Edward IV's marriage to Elizabeth Woodville) Warwick was empowered to act as the king's proxy in respect of a foreign marriage. It was formerly supposed that Warwick between the date of the king's secret marriage and the date of its publication (see above, n. 10) undertook during the summer of 1464 a mission abroad (C. L. Scofield. 'Movements of the earl of Warwick in the summer of 1464', E.H.R., xxi (1906) 732–7) in the course of which he might have negotiated the marriage of Edward IV. More recently it has been demonstrated (A. L. Brown and B. Webster. 'Movements of the earl of Warwick in the summer of 1464—a correction', E.H.R., lxxxi (1966) 80–2) that the documents adduced by Miss Scofield as evidence of Warwick's mission in 1464 related to a mission of his predecessor Richard Beauchamp, earl of Warwick, *temp*. Henry V. In the first parliament of Richard III, 23 January–22 February 1484, a pre-contract was officially declared to have existed between Eleanor Butler and Edward IV invalidating the king's marriage to Elizabeth Woodville (*Rotuli Parliamentorum*, vi. 241a). The fact that Mancini does not report this may indicate that by the time he left England no official charge to invalidate Edward's IV's marriage had been formulated. Such a delay would be in keeping with the improvised character of Richard III's usurpation. The Croyland chronicler writing slightly later (Sir Goronwy Edwards, 'The second continuation of the Crowland chronicle: was it written in ten days?' B.I.H.R., xxxix (1966) 117–29), declared that a petition purporting to have been prepared *in partibus borealibus* but actually prepared in London, alleging a pre-contract of Edward IV and Eleanor Butler furnished the pretext for Richard III's assumption of the crown on 26 June 1483 (*Historia croylandensis*, p. 567; a slightly different wording in George Buck, *History of the life and reigne of Richard III*, London, W. Wilson, 1646, fol., p. 24).

Comines (*Mémoires*, ii. 232, 305) gave a circumstantial account, but

one which has not been verified: a balanced discussion of the pros and cons is given by Professor M. Levine, 'Richard III: usurper or lawful king?', *Speculum*, xxxiv (1959) 391–401.

98. Cf. Basin, *Historia Caroli VII et Ludovici XI*, ed. Quicherat, iii, 135.

99. For a short time following the death of his only legitimate son in April 1484 Richard III recognized Edward, earl of Warwick as heir to the throne but quickly replaced him by John de la Pole, earl of Lincoln (Ross, *Historia regum Anglie*, pp. 217–18). See above, n. 75.

100. On 25 June 1483 the duke of Buckingham accompanied by lords, knights, and gentlemen together with the mayor, aldermen, and chief commoners of the city waited on the Protector at Baynard's Castle, house of Cecily, duchess of York, to present a petition begging the Protector to assume the crown (*Rotuli Parliamentorum*, vi. 240; *Historia croylandensis*, p. 567; More, *Richard III*, pp. 77–80).

101. A convocation had been summoned for 18 April 1483 (Nichols, *Grants of Edward V*, p. xxxviii) but it did not meet. On 16 May a signet letter was addressed to the archbishop of Canterbury bidding him assemble a convocation of the clergy of his province at St. Paul's London (*ib.*, p. 13).

102. Mancini was under the impression that the gathering, which he witnessed, was a parliamentary assembly, which it may have resembled though legally speaking no parliament was held between 22 Edward IV at Westminster January–February 1483 and 1 Richard III at Westminster January–February 1484. If, as seems probable, Mancini was in England during the closing months of Edward IV's reign he may have witnessed the 1483 parliament at Westminster. Although Mancini had a confused notion of the structure of parliament, which he seems to think consisted of the lords, the higher clergy and the Londoners, he at least recognized parliament's legislative powers. Comines who claimed to know something about England was scarcely better informed (*Mémoires*, ii, 8, 245, 305).

103. Richard III commenced his reign 26 June 1483, on which day he occupied the king's chair in the court of King's Bench at Westminster (*Historia croylandensis*, p. 566; *Great Chronicle*, p. 232; C. A. J. Armstrong, 'Inauguration ceremonies of the Yorkist kings and their title to the throne', *Transactions of the Royal Historical Society*, 4, xxx [1948] 59, n. 5). According to the Year Book however Richard claimed the throne on the day following St. John's day, *viz.* 25 June: 'a Crastino Johannis . . . a quel iour Richard Plantagenet, frere le roy Edward IV. . . . claima destre roy d'Engleterre et a mesme le iour proclaima le iour de sa coronacion par force de quel touts les courts le roy fuerent dis-

continues'. Year Book Edward V, *Incipit annus primus Edwardi Quinti*, fol., J. Rastell [? 1520] nos. 12 and 13; *Short-Title Catalogue*, no. 9895. *Anni Regum Edwardi quinti, Richardi tertii, Henrici septimi et Henrici octavi*, fol.; The Company of Stationers, 1620, p. 8, *Short-Title Catalogue*, no. 9904. The first privy seals of Richard's reign, four of them, are all dated 28 June 1483 (P.R.O., Chancery Warrants, Privy Seal, 1, Ric. III. C.81/886) the most important grantees were William earl of Arundel and William Catesby (*Calendar of Patent Rolls 1476–85*, p. 358). Doubt as to the commencement of Richard's regnal year persisted in outlying parts and he addressed a letter under his signet Nottingham 12 October 1484 to Ireland certifying that he began his reign on 26 June 1483 when 'we entred into owre just title taking upon us oure dignitie royall and supprane gouvernaunce of this oure royme of England', reproduced *Reports from the Commissioners ... respecting the Public Records of Ireland, 1810–1815*, pl. ix, no. 2.

104. The force, which the dukes of Gloucester and Buckingham assembled about London, prior to the former's coronation, was considered exceptionally large by contemporaries: 'Evocatis ab Aquilone, Wallia et ceteris quibusve partibus sub eorum ditione hominibus armatis in numero terribili et inaudito', *Historia croylandensis*, p. 566. An unknown correspondent wrote shortly before 21 June to Sir William Stonor 'Yt is thought ther schalbe xx thousand of my lord protectour and my lord of Bukyngham men in London this weeke' (*Stonor Letters*, ii. 160–1). This armed force was composed firstly of the followers of Gloucester and Buckingham who accompanied them when they entered London with Edward V. At that time Lord Hastings had expected them to bring 2000 men, the same number as was to accompany the king (*Historia croylandensis*, p. 565); but actually they entered London with 500 retainers (see above, p. 82, l. 13). Secondly there were the northerners. On 15 June the mayor of York received a letter from the Protector dated London 10 June asking for as many armed men as possible to be sent (*York civic Records*, p. 73). The bearer of this letter, Richard Ratcliff, was entrusted by the Protector with a similar note to Ralph Nevill (*Paston Letters*, vi. 71–2). The force so raised is unlikely to have reached London before 1 July since its leaders, the earl of Northumberland and Richard Ratcliff, had by 25 June advanced no farther than Pontefract (see above, n. 85). The *Great Chronicle* (p. 233) estimates its size as between 4000 and 5000 men, Fabyan (*Chronicles*, p. 669) and the *Chronicles of London* (p. 191) at no more than 4000. The troops alarmed not only the author of the Croyland chronicle, but also the university of Cambridge ('Item solvi uni viro conducto per vicecancellarium ad cogendum certos rumores de adventu virorum boreal-

ium...v sol'. *Grace Book A containing the Proctors' Accounts and other records of the University of Cambridge 1454–88*, ed. S. M. Leathes, Cambridge Antiquarian Society, Luard Memorial Series, 1897, p. 170) and the authorities of the city of London, for the Goldsmiths' Company contributed to the cost of the watch 'at the coming of the Northern men when they mustered at Fynesbery Fields' (*Memorials of the Goldsmiths' Company... 1335–1815*, ed. W. S. Prideaux, London, 1896–97, i. 27). According to Fabyan (*loc. cit.*) the troops were mustered on Moorfields, but on Finsbury fields according to John Stow, *A Summarie of the Chronicles of England*, London, 1575, p. 395. Their presence was required by the Protector as a security for his coronation; and according to Fabyan (*loc. cit.*) they were sent home directly he was crowned. Edward IV had also overawed London with armed men immediately preceding his occupation of the throne on 4 March 1461 (C. A. J. Armstrong, 'Inauguration ceremonies of the Yorkist kings and their title to the throne', *Transactions of the Royal Historical Society*, 4, xxx (1948) 55.

105. In 1478 an act had been passed in defence of archery against competition from other sports (*Rotuli Parliamentorum*, vi. 188).

106. The leather tunic, or Jack, was a peculiarly English form of defensive equipment. The city of York decided 16 June 1483 to pay a wage of 12*d*. a day to each man of the contingent sent to London in support of the Protector provided 'that every socher shall pay for hys aun jaket' (*York civic Records*, p. 74).

107. The equipment of the troops made a poor impression on Fabyan, (*Chronicles*, p. 669) followed by Hall (*Chronicle*, p. 375).

108. On the use of horses in England for civil and military purposes: see Du Clercq (*Mémoires*, iii. 118), the Bohemian nobleman Rožmitála, who with his companions visited England in 1466 (*Commentarius brevis et iucundus itineris*, p. 36) and the Venetian diplomatic report *circa* 1497 (*Relation or rather a true account of the Island of England*, p. 46).

109. The relevant extracts from the Wardrobe Accounts published under the heading 'To our soverayne lord the king for his apparaill, the vigil afore the day of his most noble coronacion, for to ride in from his toure of London unto his palace of Westminster' in *Archaeologia*, i. (1770) 361–83.

110. About 2½ English miles.

111. See above note 73. Thomas Bourchier did not attend the coronation banquet. The place on the king's right which belonged traditionally to the archbishop of Canterbury was occupied on this occasion by William Dudley, bishop of Durham (*Excerpta historica*, p. 382).

112. Richard III's coronation took place 6 July 1483. For a narrative relation see *Excerpta historica*, p. 379–84. For the unusual coronation oath *Registrum Thome Bourgchier*, p. 60–1. The claim of the city of London in *Report to the Court of Common Council from the Committee for General Purposes. Presented 18 August 1831*, no. xii, p. 34. Claim of the Cinque Ports in H.M.C. *Calendar of the White and Black Books of the Cinque Ports*, ed. F. Hull, 1966, p. 641. The date of the coronation had probably been notified abroad in advance of the event, since the English merchants at Bruges provided a lavish entertainment in honour of the coronation on 7 July. They could not celebrate on 6 July as on that day the child count of Flanders, Philip the Fair, paid a state-visit to Bruges and the municipality monopolized all festivities on his behalf (*Het Boeck van al't gene datter geschiedt is binnen Brugghe sichtent jaer 1477*, ed. C. C[arton] *Maatschappy der Vlaemsche Bibliophilen*, Ghent, 3, ii (1859) 56.

113. Gordon C. Home, *Old London Bridge*, London, 1931. *esp.* pp. 106–36.

114. For this and the subsequent notes 115 to 117 see I. Darlington and J. Howgego, *Printed maps of London 1553–1850*, London, 1964. For the fifteenth century topography and for Mancini's description two map-views are especially relevant:

(i) *circa*, 1544, the drawing of Antonius van den Wyngaerde reproduced by the *London Topographical Society*, no. 5, 1881–2, on which see Darlington and Howgego, *op. cit.*, p. 7.

(ii) *post*, 1561, the so-called Agas woodcut reproduced *London Topographical Society*, no. 7, 1905. See also Darlington and Howgego, *op. cit.*, pp. 12–19, 54–5.

In both these map-views the Thames waterfront with its warehouses is prominent.

115. This was Thames Street running in an almost straight line from the Tower on the east to Blackfriars on the west. Its route is traced by Stow (*Survey of London*, i. 106, 132–3, 135–7, 188, 205, 210–11). The raw materials and goods noted by Mancini were all bulky and heavy imports accounted for by the proximity (i) of the Hanseatic 'Steelyard' lying between Thames Street and the river; (ii) by the neighbouring halls of the Fishmongers, Ironmongers, and Vintners (Stow, *op. cit.*, i. 81, 206, 213–15, 232–5, 240–2).

116. This intermediate throughfare was less straight and less readily distinguishable on the map-views than the other two. Its broadest and straightest section, Candlewick Street, was the part which attracted the attention of Mancini, for here the sale of cloth was supreme: 'thrwghe-out all Canywike-strete, Drapers to me they gunne call anon

great chepe of clothe' (*London Lickpenny, Anglia*, xliii [1919] 65). St. Swithun's church standing in the same street was a burial place for drapers (Stow, *Survey of London*, i. 223–4).

117. A route running from Aldgate on the east to Newgate on the west. Its central section known as [West] Cheap was the finest way in the city and was known simply as 'the street'. Many goldsmiths were settled here (T. F. Reddaway, 'London Goldsmiths *circa* 1500', *Transactions of the Royal Historical Society*, 5, xii [1962] 52) who often chose their burial in the neighbouring churches (Stow, *Survey of London*, i. 81, 305, 322, 345). The goldsmiths excited the admiration of foreigners: e.g. in 1466 Rožmitála (*Commentarius brevis et iucundus itineris*, p. 37) and in 1497 the Venetian diplomatic report (*Relation or rather a true account of the Island of England*, pp. 42–3. corrected by E. Jeffries Davis 'The Goldsmiths in La Strada, London, 1497', *History*, xvii [1932] 47–8). For the sale of other precious stuff mentioned by Mancini see *London Lickpenny* (*Anglia*, xliii [1919] 65).

118. This observation applies to merchants' houses of the period in London and in other English towns. C. L. Kingsford, 'A London merchant's house and its owners', *Archaeologia*, lxxiv (1923) 149; W. A. Pantin, 'Merchants' houses and warehouses of King's Lynn', *Medieval Archaeology*, vi and vii (1962–3) 173–81; and 'Medieval English Town-House plans', *ib.*, pp. 202–39.

119. Foreigners noticed the fondness of the English for prophecies. Comines (*Mémoires*, ii. 65) states that when Edward IV and Louis XI met at Picquigny, 29 August 1475, the chancellor of England, began his address with a prophecy 'dont les Angloys ne sont jamais despourveuz, laquelle disoit que en ce lieu de Pequigny se devoit faire une grand paix....' For another prophecy current in London in May 1483 see *Great Chronicle*, p. 230. For the historiographical relevance of prophecies see Kingsford, *English Historical Literature*, pp. 236, 237, 262, 358.

APPENDIX

RICHARD III AS SEEN BY ANOTHER FOREIGN TRAVELLER, NICOLAS VON POPPELAU

THE reminiscences of Nicolas von Poppelau are a valuable supplement to the work of Mancini. Nicolas came to England in 1484, and wrote down his travel diary some time between then and his death, which probably occurred between 1490 and 1494.[1] The original manuscript, written perhaps in Latin,[2] does not seem to have survived; but there are German copies dating from the seventeenth or eighteenth centuries,[3] and the contents have been frequently printed in Silesia. Possibly the earliest and most reliable extract from the journal of Nicolas was that made by a Silesian historian, Samuel Benjamin Klose (1730–98), for his history of Breslau called, *Darstellung der inneren Verhältnisse der Stadt Breslau vom Jahre 1458 bis zum Jahre 1526*: this has been edited by G. A. Stenzel as vol. iii of *Scriptores Rerum Silesiacarum*.[4]

Nicolas belonged to a noble Silesian family, and may be regarded as the last of knights-errant, or one of the first modern diplomatists. He was equally suited to either calling, as he combined literary and oratorical talent with almost superhuman strength. On his travels he carried with him a great lance, that none but himself could wield; others, who attempted to do so, were borne by its weight to the ground, if they did not find it impossible even to lift. Clearly his travels were originally undertaken from motives of adventure and chivalry, and it was only after his successful visit to the countries of western and eastern Europe that the emperor Frederick III saw the advantage of sending him as an ambassador to Russia.

Poppelau arrived in London on 16 April 1484, having come from

[1] Joseph Fiedler, *Nikolaus Poppel, erster Gesandter Österreichs in Russland*, Sitzungsberichte der kaiserlichen Akademie der Wissenschaften [Vienna], Philosophisch-historische Classe, xxii [1856], 218–19.

[2] The earliest reference to the manuscript journal of Nicolas is under the title of *Itinerarium Poppelianum* (Johannes Sinapius, *Schlesischer Curiositäten erste Vorstellung, darinnen die ansehnlichen Geschlechter des Schlesischen Adels*, etc., 2 parts, Leipzig, 1720–8, i. 718).

[3] Fiedler, p. 190, note. Ludwig Petry, *Die Popplau*, Breslau, 1935, pp. 142–3.

[4] Breslau, 1847. The account of Poppelau's visit to England, from which the following is taken, occurs on pp. 363–6.

Middelburg by way of Canterbury. His stay in London was brief, and he set out for the north through Cambridge, Stamford, Newark, and Doncaster, reaching Pontefract on 1 May 1484.[1] Here he presented to Richard III letters of introduction from the emperor, and delivered a Latin oration that drew forth the admiration of all; the king took him graciously by the hand and ordered a chamberlain to conduct him to his lodgings. The following day Nicolas attended the mass at which the king was present, and listened to the magnificent music. Leaving the church he joined the king's retinue and went to watch Richard at dinner. Afterwards the king spoke quite alone with Poppelau, and asked him a great deal about the emperor and the princes of the empire. Finally he came to speak of the Turks, and when Nicolas told of the victory over the Turk gained by the king of Hungary before St. Martin's day 1483, Richard was delighted and cried out, 'I wish that my kingdom lay upon the confines of Turkey; with my own people alone and without the help of other princes I should like to drive away not only the Turks, but all my foes.'[2] Poppelau remained another eight days at court, and always dined at the royal table: he received from Richard a golden necklace, which the king took from the neck of a certain lord.

Of the king's appearance he has left the following description. Richard was three fingers taller than himself, but a little thinner and not so thick set, also much more lean; he had delicate arms and legs, also a great heart.[3] Having regard to Poppelau's extraordinary strength, it is natural to suppose that he was a big man, and if Richard was three fingers taller his height was doubtless considerable. If the king's limbs were really so frail, it is easy to see how the legend arose of Richard's withered arm. Hostile caricature

---

[1] On 1 May 1484 Richard was at York, later he went to Middleham, where he stayed till at least 10 May (British Museum, MS. Harleian 433, ff. 172–3). Probably Poppelau confused the two castles of Pontefract and Middleham.
[2] 'Iche wünschte, dass mein Königreich an der Türkischen Grenze läge, ich wolte gewiss mit meinem Volk allein, ohne Hülfe andrer Fürsten, nicht nur den Türken, sondern auch alle meine Feinde leicht austreiben' (*Scriptores Rerum Silesiacarum*, iii. 365).
[3] 'Konig Richard [war] drei Finger länger, doch ein wenig schlanker und nicht so dik als er [i.e. Nicolas von Poppelau], auch gar viel dürrer, hatte ganz subtile Arme und Schenkel, auch ein grosses Herz' (ibid.).

would have little difficulty in making a hunch-back of a tall and emaciated man, who not improbably stooped as well.

Nicholas had far less regard for the English than for their sovereign. In his opinion they surpassed the Poles in ostentation and pilfering, the Hungarians in brutality, and the Lombards in deceit. Their virtue consisted in wealth and hospitality, but their cooking was poor: moreover, the avarice of the people made everything in England dear; and the women, though very beautiful, seemed to Nicolas astoundingly impudent.

INDEX

Acciaiuoli, Ludovico, 112, n. 23.
Acquila, Matteo dill', 29.
Aegidius Romanus, 9, n. 2.
Æmilius, Paulus, 51.
Alabanti, Antonio, 9, n. 2.
Albiano, Renaldo 26, n. 4.
Alcock, John, bishop of Worcester, 127, n. 90.
Alexander VI, 38, n. 3, 47.
Alfonso V, king of Aragon and of Naples, 29.
Andreas Bernard, 107, n. 7.
Anglia, see England.
Anjou, Margaret of, wife of Henry VI, 109, n. 11, 122, n. 68.
Anne, daughter of Richard earl of Warwick, wife of Richard III, queen of England, 125, n. 76.
Apollo, 50.
Aquinas, St. Thomas, 9, n. 2, 47, 49.
Aragon, house of, see
  Alfonso V, king of Aragon and Naples.
  Federigo, prince of Taranto, subsequently king of Naples.
  Ferdinand, prince of Capua.
  Ferrante, king of Naples.
  John.
Argentine, John, 19, 20, 53, 92, 93, 127, n. 89.
Ariminensis, Gregorius, see Rimini, Gregorio da.
Aristotle, 47.
Armorici, see Brittany
Arras, peace of 1482, 106, n. 3.
Arthur, prince of Wales, 127, n. 89.
Arundel, William Fitz-Alan, earl of, 131, n. 103.
Astinco, see Hastings.
Augustine, St., 10, n. 4.
Austria, house of,
  origins, 53, n. 1.
  Frederick III, king of Romans and emperor, 3, 136.
  Margaret of, 106, n. 3.
  Maximilian, king of the Romans, 8, 38, n. 4, 106, n. 3.
  Philip the Fair, 134, n. 112.

Bacone, Johannes de, 9, n. 2.
Balbus, Hieronymus, 41, 42, 48, n. 4, 49.
Barclay, Alexander, 11, n. 1.
Basin, Thomas, bishop of Lisieux, 15, n. 1, 42, n. 7, 104, n. a.
  Historia, 107, n. 5, 110, n. 13, 131, n. 98.
Beaugency, 5, 23, 104, 105.
Bedford, John duke of, 108, n. 8.
Benevento, 29, 37, 46, 47.
Berbiciensium dux, see Warwick, Richard Neville, earl of.
Blois, 10, 23.
Bologna, 29, n. 5.
—, Urbano da, 9, n. 2.
Bolumbrello, Antonello, 34.
Boulogne-sur-mer, 118, n. 57.
Bourbon, Gilbert de, count of Montpensier, 47.
Bourchier, Thomas, cardinal archbishop of Canterbury, 17, 88, 89, 100, 101, 116, n. 49, 119, n. 59, 121, n. 64, 124, n. 73, 74, 131, n. 101, 133, n. 111.
Brackenbury, Sir Robert, 19, n. 1.
Brampton, Edward, 121, n. 67.
Briçonnet, Guillaume, 27.
— Jean, 26, n. 4.
Britannia, Britanni, see England, Englishmen.
Brittany, 24, 54, 86, 87, 119, n. 59.
  Joan, dowager duchess of, second wife of Henry IV, king of England, 110, n. 13.
Bruges, 111, n. 22, 112, n. 23, 134, n. 112.

140 INDEX

Brussels, Arnold of, 33.
Buck, Sir George, 130, n. 97.
Buckingham, Henry Stafford, second duke of, 74, 75, 76, 77, 82, 83, 90, 91, 94, 95, 96, 97, 98, 99, 107, n. 6, 114, n. 39, 41, 43, 116, n. 46, 119, n. 59, 121, n. 64, 124, n. 74, 129, n. 96, 131, n. 100, 132, n. 104.
Burdett, Thomas, 110, n. 17.
Burgundy,
   Charles duke of, 27, 28, 34, 36, 111, n. 22.
   Mary duchess of, 5, 26, 34, 106, n. 3.
Butler, Eleanor, 130, n. 97.

Calabria, Nicolas of, 26.
Calais, 106, n. 2, 114, n. 39, 119, n. 59.
Cambridge, university of, 126, n. 82, 132, n. 104, 137.
Canaries, 33.
Canterbury, cardinal archbishop of, see Bourchier, Thomas.
   city of, 121, n. 67, 137.
   cantuar: cardinalis, see Bourchier, Thomas.
Cardonne, Jean Francois de, 26, n. 4, 28.
Carmeliano, Pietro, 4, 19.
Catesby, William, 125, n. 80, 131, n. 103.
Catherine, daughter of Charles VI of France and wife of Henry V king of England, 109, n. 12.
Cato, Angelo, archbishop of Vienne, 3, 4, 5, 17, 23, 24, n. 2, 26-51.
   dedication of the *De Occupatione* to, 56, 57, 104, 105.
   medals of, 29, n. 1, 49, 50.
   mss. consulted or owned by, 33, 48, 49.
   physician, 13, 29, 33, 35, 37, 49.
   published works of, 31-4, 41.
   unpublished works of, 30, n. 5, 43, 47, 49.
— Lucrezio, 30, 46.

Charles VII, king of France, 22, 35, n. 1.
Charles VIII, king of France, 6, 22, 23, 25, 38, 39, 42, 43, 44, 46, 47, 48, n. 4, 104, n. a. 106, n. 3, 118, n. 57.
Chiaramonte, Tristram da, 43.
Chronicles of London, 120, n. 60, 124, n. 74, 125, n. 81, 126, n. 84, 128, n. 92, 93, 129, n. 95, 96, 132, n. 104.
Cicero, 50, n. 1.
Cinque Ports, Coronation claim of, 134, n. 112.
Clarence, George duke of, 62-63, 64, 65, 67, 68, 70, 71, 88, 89, 96, 97, 110, n. 15, 16, 17, 111, n. 18, 113, n. 32.
   Isabelle, duchess of, 125, n. 76.
Cléry, Notre-Dame de, 23, 39.
Cobham, John Brooke, Lord, 121, n. 67.
Comines, Phillipe Sire de, 15, n. 1, 17, 35, 36, 38, 54.
   Mémoires of, 26, 28, 37, 39, 42, 46, 52, 56, n. a, 107, n. 5, 108, n. 10, 111, n. 18, 113, n. 33, 130, n. 97, 131, n. 102, 135, 119.
Cora, Ambrosius, 10, n. 4.
Cordis, dominus de, see Crèvecouer.
Cornazzano, Antonio, 108, n. 10.
Courtin, Martin, 38, n. 5.
Coventry, 107, n. 6, 108, n. 8.
Crèvecoeur, Philippe de, 80, 81, 118, n. 57, 58.
Croyland, chronicle of; *Historia croylandensis*, xvii, xviii, 107, n. 7, 110, n. 16, 111, n. 22, 114, n. 39, 40, 41, 43, 115, n. 45, 116, n. 46, 47, 48, 50, 51, 117, n. 52, 120, n. 61, 63, 124, n. 74, 126, n. 85, 128, n. 92, 130, n. 97, 132, n. 104.

Dauphiné, 45.
De Passione Domini, 1, 7, 11, 12, 13, 14.

INDEX

De quatuor Virtutibus, 1, 6, 11, 12, 13, 14.
Dorset, see Grey, Thomas, marquess of.
Dover, 121, n. 67, 129, n. 94.
Dudley, William, bishop of Durham, 133, n. 111.
Dürer, Albert, 14.
Dymmock, Andrew, 115, n. 45.

Ebor: archiepiscopus, see Rotherham, *dux*, see York.
Edward IV, king of England, 5, 15, 16, 18, 21, 22, 58, 59, 60, 61, 64, 65, 66, 67, 68, 69, 80, 81, 88, 89, 90, 91, 94, 95, 96, 97, 104, 105, 106, n. 2, 3, 107, n. 5, 7, 108, n. 8, 10, 109, n. 11, 12, 110, n. 14, 15, 111, n. 20, 112, n. 23, 27, 113, n. 28, 35, 114, n. 42, 43, 117, n. 54, 118, n. 56, 119, n. 59, 120, n. 61, 120, n. 63, 121, n. 64, 122, n. 68, 127, n. 91, 128, n. 92, 128, n. 93, 130, n. 97, 132, n. 104, 135, n. 119.
Edward V, king of England,
 prince of Wales, 15, 16, 18, 19, 58, 59, 70, 71, 127, n. 89, 90.
 king, 15, 16, 18–21, 72–83, 93–97, 106, n. 2, 107, n. 6, 114, n. 40, 41, 42, 115, n. 44, 45. 116, n. 46, 51, 119, n. 59, 120, n. 60, 120, n. 63, 121, n. 64, 126, n. 86, 127, n. 87, 127, n. 91, 129, n. 94, 132, n. 104.
Elizabeth, queen of England, wife of Edward IV, see Woodville.
Ely, bishop of, see Morton, John.
England, English affairs, Englishmen, 4, 54, 56, 57, 78, 79, 100, 101, 104, 105, 109, n. 12, 133, n. 108, 138.
Exeter, Henry Holland, duke of, 117, n. 54.

Fabyan, Robert, *Chronicles*, 108, n. 10, 111, n. 18, 116, n. 46, 117, n. 52, 120, n. 60, 124, n.

74, 125, n. 81, 126, n. 84, 128, n. 93, 129, n. 95, 96, 132, n. 104, 133, n. 107.
Federigo,
 Frederick III, king of Naples, 1496–1501, 106, n. 1.
 prince of Taranto, 27, 28, 30, 34, 36, 37, 43, 46, 56, 57.
 Ciarletta, daughter of, 46.
Ferdinand, prince of Capua, subsequently king of Naples, 1495–96, 49, n. 6.
Fernand, Jean, 41.
Ferrante of Aragon, king of Naples, 29, 30, 33, 34, 43, 46, 48, n. 4.
Fiorentino, Adriano, 46, 49, n. 6.
Flamingi, see Flemings.
Flanders, 106, n. 3, 109, n. 12, 112, n. 23.
Flemings, 58, 59, 66, 67.
Florence, 40, 112, n. 23.
Fotheringay, 109, n. 12.
France, Frenchmen, 58, 59, 80, 81, 104, 105, 107, n. 7, 118, n. 56.
Franci, see Frenchmen.
Frederick III, king of the Romans and emperor, see Austria.
Fribois, Noel de, 22.
Fulford, Sir Thomas, 121, n. 67.

Gaguin, Robert, 3, 6, 7, 8, 9, 24, 41.
Gallia, Galli, see France, Frenchmen.
Gaunt, John of, duke of Lancaster, 109, n. 12.
Genoa, Genoese, 84–7, 122, n. 68.
Gloucester, Anne duchess of, queen of England, wife of Richard III, 88, 89.
Godefroy, Charles, 53, n. 1.
— Denis, 52, 56, n. a.
— Denis-Charles, 53.
— Theodore, 52.
Grafton Regis, 108, n. 10.
— Richard, *Chronicle*, 108, n. 10, 114, n. 43, 123, n. 72, 125, n. 80, 126, n. 82.
Grandson, battle of, 27, 35, 36.
Grassis, Paris de, 35, n. 5.

142 INDEX

Great Chronicle of London, xviii, 108, n. 10, 111, n. 18, 114, n. 43, 116, n. 46, 117, n. 52, 119, n. 59, 120, n. 60, 63, 124, n. 73, 74, 125, n. 76, 80, 81, 126, n. 84, 85, 127, n. 87, 88, 128, n. 92, 93, 129, n. 96, 132, n. 104, 135, n. 119.
Grey, George, son of Thomas marquess of Dorset, 113, n. 35.
— Sir John, first husband of Elizabeth Woodville, 108, n. 9.
— Richard, 64, 65, 92, 93, 108, n. 9, 113, n. 30, 116, n. 46, 126, n. 85.
— Thomas, Marquess of Dorset, 64, 65, 78, 79, 80, 81, 90, 91, 108, n. 9, 113, n. 30, 32, 35, 117, n. 52, 119, n. 59, 126, n. 84.
Grosellus, Johannes, see Russell, John, bishop of Lincoln.
Guainerius, Antonius, 31, n. 5.
Guelders, Charles of Egmond, duke of, 45, n. 5.
Gutenberg, 41.

Hall, Edward, *Chronicle*, 107, n. 5, 108, n. 10, 118, n. 57, 133, n. 107.
Hansards, 112, n. 23, 117, n. 54.
Harfleur, 25.
Hastings, William Lord, 5, 18, 19, 53, 68, 69, 70, 71, 72, 73, 88, 89, 90, 91, 92, 93, 94, 95, 96, 97, 113, n. 35, 114, n. 39, 115, n. 45, 116, n. 51, 119, n. 59, 124, n. 74, 77, 127, n. 87, 128, n. 93, 132, n. 104.
Haute, Richard, 116, n. 46.
'*Hearne's Fragment*', 108, n. 10.
Henry IV, king of England, 110, n. 13.
Henry V, king of England, 109, n. 12, 114, n. 38.
Henry VI, king of England, 60–1, 62, 63, 80, 81, 90, 91, 109, n. 12, 117, n. 53, 118, n. 56, 122, n. 68.

Henry VII, king of England, 21, 25, 107, n. 7, 123, n. 71.
earl of Richmond, 24, 25, 122, n. 68, 125, n. 75.
Henry VIII, king of England, 107, n. 7.
Henry II, king of France, 15, n. 1, 26.
Holwell, John, 121, n. 67.
Hungary, king of. Matthias Corvinus, 137.
Hungerford, Mary, Lady, wife of Sir Edward Hastings, 113, n. 35.

Innocent VIII, 43.
Innocents, Holy, 21.
Ireland, 131, n. 103.
Isabelle, daughter of Charles VI of France and wife of Richard II king of England, 22.

John of Aragon, son of Ferrante, king of Naples, 30, 32.
Julius II, 35, n. 5.

Kemp, Margery, 20, n. 5.
Knole, 124, n. 73.

La Marche, Olivier de, 111, n. 18.
Landais, Pierre, 38, n. 5.
Langeac, Jaques de, vicomte de Lamothe, 42, n. 7, 43.
Le Glay, A., 53.
Lille, 50, 52, 53.
Lincoln, bishop of, see Russell, John.
John de la Pole, earl of, 131, n. 99.
Lombez, bishop of, 38, n. 5.
London, see also *Chronicles* of and *Great Chronicle*, 13, 15, 16, 18, 58, 59, 70, 71, 74, 75, 78, 79, 84, 87, 94, 95, 101, 112, n. 23, 114, n. 39, 41, 42, 115, n. 44, 45, 116, n. 46, 51, 118, n. 58, 119, n. 59, 120, n. 63, 121, n. 64, 123, n. 69, 132, n. 104, 133, n. 106, 134, n. 112, 136, 137.

Baynard's Castle, 125, n. 80.
City Council, 124, n. 74.
Crosby Place, 125, n. 80.
Finsbury, 132, n. 104.
Guildhall, 129, n. 96, 131, n. 100.
Moorfields, 132, n. 104.
St. Pauls, 116, n. 51, 120, n. 60, 131, n. 101.
Topography of, 134, n. 114, 115, 116, 135, n. 117.
Tower of, 19–21, 90–3, 96, 97, 101–3, 114, n. 38, 117, n. 54, 127, n. 87, 128, n. 92, 134, n. 115.
Lorraine, René II, duke of, 43.
Louis XI, king of France, 2, 3, 4, 17, 22, 23, 27, 34, 37, 38, 39, 40, 42, 58, 59, 66, 67, 106, n. 3, 112, n. 27, 118, n. 56, 130, n. 97, 135, n. 119.
Louis XII, king of France, duke of Orleans, 10, 42.
Louis XIV, king of France, 52.
Ludlow, 106, n. 2, 115, n. 44.
Luxembourg, Jacquetta of, 108, n. 8.
Lyons, 41, 44, 45, 118, n. 57.

Machlinia, William de, 106, n. 3.
Maillezais, bishopric of, 39.
Mancini, Dominic.
   family of, 1.
   his historical method, 15–18, 20, 107, n. 7, 108, n. 10, 113, n. 36, 116, n. 46, 129, n. 96, 131, n. 102.
   laureate, 3.
   member of a religious order, 2, 8.
   poetical works (see also *De Passione Domini* and *De quatuor Virtutibus*), 1, 2, 3, 6–8, 10, 11.
   visit to England, 3–5, 20, 23, 112, n. 23, 127, n. 91.
Mancini-Mazzarini, Philippe Julien, duke of Nevers, 1.
Marchio, see Grey, Thomas, marquess of Dorset.

Mazarin, Cardinal, 1.
Medici, Bank of the, 112, n. 23, 27
Mesue, Johannes, 29, n. 1, 34, 49
Middleham, 126, n. 85, 137, n. 1.
Milan, duke of, Galeazzo-Maria Sforza, 122, n. 68, 125, n. 81
Ludovico Sforza, 44, 48, n. 4.
Milet, Guillaume, 2, 10.
Molinet, Jean, *Chroniques*, 106, n. 3, 107, n. 5, 110, n. 15, 111, n. 18, 118, n. 57, 120, n. 61.
Morat, battle of, 27, 28, 34, 37.
More, [St.] Sir Thomas, *History of Richard III*, 108, n. 10, 110, n. 13, 15, 111, n. 18, 19, 113, n. 29, 31, 33, 35, 115, n. 44, 116, n. 46, 48, 51, 117, n. 52, 119, n. 59, 120, n. 60, 62, 63, 121, n. 64, 65, 124, n. 74, 125, n. 80, 81, 126, n. 82, 83, 128, n. 93, 129, n. 96, 131, n. 100.
Morton, John, bishop of Ely, 17, 19, 68, 69, 70, 71, 88, 89, 90, 91, 125, n. 80, 126, n. 82.

Nancy, 27.
Naples (city and university), 26, 29, 31–4, 43, 46, 47, 48, 49 n. 6.
Nassau, Engelbert II, count of, 45, n. 5.
Neumeister, Johann, 41.
Nevill, Ralph, 132, n. 104.
Newark, 137.
New Romney, 129, n. 94.
Nigrono, Joannes, Ambrosius de, 123, n. 70.
Norfolk, Anne, heiress of, daughter of John Mowbray, 127, n. 91.
   John Howard, duke of, 124, n. 74, 127, n. 91.
Northampton, 114, n. 43, 116, n. 46, 49, 119, n. 59, 121, n. 64.
Northumberland, Henry Percy, earl of, 126, n. 85, 132, n. 104.
Nottingham, 114, n. 43, 131, n. 103.

Orleans, 23, 104, 105.
Orvieto, 47.
Oxford, university of, 126, n. 82.

Padua, 20.
Paris (city and university), 2, 3, 23, 24, 41, 43, 44, 51.
Parlement, 45.
Parliament, 112, n. 23, 24.
Parron, William, 21.
Pavia, 33.
Payne, John, mayor of Southampton, 112, n. 23.
Pazzi, conspiracy of (1478), 40, 125, n. 81.
Penchenet, or Peuchenat, Raphael de, 48.
Penketh, Thomas, 9, 128, n. 93.
Persivall, 114, n. 43.
Pharès, Symon de, 27, n. 2, 37, 44, 45.
Piccolomini, Aeneas Sylvius, (pope Pius II), 15.
Picquigny, 135, n. 119.
Plato, 41, 49, 50 n. 1.
Pole, de la, William, duke of Suffolk, 20, n. 5.
Politian, 12.
Pont-à-Mousson, 34.
Pontano, Giovanni, 46.
Pontefract, 120, n. 61, 132, n. 104, 137.
Poppelau, Nicolas von, 16, n. 2, 136-7.
Portinari, Tommaso di, 112, n. 23.
Portugal, 33.

Raffael, 35, n. 5.
Ransano, Pietro, 32.
Ratcliff, Richard, 132, n. 104.
Reading, 108, n. 10.
Rély, Jean de, 6.
Rhodera, Thomas, see Rotherham, Thomas, archbishop of York.
Richard II, king of England, 22.
Richard III, king of England, 21, 22, 24, 54, 56-9, 96-9, 122, n. 68, 123, n. 70, 71, 126, n. 82, 127, n. 91, 128, n. 93, 129, n. 96, 130, n. 97, 131, n. 99, 131, n. 103, 134, n. 112.
appearance of, 137, 138.

duke of Gloucester, 5, 15-19, 60-5, 70-7, 80-9, 94, 95, 107, n. 6, 7, 109, n. 12, 110, n. 13, 14, 111, n. 20, 113, n. 30, 32, 36, 114, n. 39, 40, 41, 43, 115, n. 44, 116, n. 46, 51, 118, n. 56, 58, 119, n. 59, 120, n. 61, 121, n. 64, 124, n. 73, 126, n. 85, 132, n. 104.
Protector of England, 82, 83, 120, n. 63, 121, n. 66, 67, 123, n. 72, 124, n. 74, 125, n. 80, 127, n. 87, 91, 131, n. 100, 132, n. 104.
Riessinger, Sixtus, 32.
Rimini, Gregorio da, 2-3, 5, 9, 10, 49.
Rivera and Rivers, earl, see Woodville, Anthony.
Robert, III, king of Naples, 33.
Rochefort, Guillaume de, chancellor of France, 6, 22, 23, 24, 41.
Gui de, brother of the chancellor, 23, 41.
Rome, 37, 43, 44, 45, 46, 47, 48.
Ara Coeli, 1.
Capitol, 1.
S. Maria del Popolo, 40.
S. Maria-in-via-Lata, 1.
Sistine chapel, 40.
Ross, John of Warwick, xviii, 110, n. 16, 115, n. 44, 116, n. 46, 48, 117, n. 52, 121, n. 65, 126, n. 85, 127, n. 90, 131, n. 99.
Rotherham, Thomas, archbishop of York, 5, 17, 53, 68, 69, 70, 71, 84, 85, 88, 89, 121, n. 64, 124, n. 74, 125, n. 78, 126, n. 82.
Rouen, 109, n. 12.
Roye, Jean de, *Journal*, 107, n. 5, 111, n. 18.
Rožmitála, Jaroslav, 133, n. 108, 135, n. 117.
Russell, John, bishop of Lincoln, 84, 85, 121, n. 64, 65.
Rying, Bertold, 33, 34.

INDEX

St. Albans,
 first battle of, 1455, 114, n. 43.
 second battle of, 1461, 108, n. 9.
Saluzzo, 44.
Sandwich, 121, n. 67.
Sanseverino,
 Antonello, prince of Salerno, 48, n. 4.
 Federico, bishop of Maillezais, 6.
 Roberto, 6.
Sauvage, Denis, historiographer to Henry II of France, 15, n. 1, 26, 28.
Savoy,
 Anne of, daughter of Amadeus IX, 35, 46, n. 7.
 Bona, of, 130, n. 97.
 Charlotte of, queen of France, wife of Louis XI, 35, n. 1.
 Yolande, duchess of, daughter of Charles VII king of France, 35, n. 1.
Scotland, 111, n. 20, 122, n. 68.
Scots, 82, 83.
Scotus, Duns, 9, n. 2.
Shaw, Edmund, mayor of London, 127, n. 88.
— Dr. Ralph, 128, n. 93.
Sheriff Hutton, 126, n. 85.
Silesia, 136.
Silvaticus, Matthaeus, 30, n. 1, 31, n. 4, 32, n. 7, 33, 49.
Sixtus, IV, 5, 10, n. 4, 28, 31, n. 3, 37, 39, 40, 48, 51.
Stallworth, Simon, 119, n. 59. 123, n. 72, 124, n. 74.
Stamford, 137.
Stonor, Sir William, 132, n. 104.
Stony-Stratford, 114, n. 41, 115, n. 44, 116, n. 46, 50, 117, n. 52, 119, n. 59.
Supino, 29, 50, n. 1.
Surigone, Stefano, 4.
Sutton, Sir Richard, 126, n. 85.

Tangiers, 33.
Tardif, Guillaume, 41, 42, 48, n. 4.
Terrena, Guido, 9, n. 2.

Tetzel, Gabriel, 15, n. 5.
Tewkesbury, abbey, 117, n. 54.
Tiptoft, John, earl of Worcester, 21.
Tours, 22, 23, 24, 27, 106, n. 1, 118, n. 58.
Trebizond, 33.
Trithemius, Johannes, abbot of Sponheim, 7, 8, 9, 26.
Troyes, 51.
Turks, 137.

Ursins, Jean Jouvenel des, 22.

Vaudrey, Claude de, 6.
Vaughan, Sir Thomas, 116, n. 46, 120, n. 61.
Vergil Polydore, 18.
 Anglica Historia, xviii, xix, 107, n. 5, 107, n. 7, 111, n. 18, 112, n. 26, 113, n. 36, 114, n. 39, 40, 116, n. 46, 51, 117, n. 52, 123, n. 72, 124, n. 74, 125, n. 81, 126, n. 83, 128, n. 93, 129, n. 96.
Vienne, archbishopric of, see also Cato, Angelo, 31, 38, 39, 40, 42, 44, 47.

Wales, 70, 71, 74, 75.
 Marches of, 114, n. 43.
Welshmen, 82, 83, 120, n. 61.
Warwick, Edward earl of, son of George duke of Clarence, 88, 89, 96, 97, 113, n. 32, 125, n. 75, 131, n. 99.
 Richard Beauchamp, earl of, 130, n. 97.
 Richard Neville, earl of, 96, 97, 109, n. 12, 119, n. 59, 128, n. 92, 130, n. 97.
Wellis, John, 121, n. 67.
Westminster, 18, 78, 79, 100, 101, 102, 103, 106, n. 2, 107, n. 5, 108, n. 8, 116, n. 51, 117, n. 54, 121, n. 64, 123, n. 72, 124, n. 74, 126, n. 84, 127, n. 87, 129, n. 94, 131, n. 102.
Windsor, 109, n. 12.

146 INDEX

Woodville,
 family of, 110, n. 15, 111, n. 21, 113, n. 32, 114, n. 39, 42, 115, n. 45.
— Anthony, earl Rivers, 17, 64, 65, 66, 67, 74, 75, 78, 79, 85, 92, 93, 113, n. 31, 32, 115, n. 45, 116, n. 46, 120, n. 61, 126, n. 85.
— Catherine, wife of Henry duke of Buckingham, 114, n. 43.
— Sir Edward, 19, 64, 65, 80, 81, 84, 85, 86, 87, 113, n. 30, 119, no. 59, 121, n. 67.
— Elizabeth, wife of Edward IV, queen of England, 15, n. 5, 28, 60, 61, 62, 63, 64–5, 66, 67, 70, 71, 74, 75, 76, 77, 78, 79, 80, 81, 88, 89, 96, 97, 108, n. 8, 10, 109, n. 11, 110, n. 14, 15, 114, n. 40, 42, 115, n. 45, 117, n. 52, 119, n. 59, 120, n. 63, 121, n. 64, 124, n. 74, 130, n. 97.
— Lionel, chancellor of Oxford university, 111, n. 21.
— Sir Richard,, created Lord Rivers, 108, n. 8.

York,
 city of, 106, n. 2, 114, n. 43, 115, n. 44, 128, n. 92, 129, n. 94, 132, n. 104, 133, n. 106, 137, n. 1.
 county of, 113, n. 36, 116, n. 46.
 Cecily, duchess of, *ob*: 1495, mother of Edward IV and Richard III, 60, 61, 96, 97, 121, n. 64, 131, n. 100.
 Elizabeth of, eldest daughter of Edward IV, 106, n. 3.
 Margaret, duchess of Burgundy, sister of Edward IV, 112, n. 23.
 Richard, duke of, *ob*: 1460, father of Edward IV and Richard III, 62, 63, 94, 95.
 Richard, duke of, younger son of Edward IV, 20, 60, 61, 70, 71, 78, 79, 88, 89, 117, n. 52, 124, n. 74, 127, n. 87, 91.

OF ASSOCIATED INTEREST

HISTORIC DOUBTS
ON THE LIFE AND REIGN OF
RICHARD THE THIRD

HORACE WALPOLE

WITH AN INTRODUCTION AND NOTES BY
P. W. HAMMOND

ISBN 0-86299-299-0   256pp
216mm × 135mm   £5.95

OF ASSOCIATED INTEREST

Richard III

Keith Dockray

A Reader in History

ISBN 0-86299-313-X 144pp
216mm × 135mm £5.95

OF ASSOCIATED INTEREST

THE TRIAL OF RICHARD III

Richard Drewett and Mark Redhead

Based on the London Weekend Television Production for Channel 4

ISBN 0-86299-198-6   176pp
215mm × 150mm   £5.95